AFRICA IN THE
NEW INTERNATIONAL ORDER

≡IGCC

A project of the University of California
Institute on Global Conflict and Cooperation

AFRICA in the New International Order

Rethinking State Sovereignty and Regional Security

EDITED BY

EDMOND J. KELLER & DONALD ROTHCHILD

LYNNE
RIENNER
PUBLISHERS

BOULDER
LONDON

Published in the United States of America in 1996 by
Lynne Rienner Publishers, Inc.
1800 30th Street, Boulder, Colorado 80301

and in the United Kingdom by
Lynne Rienner Publishers, Inc.
3 Henrietta Street, Covent Garden, London WC2E 8LU

Library of Congress Cataloging-in-Publication Data
Africa in the new international order : rethinking state sovereignty
    and regional security / Edmond J. Keller and Donald Rothchild, eds.
        p.   cm.
    Includes bibliographical references and index.
    ISBN 1-55587-624-2 (alk. paper)
    ISBN 1-55587-631-5 (pbk. : alk. paper)
    1. Africa—Foreign relations—1960–   2. United Nations—Africa.
3. Regionalism (International organization) 4. Sovereignty.
5. Security, International. I. Keller, Edmond J. (Edmond Joseph),
1942–   . II. Rothchild, Donald S.
JX1582.A46   1996
327.1'7'096—dc20   95-26190
                                                                      CIP

British Cataloguing in Publication Data
A Cataloguing in Publication record for this book
is available from the British Library.

Printed and bound in the United States of America

The paper used in this publication meets the requirements
of the American National Standard for Permanence of
Paper for Printed Library Materials Z39.48-1984.

5 4 3 2

This book is dedicated to
Olusegun Obasanjo,
statesman, scholar, and patriot,
and to all the heroes and martyrs
for African peace, democracy, and social justice

CONTENTS

PREFACE

The inspiration for this project came from the realization that the end of the Cold War represented a watershed in how African states interacted with the world community and one another. By the early 1990s, it had become clear that domestic conflicts in some African states could spill over and cause problems for regional, even global, security. Outside actors appeared less and less interested in a close relationship with Africa and therefore could not be relied upon to act as third-party resources when conflicts became intense.

We recognize that there are a number of monographs that examine Africa's interstate politics with a discerning eye, but many of them have an outsider's perspective. What we attempt to do in this volume is adopt a more comprehensive approach, involving leading Africans and non-Africans in a dialogue on the implications of current changes, assessing how Africa's states and leaders are responding to their new reality, and pointing to possible alternative interpretations and strategies.

The book grew out of an international conference, "The End of the Cold War and the New African Political Order," held in 1994 at the University of California, Los Angeles, under the auspices of the James S. Coleman African Studies Center. Many individuals and organizations played critical roles in that successful conference. We are deeply indebted to the U.S. Institute of Peace and the University of California's Institute for Global Conflict and Cooperation for their generous grants in support of the undertaking; their backing made it possible for us to invite participants from all over the world.

In addition to those presenting papers, the other participants at the conference made an important contribution; these invitees included Ruth Iyob, Gwendolyn Mhlelela, Margaret Lee, William Cyrus Reed, Michael Lofchie, Richard L. Sklar, Guy Martin, Gerald J. Bender, Patricia Maselu, Georges Nzongola-Ntalaja, C. R. D. Halisi, Roy Pateman, and Lako Tongun. Muadi Mukenge, Alice Nabalamba, and their staffs earned our appreciation for the effective way they organized the conference. We also wish to

thank Barbara Thomas-Woolley and Lisa Sharlach for their helpful editorial work on the manuscript. Finally, we wish to express our gratitude to
Ethel Enoex for her tireless efforts on the final version of the manuscript.

Edmond J. Keller
Donald Rothchild

Introduction:
Toward a New African Political Order

EDMOND J. KELLER

At the dawn of the 1990s, the world was witnessing momentous changes. The Berlin Wall had collapsed, and Germany was united for the first time since the end of World War II. The Polish Solidarity Movement had used organized labor in a ten-year struggle to topple communism, and the people of Czechoslovakia had fashioned their own "velvet revolution." The late 1980s had been characterized by a "new thinking" in the Soviet Union, and by the end of that decade, Soviet communism had completely lost its moral power—not only abroad but at home as well. No outside observers were prepared for the rapid and complete manner in which the Soviet bloc was shattered: The world had come to assume unquestioningly that the Cold War would always be with us. However, almost overnight a unipolar world was created, a result of the fact that the United States and what was left of the former Soviet bloc had decided to cooperate rather than compete on the world stage.

Africa was not immune to these dramatic shifts in the world economic and political order. Around the same time that sea changes began to occur in the Eastern bloc, Africa was embroiled in economic and political crises. Poor governance and bad policy choices had, over the first three decades of African independence, created circumstances that had become unbearable to the citizens of many African countries, which led to the emergence of popular movements for political and economic reform.

Faced with a severe economic crisis, intensifying pressures from abroad for economic and political reform, escalating popular protest demanding an end to authoritarian and corrupt rulership, and the uncertain implications of the demise of the Cold War, African leaders were forced to ask soberly the questions: If the Cold War has ceased, what does this mean for Africa? Will there be a peace dividend that will enable Africa to recover from its debilitating economic crisis? Or will Africa simply be relegated to the dustbin of history? General Olusegun Obasanjo, former Nigerian Head of State and current Chairman of the Africa Leadership Forum, addresses this issue in Chapter 1.

Today it is generally assumed that we have entered an era in which a new international order is emerging. However, the question remains—where does Africa stand as a result of this transformation? To be sure, the two superpowers are no longer poised to launch mutually destructive nuclear attacks on each other's territory; nor do Russia and the United States now seek to undermine each other through surrogates in the Third World. But does this imply that there will be a peace dividend for the world at large, let alone for Africa? These and other related questions will be addressed in this volume. The contributors critically assess the bases for inter- and intrastate conflict in Africa; the past, present, and prospective modalities of conflict resolution; and the past, present, and possible future roles of external actors in African conflicts.

Given the end of the Cold War and the elimination of superpower competition for clients in the South, African nations are faced with challenges of epic proportions, not the least of which are the achievement of peace, security, development, and democracy. Whereas in the past the tendency was for African intellectuals to identify the source of their ills as external to the continent,[1] today there is a mood of introspection and a growing resolve to find African solutions to African problems. In their respective chapters, Ibrahim Gambari and Solomon Gomes flesh out the dimensions of this new thinking in Africa. The once sacrosanct concept of state sovereignty is now being reconsidered, and an effort is being made to clearly articulate new norms of external intervention where severe internal insecurity exists.

Also, there is now frank talk in the corridors of power in Africa and at the UN about the need to fight the trend toward the marginalization of Africa. In large measure, this looming marginalization is attributed to the new world order. Speaking of the 1992 annual meeting of the World Bank and the International Monetary Fund (IMF), one African delegate remarked, "This year's meeting was the first truly global meeting. . . . For the first time in history, there is no demarcation between East and West. What that means is that the focus is now being put on the incoming states [that is, countries such as Russia and Ukraine]." The delegate went on to caution, "If Africa is not careful, it is going to be marginalized."[2]

Rather than wringing their hands in despair, some African leaders have taken up the challenge. For example, at the Kampala forum in 1991, former Tanzanian president Julius Nyerere asserted, "Nobody can marginalize us if we don't want to marginalize ourselves. You can marginalize 500 million chickens, but how do you marginalize 500 million people?"[3] In a similar vein, Ugandan president Yoweri Museveni remarked in 1992, "A little neglect would not be bad. . . . The more orphaned we are, the better for Africa. We will have to rely on ourselves."[4]

In Chapter 1 Obasanjo contends, "The African situation is not a 'basket case,' rather, it is a 'calabash case.'" That is, there are sets of common problems relating to democracy, stability, development, and security that if approached in the traditional manner can be resolved through negotiations.

In order for Africa to successfully meet the challenges of the new order, it will first have to resolve its emerging "insecurity dilemma."[5] In the postcolonial era, Africa has generally been viewed by outsiders as an area that had no external threats and therefore no security dilemma. To the extent that security is considered a problem on the continent, it is generally viewed as a result of domestic conflict and regional insecurities.[6] Factors such as drought, famine, and internal wars have often led to human dislocations within African states as well as across their borders. Since 1960, Africa has witnessed more than a score of civil wars, and over the past decade between 2 million and 4 million people have died in such wars. In 1993 alone there were 5.2 million refugees and 13 million displaced persons in Africa. Domestic insecurity in Africa, then, has had an increasingly high propensity to spill over borders, resulting in new regional security dilemmas. For example, in a matter of weeks, the 1994 civil war in Rwanda resulted in 500,000 deaths, and more than 3 million refugees fled to Zaire and Tanzania. Until now, African states have dealt with these types of situations haphazardly and ineffectively. However, it is now clear that the new order requires a reassessment of the modalities employed by the African community of states in dealing with severe domestic conflicts that cause regional insecurity.

One of the main defining features of the new world order is the emergence or resurgence of nationalism among large ethnic groups that were previously incorporated into multiethnic states. This movement can be seen not only in the former Soviet Union and the former Yugoslavia but also in such countries as Ethiopia, Somalia, Sudan, and Rwanda. What is so important about contemporary domestic and regional conflicts in Africa is that they now have the tendency to become internationalized. The current conflicts in the Horn and Rwanda, for example, have created flows of refugees and armed combatants across national borders, catastrophic famine, and gross violations of human rights.

What were once thought to be mere domestic conflicts, out of the purview of international organizations such as the UN and regional organizations such as the Organization of African Unity (OAU), have now been internationalized. For example, as Terrence Lyons notes in Chapter 6, the United States spearheaded a move by the UN to support a referendum to decide the status of the former Italian colony of Eritrea, which had been embroiled in a thirty-year civil war. Anna Simons, in Chapter 5, cogently describes the creation of the myth of a Somali nation-state that was finally exposed with the collapse of the Somali state after a decade of civil war. In Chapter 7, Francis Deng and Khalid Medani trace the roles of the colonial heritage and the Cold War in bringing Sudan to the brink of partition. Robert Mortimer and Margaret Vogt, in Chapters 10 and 11, respectively, show how Liberia was thrown into chaos caused by internal conflict that ultimately affected the entire West African region. In each of these cases, external actors have been drawn into what were technically civil wars in order to restore peace and security.

The Colonial Legacy, the Cold War, and Africa

The Colonial Inheritance

Most of Africa's fifty-three states are multiethnic, artificial creations, largely the product of the European scramble for Africa in the late 1800s. The colonial powers divided the peoples in the territories they claimed according to administrative convenience rather than precolonial social or political arrangements. Consequently, during the colonial period, African peoples were thrown together with other ethnic groups with which they had had few, if any, prior relationships. For example, Ethiopia has as many as 70 distinct ethnic groups, Eritrea 9, and Tanzania 120! In each of these cases, the modern nation-state was cobbled together in the later years of the nineteenth century, without much attention paid by leadership to the creation of a sense of national political integration among disparate constituent ethnic groups. Similar patterns can be found in most other contemporary African states.[7]

The colonial powers organized their possessions into what looked like states, and following World War II, they began to encourage the creation of a fiction of multiethnic nations founded on the remnants of colonial states. During the struggle for independence, nationalist leaders readily accepted this fiction as the surest and quickest route to the demise of colonial rule.[8] The slogan in many places became "We must die as tribes so that we can be born as a nation."

Most African societies have come to accept the legitimacy of colonially created states, but in some instances, groups claiming the right to national self-determination have risen to challenge such arrangements. In some cases, ethnic groups claiming to be nationalities and questioning the legitimacy of their inclusion into a particular postcolonial nation-state have attempted to disengage from the state and to exercise their "exit option."[9]

Lyons and Simons describe such a case in their examinations of the irredentist movement of ethnic Somalis in Ethiopia, in which the Ogadeni Somali claim to be part of a historic Somali nation that was divided by colonialism. Lyons also describes the quest for national self-determination of the Oromo peoples, who claim to have been colonized by Imperial Ethiopia. Deng and Khalid describe the plight of the peoples of southern Sudan, who have been forced by an intransigent northern Islamic government to "sue for divorce." In such situations, severe domestic conflicts have grown into regional security dilemmas, or at least have the potential to do so.

The threat to regional security is sometimes a military one, but in Africa, regional insecurity can most often be traced to a wide variety of deprivations (e.g., famine, disease, and pestilence) stimulated by domestic conflict.[10] For example, drought and famine in Ethiopia in the mid-1980s created refugee flows across that country's borders with Kenya and Sudan.[11] If domestic problems spill over into a neighboring state and threaten the ability of that state to meet the basic needs of its own citizens, then the problem has been regionalized. The anarchy that has been raging in Somalia since 1990 and most recently the troubles in Rwanda are examples of such regionalization.

As is noted by William Zartman (Chapter 4), Gambari, and Gomes, Africa as a region has historically perceived a vested interest in maintaining the collective security of the continent and its various subregions and the national security of individual member states. The OAU was founded in 1963 specifically to provide a mechanism for the effective resolution of disputes and violations of the territorial integrity of member states. The assumption was that wars between states posed the most serious threat to national security. The principle of *uti possidetis juris* was adopted by the body, and it was asserted that the colonial boundaries inherited by individual states at independence would remain inviolable. This move was seen by most African leaders as a hedge against secessionism and irredentism; at the same time, it was an effort by the majority of the member states to avoid dealing directly with already existing disputes involving Algeria and Morocco, Somalia and Ethiopia, Somalia and Kenya, and Ethiopia and Eritrea.

What the signatories of the OAU charter apparently failed to realize was that during the course of modernization, structural inequalities rooted in the colonial past might serve to sharpen ethnic differences and thereby create the seeds for domestic conflicts that could become internationalized. These inequalities are clearly the basis for the civil conflicts in Liberia, Somalia, Ethiopia, and Sudan. Ethnically based grievances have coupled with the widespread availability of light weapons in the aftermath of the Cold War and have grown out of hand, turning into incidents of regional insecurity.

Cold War Effects

The Cold War competition between the superpowers greatly contributed to several of the incidents of militarily based regional conflict addressed in this volume. Jeffrey Lefebvre, Peter Schraeder, Lyons, and Simons clearly spell out the dynamics of this process. In the Conclusion, Donald Rothchild cogently maintains that the militarization of territorial disputes between Ethiopia and Somalia, the escalation of the Eritrean war of national liberation, and the proxy wars in Angola and Mozambique, coupled with destabilization efforts on the part of South Africa in Mozambique, Angola, and Namibia, were all directly connected to the Cold War competition of the superpowers on the continent.

Despite the historic roots of domestic and regional conflicts in Africa, a new dimension was added during the Cold War. For example, in the 1970s and 1980s, the superpowers were heavily involved in supporting clients in the Horn. Over a thirteen-year period, Soviet military assistance to Ethiopia is estimated to have been as high as $11 billion.[12] Following its break with Ethiopia in 1977, the U.S. President Jimmy Carter's administration embarked upon an "encirclement strategy," attempting to contain Soviet expansionism in the Horn and the Middle East by engaging in military alliances with Ethiopia's neighbors: Egypt, Sudan, Kenya, Somalia, and Oman. In addition to assisting these countries in upgrading their military facilities and capabilities, the United States engaged these countries in joint military exercises. The territories of U.S. clients in the Horn were used as a stage for the U.S. Rapid Deployment Force, which was designed to facilitate the efficient projection of U.S. military power into the Middle East and Persian Gulf.[13] These developments caused Soviet clients in the region, Ethiopia and South Yemen, to come together in a show of solidarity and to resolve jointly to repulse any efforts on the part of the United States or its proxies to intervene in their affairs. The resulting tensions did not abate until the Cold War began its meltdown in the mid-1980s.

In the process of pursuing what they considered their own vital interests, the superpowers contributed to an escalation of a regional arms race in the Horn. While the Soviets and the Americans jockeyed to check each other, the Ethiopians and Somalis tried to outfox each other. The negative consequences for regional security were momentous. The size of the Ethiopian armed forces grew from 54,000 in 1977 to more than 300,000 a decade later; by 1991, the Ethiopian army was estimated to be over 600,000 strong. Somalia's army swelled from about 32,000 in 1977 to 65,000 in 1987.[14] The growth of the military of Sudan was less dramatic, but in the 1980s, internal military activities grew significantly as the Ethiopian-supported Sudan People's Liberation Army was able to capture and control large portions of southern Sudan.

In the same period, Ethiopia's defense budget grew from $103 million to almost $472 million. Between 1977 and 1985, Somalia's defense expenditures rose from $36 million to $134 million, and Sudan's from $237 million to $478 million. This level and pattern of growth in military expenditures could not have taken place if the countries of the Horn had not been able to rely upon superpower patrons for ever increasing levels of military assistance.

Significantly, however, the desire for more and more arms on the part of the countries of the Horn seems to have been inspired primarily by internal conflict rather than by the need to protect the border zones of each country. As is noted in the chapters by Zartman and Simons, the devastating defeat of the Somali army and the irredentist Western Somali Liberation Front in the Ogaden War of 1977–1978 caused internal opposition to surface against Somali president Siad Barre. Over the next decade, the internal crisis escalated until the entire country was in turmoil. Amidst anarchy, the Barre regime was forced to abdicate in January 1991. Northern Somalia, which had been a British colony before uniting with formerly Italian Somaliland in 1960, broke away from the Republic of Somalia and formed the Somaliland Republic. The rest of the country was reduced to chaotic clan warfare. What was worse, the possible level of destruction was heightened tremendously by the availability of heavy and light arms and equipment left over from the largesse of the superpowers during the Cold War.

The 1980s also witnessed an increase in the capacity and efficiency of the Eritrean national liberation movement. After being routed by the Ethiopian army in the late 1970s, the Eritrean People's Liberation Army (EPLA) was able to regroup and by 1987 begin to make serious inroads toward liberating Eritrea from Ethiopian control. The success of the EPLA was enhanced by the fact that the Tigrean People's Liberation Front and the Ethiopian People's Democratic Movement formed a united front, the Ethiopian People's Revolutionary Democratic Front (EPRDF). By 1991 the EPRDF, operating inside the Ethiopian central highlands and with the logistical and tactical support of the EPLA, was able to capture huge tracts of territory and to demoralize the Ethiopian army. In May 1991, Ethiopia's president Mengistu Haile Mariam fled into exile, and his army of 600,000 collapsed. The EPRDF rebels were able to seize control of Ethiopia's capital, Addis Ababa, without significant resistance.

Whereas Ethiopia had become dependent on the Soviets for arms, ammunition, and equipment, both the EPLA and the EPRDF relied upon captured military hardware to fuel their efforts. In addition, when massive defections from the Ethiopian army began after 1989, the rebel groups expanded their ranks with these defectors.

By 1987 it was clear to the Soviets that it was unwise for Mengistu to continue to deal with the opposition with the military force. Following their humiliating withdrawal from Afghanistan, the Soviets began to rethink the viability of the Brezhnev Doctrine, designed to spread Soviet influence throughout the Third World. Instead, "New Thinking" advocated disengagement from military competition with the United States in the Third World and the promotion of political resolution of internal conflicts. The era of glasnost inaugurated by Soviet president Mikhail Gorbachev had a dramatic impact on Ethiopia's capacity to maintain its military program against its internal opponents. Gorbachev informed the Mengistu regime that his country would have to see both dramatic changes in Ethiopia's agricultural policies and political liberalization if good relations were to continue. He also refused to continue unqualified military and economic support for the Mengistu regime.

The result of these measures was that by the end of the 1980s, Ethiopia could no longer rely upon its superpower sponsor for the assistance it needed to repress internal opposition. Ultimately, the regime collapsed, and a power vacuum was averted as the forces of the EPRDF, with international political support, assumed power and prevented the country from falling into anarchy.

Rothchild notes that regional security in southern Africa had been a problem ever since the early 1960s, when wars of national liberation erupted in the Portuguese colonies of Angola and Mozambique, and since black opposition parties in South Africa such as the African National Congress (ANC) and the Pan-Africanist Congress (PAC) were banned and driven underground. For more than two decades, the Portuguese, with tacit support from NATO allies, doggedly attempted to hold on to their southern African colonies. Portugal's aims complemented those of South Africa, which feared that independent Angola and Mozambique might make it easier for black liberation movements to wage war on its own territory. However, by the early 1970s, the Portuguese populace and the military were tired of war. A military coup led to the independence of all Portuguese colonies in Africa in 1975.

Independent Angola and Mozambique quickly assumed active involvement in the Front Line States organization, formed to press for the complete independence of all countries in the region. Whereas throughout the 1960s, South Africa had periodically invaded or infiltrated its neighbors in an effort to undermine the planning and training of the armies of the ANC and PAC, after 1975, it projected its military into southern Angola and supported a destabilization campaign in Mozambique.[15] Its presence in Angola was largely an effort to crush the army of the Southwest African Peoples' Organization, which was fighting for the independence of Namibia, and to support the efforts of Jonas Savimbi's National Union for the Total Independence of Angola to overthrow the Marxist government in Luanda.

The net effect of South Africa's military activities to maintain domestic order and security was an exacerbation of regional insecurity, which did not let up until the international sanctions and disinvestment initiated in the mid-1980s against South Africa began to have their effect. These sanctions, coupled with enlightened white leadership in South Africa, led to a reduction in the country's attempts to destabilize neighboring countries.

With the end of the Cold War, the superpowers no longer are locked in potentially deadly military competition in Africa. Lefebvre, in Chapter 13, finds that Russia is seeking to promote trade and investment in Africa and at the same time maintain its credibility as a major world power. In Chapter 12, Schraeder observes a complementary shift in the United States' involvement in Africa. Military assistance is now being de-emphasized in favor of promoting good governance, democracy, and economic reform. In South Africa, the end of the Cold War gave impetus to the dismantling of apartheid, and a new South Africa is in the process of being built. In Chapter 8, Marina Ottaway describes how the threat to domestic and regional security represented in potential ethnic conflict in South Africa was minimized by a process of political pact making that resulted in majority rule and power sharing. In Chapter 9, Denis Venter provides insight into the implications that the newly emerging international and South African orders will have for regional security. He suggests that South Africa will become a highly engaged, positive force in African development both in the southern region and on the continent as a whole. Not only has South Africa taken a leadership role in creating a new regional security mechanism, it has joined in OAU and UN conflict prevention and resolution exercises.

Superpower competition in the Horn and southern Africa was accompanied by a general increase of external support for would-be opposition groups; this is clearly seen in the case of Liberia. The Liberian civil war was fueled by the repressive, autocratic, and corrupt regime of Samuel K. Doe, which by the mid-1980s had become ethnically based. In the process, groups other than Doe's Krahn and Mandingo were discriminated against and oppressed.[16] Liberian opposition forces were able to purchase arms on the international market and to utilize neighboring countries to launch their internal war. Eventually, the Economic Community of West African States (ECOWAS) Monitoring Group (ECOMOG) attempted to broker a cease-fire but quickly became a party to the conflict. By 1994, after almost five years, the situation had become somewhat stabilized. Vogt and Gambari both suggest that ECOMOG might provide a prototype of a future all-Africa peacekeeping force.

Even though France is not a superpower actor in the strictest sense of the word, it is a middle-range Western power with historical interests in Africa. Until recently, France has been extremely active in carving out a role for itself in Africa through its economic and military activities. Zartman notes that the disengagement of Great Britain and Belgium from Africa after the independence period left France by default the only European actor in the region willing to accept an interventionist role. In the early 1960s, France intervened to prop up regimes in Congo, Cameroon, Gabon, Mauritania, Niger, and Chad. However, the French military presence on the continent had dropped from 60,000 in 1960 to 5,000 in the late

1960s. Also, direct military intervention in African domestic and regional affairs became less common. However, one particularly bold and controversial intervention to remove an African head of state occurred in 1979 in the Central African Republic.[17]

In the 1970s and 1980s France extended its involvement beyond Francophone Africa. Sheldon Geller has argued that in part this was because France felt it had a historic mission to be the most active European power in Africa and also to counter the expansion of the two superpowers on the continent.[18] France has seemed most interested in maintaining political stability so as to protect French economic interests. These interests are one reason that France provided leadership in restoring order to Zaire's Shaba province in 1977 and 1978 and intervened in Chad to halt Libyan expansionism between 1977 and 1980.

After President François Mitterrand assumed office, France sharply curtailed its tendency to intervene militarily in African affairs. An exception was its 1990 intervention in Chad to check the advance of Libya once again, which resulted in a peace agreement leading to the withdrawal of all foreign troops from Chadian soil.[19] Ultimately, after losing its border dispute case before the International Court of Justice in 1994, Libya gave up its claim to the disputed territory in northern Chad.[20]

Since the end of the Cold War, there has been a significant shift in French policy toward Africa. France is now less interested in military intervention than it is in creating an enabling environment for liberalized economic policies. Therefore, France, at least in theory, now makes its foreign aid conditional on good governance practices and progress toward democratization.

The Challenge of the New African Order

The end of the Cold War and the simultaneous emergence of a new world order have profound implications for Africa. The international state system is now being forced to rethink the notion of state sovereignty and is being challenged to establish new rules to govern when and how international and regional organizations should intervene in domestic conflicts that have international implications. This challenge is also part and parcel of what can be termed the "new African order." Can we avert a future Somalia, Sudan, Liberia, or Rwanda? When ethnic and other forms of domestic conflict spill over borders, will Africa have the capacity to restore peace and order? Given the fact that the Cold War has ended, what role will there be for external actors such as the United States, Russia, or France in peacemaking, peacekeeping, and development in the new African order? Will there be a "Marshall Plan" for Africa? Or will Africa simply be put up for triage? It is certainly fair to ask what national interests the United States or Russia have in Africa today. Also, in light of contemporary realities, will the UN and the OAU redefine when and how they become involved in the settlement of severe internal conflicts with international or regional ramifications? Only when human rights are being violated? Should the norms of intervention be changed, or should the world community continue to look upon domestic disputes as being out of the domain of international and regional actors?

The answers to these and related questions are not yet clear. However, there is now much discussion about how issues raised here should be addressed. Traditional modalities for conflict management in Africa are being reexamined and new ones are being proposed.

Except for France, extra-African actors have generally shied away from unilateral intervention in modern Africa. The preferred mode of intervention by such actors has been through support of UN operations. The UN, like the OAU, has historically supported the idea of the inviolability of the national boundaries of African states that existed at the time of independence. However, interstate conflict is less a problem now than are severe internal conflicts, particularly those that bring states to the brink of collapse. The reality is that today, domestic conflict is the most serious threat to regional and national security, and it will continue to be in the foreseeable future.

Rothchild notes that sixteen of the thirty-five internal wars currently being waged throughout the world—with battle deaths exceeding 1,000 per year—are taking place in Africa. The Cold War is over, the superpowers are no longer there to step in to support one regional client or the other, and Africa is generally being left to its own devices.[21] To the extent that external intervention by non-African actors will continue, it will be mainly for humanitarian and economic reasons rather than for ideological ones. African leaders will seriously have to revisit such issues as state sovereignty and the norms of intervention by external actors.

The chapters in this volume make it abundantly clear that continuing armed conflicts in Somalia, Sudan, Liberia, and elsewhere make it necessary to find new ways of addressing both domestic and regional conflicts in Africa. New institutions have to be developed in order to avert such debilitating conflicts and to resolve them once they erupt. Such a realization is reinforced by the actions of the activist UN secretary-general Boutros Boutros-Ghali, who envisions a much more interventionist role for the UN, and by the visionary leadership of OAU secretary-general Salim Ahmed Salim.

In 1991, the Africa Leadership Forum, the OAU, and the UN Economic Commission for Africa jointly sponsored a historic conference in Kampala, Uganda. The final report of the gathering proposed the establishment of a permanent Conference on Security, Stability, Development and Cooperation and called for the establishment of a continental peace-keeping machinery and the drastic lowering of military expenditures by African states. This theme was picked up by OAU secretary-general Salim, and over the next three years, plans were made for the establishment of an OAU Conflict Management Mechanism. The Mechanism is now in place but faces enormous challenges in securing an appropriate level of funding and implementing its plans.

At its 1995 summit, the OAU made great strides on both fronts. First, the secretary-general threatened to cut off speaking and voting rights for the leaders of countries behind in their OAU dues, which resulted in the immediate infusion of some $20 million and prompted Salim to remark, "After six years in this job, for the first time I am very optimistic about the financial situation of this organization."[22] Second, the leaders in attendance, demonstrating a firm commitment to the Mechanism, agreed to place their armed services on standby for possible intervention in increasingly unstable Burundi. These actions were preceded by the inauguration of the Cairo Center for African Crisis Solving, which hosted a one-month training program for twenty-eight military officers from fourteen African countries on conflict prevention and management. A similar center is projected for Harare, Zimbabwe. Eventually, the OAU plans to create elements of a continental "rapid deployment force" based in these two hubs. Troops would be drawn from standing national armies and trained and deployed from either center. The force is expected to operate under the aegis of the UN.[23]

The primary objective of the Mechanism is said to be "the anticipation and prevention of conflicts." In situations where conflicts have occurred, the Mechanism is supposed to be responsible for undertaking peacemaking and peace-building activities. In cases of severe conflict, there is a provision for OAU cooperation with the UN.

The establishment of the Mechanism comes at a time when the UN and bilateral aid donors are looking to Africa to do more of its own problem solving. The United States, for example, is now working directly with the OAU as well as subregional organizations such as ECOWAS and the Inter-Governmental Authority on Drought and Development (IGADD) to develop and implement enhanced African peacekeeping and peacemaking capabilities. However, the question remains: Is Africa ready for new thinking and new norms with regard to issues of state sovereignty and the legitimacy of external intervention in what were heretofore considered essentially domestic problems?

The Mechanism is an ambitious project that is destined to face enormous difficulties. First, Africa contains fifty-three of the poorest countries in the world, many of which are characterized by unstable politics and food shortages. Their militaries are small, yet they already spend too much on military purposes. How, then, will they afford to participate in the Mechanism? Who will pay for the training and upkeep of the elite troops a nation must make available to the inter-African peacekeeping force? The second potential pitfall concerns state sovereignty and the norms of external intervention. Will the OAU secretary-general be able to assert the authority assigned to him when a crisis emerges? Although African leaders tend to agree that the Mechanism is needed, it is unclear what most of them would do if the Mechanism were to intervene in their own countries.

The challenges facing the architects of the new African order are enormous. Successful construction of this new order will require leadership with vision and substantial political will. This is Africa's only hope.

Notes

I would like to thank Donald Rothchild, Barbara Thomas-Woolley, and Kiron Skinner for their comments and helpful suggestions on an earlier version of this chapter.

1. See, for example, Emmanuel Hansen, ed., *Africa: Perspectives on Peace and Development* (London: Zed Books, 1987).

2. William Acworth, "African Delegates Resist Marginalization at World Bank, IMF Meeting," *AFRICA: NEWS,* September 28–October 11, 1992, p. 3.

3. Mwalimu Julius Nyerere, "Lessons from the Past," *Africa Forum* 1,3 (1991), p. 51.

4. Lance Morrow, "Africa: The Scramble for Existence," *Time,* September 7, 1992, p. 46.

5. See Brian L. Job, ed., *The Insecurity Dilemma: National Security of Third World States* (Boulder, Colo.: Lynne Rienner, 1992).

6. Robert H. Jackson, "The Security Dilemma in Africa," in Job, ed., *The Insecurity Dilemma,* p. 93.

7. See Crawford Young, "The African Colonial State and Its Political Legacy," in Donald Rothchild and Naomi Chazan, eds., *The Precarious Balance: State and Society in Africa* (Boulder, Colo.: Westview Press, 1988).

8. Basil Davidson, *Black Man's Burden: Nationalism and the Curse of the Nation-State in Africa* (New York: Random House, 1992).

9. See Rothchild and Chazan, eds., *The Precarious Balance;* and Albert O. Hirschman, *Exit, Voice and Loyalty* (Cambridge: Harvard University Press, 1970).

10. See Patrick Morgan, "The Study of Regional Conflicts: Preliminary Considerations and a Starting Point," in David Lake and Patrick Morgan, eds., *Regional Orders* (unpublished manuscript, 1994).

11. Edmond J. Keller, "Drought, War, and the Politics of Famine in Ethiopia and Eritrea," *The Journal of Modern African Studies* 30,4 (1992), pp. 609–624.

12. See Paul Henze, "Ethiopia in Transition," *Ethiopian Review,* July 1992.

13. Henry F. Jackson, *From the Congo to Soweto: U.S. Foreign Policy Toward Africa Since 1960* (New York: William Morrow, 1982).

14. International Institute for Strategic Studies, *The Military Balance,* vols. 1976/1977–1989/1990.

15. William Flannigan, *A Complicated War* (Berkeley: University of California Press, 1992).

16. Ted Robert Gurr, "Identifying Communal Groups," in T. R. Gurr, *Minorities at Risk* (Washington, D.C.: U.S. Institute of Peace, 1993), pp. 9–10.

17. See David R. Smock, ed., *Making War and Waging Peace: Foreign Intervention in Africa* (Washington, D.C.: U.S. Institute of Peace, 1993), p. 5.

18. Sheldon Geller, "All in the Family: France in Black Africa, 1958–1990," *Asian and African Studies* 26,2 (July 1992), p. 111.

19. Alain Rouvez, "French, British, and Belgian Military Involvement," in Smock, ed., *Making War and Waging Peace*, pp. 35–36.

20. *Facts on File* 54,2777 (February 17, 1994), p. 95.

21. Donald Rothchild, Chapter 14 in this book.

22. "Miracles Happen at OAU," *The Pretoria News,* June 24, 1995.

23. "OAU Discusses Rapid Deployment Force," *Agence France Presse,* Addis Ababa, June 27, 1995.

1

A Balance Sheet of the African Region and the Cold War

OLUSEGUN OBASANJO

The Cold War was characterized by uneasy peace, tension, and limited predictability in an international community dominated by rival nuclear superpowers and ideological and economic blocs; it took place from the end of World War II in 1945 until the dramatic political events in Eastern Europe of 1989–1990, culminating in the collapse of the Berlin Wall and the reunification of the two Germanies.

The Cold War was also characterized by political, ideological, and strategic confrontations between the superpowers and by a fissure between the East and the West. Allied with the United States were Canada, Japan, and the industrialized capitalist countries of Europe; all the countries of Eastern Europe, except perhaps Yugoslavia, were on the side of the Soviet Union. The superpowers' rivalry and pursuit of hegemony were structured on opposing political ideologies and included threats of military confrontation, an arms race, and a strategic balance of terror. The global polarization of the period was reflected in the existence of the North Atlantic Treaty Organization (NATO), grouping the Western alliance, and the Warsaw Pact, encamping the Eastern bloc.

On the economic front, the Soviet Union and the Socialist bloc vigorously promoted socialism through the Council for Mutual Economic Assistance, an umbrella organization for Eastern Europe. The United States and its Western allies promoted capitalism and the market economy with the Organization for Economic Cooperation and Development (OECD).

As the Cold War years advanced, growing inequalities between the industrialized nations of Europe and North America, on the one hand, and the underdeveloped countries of the Third World, on the other, introduced new tensions and new fears and added another dimension to the already tense international atmosphere. However, the inability of communism to reify its ideological exhortations brought about its eventual demise. In

15

effect, the end of the Cold War was a result of the crisis of one of its ideological pillars, that is, the crisis of communism.

Africa in the Cold War Era

In spite of the emergence of the Non-Aligned Movement in the 1950s,
most of the countries of the Third World, especially Africa, Asia, and Latin
America, did not escape the contagion of the superpower ideological polarization. Many of the nonaligned countries even had military cooperation
pacts with the superpowers or their allies and they were consequently involved in the arms race. Although the United States and Soviet Union were
not colonial powers in the classical sense in Africa, both countries largely
succeeded in carving for themselves spheres of influence by virtue of the
predominant roles they played ideologically and militarily in Africa. In
particular, the Soviet Union's economic and military assistance to Africa's
liberation struggles in the 1950s and the 1960s helped strengthen the ideological position of the East in Africa. The West, not wanting to be out-
done, encouraged even the most repressive government in the search for
allies and spheres of influence.

In a nutshell, the effects of Cold War politics on Africa were mixed. In
a positive sense, Cold War politics encouraged and assisted the course of
political emancipation from what was perceived as Western colonial domination. Cold War rivalry also impelled the superpowers and their allies to
provide competitive economic assistance for the newly independent
African states in the 1960s and 1970s. In a negative sense, the involvement
of the new states in superpower ideological politics aggravated their internal conflicts and encouraged instability. Furthermore, the readiness of the
superpowers and their allies to supply arms to Africa encouraged an un-
necessary arms buildup and diverted resources meant for development to
unproductive and wasteful ends.

At the continental level, most issues were seen through the prism of
the Cold War. Consequently, African states could not make objective decisions or reach consensus on issues vital to their interests. The division of
African states into Casablanca and Monrovia groups in the early 1960s, for
instance, was a result of the ideological polarization of African leaders at
that time along the East-West divide. Even when the Organization of
African Unity (OAU) was created in 1963, the congenial discord between
the two groups hindered the successful pursuit of such objectives as common and collective security, economic cooperation, and political union of
the continent. During the Cold War, even the most innocuous of conflicts
in Africa became seemingly intractable and protracted, often resulting in

wars of attrition or at best internecine conflicts. The only significant conflict that managed to escape Cold War meddling was the Nigerian civil war, in spite of efforts to the contrary by the superpowers. Evenhanded Nigerian leaders and the involvement of the OAU allowed Nigeria to resist superpower influence.

Whatever statistics are cited, Africa is a continent that is derelict, despondent, disillusioned, and detached from the rest of the world. In fact, I have had occasion to remark that the African coach of development has been delinked from the train of global development. Most socioeconomic indicators depict the continent as losing its shares in world trade and manufacturing, as its relative global proportions of such negative indices as poverty, infant and maternal mortality, and illiteracy are increasing. The most visible indices of Africa's increasing marginalization are its sharply declining shares in world exports, imports, foreign direct investment, and official development assistance. The persistent deterioration of Africa's terms of trade is also an index of relative regional deterioration.

Africa in the Post–Cold War Era

More than halfway through the 1990s, Africa's situation has become more precarious and the prospects for the future bleaker by the minute. Obviously, Africa cannot hope to usher in the twenty-first century as a more politically stable and economically viable region. And, as political analysts have warned, although the change from the Cold War psyche to a relaxed international environment promises a welcome alternative to the tension and confrontation of the past, the future harbors many unanswered questions and great unpredictability.

The political and economic restructuring that took place in the Soviet Union and the subsequent changes that swept through Eastern Europe have had worldwide political consequences, most significantly, the end of the Cold War, the end of superpower ideological and strategic confrontation, the dissolution of the Socialist bloc of Eastern Europe, the drastic slowing down of the arms race, and the high tide of prodemocracy and liberalization movements globally. In Africa, these consequences are manifest in the domain of conflict resolution, the renewed surge of prodemocracy agitations, and the general effects on the economic relations and prospects of African countries in the emerging world configuration.

The Soviet Union's decision to reorder its global priorities and redefine its commitments to its allies facilitated the resolution of a number of conflicts in Africa. For instance, the withdrawal of Soviet military aid and the evacuation of Cuban soldiers from Angola sped up the independence process in Namibia. Of course, this process was also encouraged by the political acumen and foresight of Namibia's leading political figures, who had opted for the adoption of a constitution that embodied, among other things, the principles of a multiparty system, a justifiable bill of rights, a free press, and a limited presidential tenure. Namibia achieved independence in a favorable international and domestic environment; so far it is a success story.

In South Africa, the withdrawal of the Soviet threat is partly responsible for the abolishment of apartheid and the establishment of the first democratic government. The "Mandela factor" is a result of a new thinking in South Africa, a reflection of global liberalization. The end of the protracted armed conflict in Ethiopia was brought about abruptly by the withdrawal of Soviet aid to the dictatorial Marxist government, and is indicative of the hollow base on which many dictatorial regimes in Africa rest.

One other significant result of recent world events on developments in Africa is the encouragement given to prodemocracy movements on the continent. The elimination of corrupt dictatorships and autocratic one-party systems and state structures, inefficient systems, and unresponsive social institutions in Eastern Europe provided moral encouragement to Africa's prodemocracy movements, which had been either suppressed or tagged subversive in the eyes of the outside world. The withdrawal of Soviet support from those regimes in Africa that camouflaged their dictatorship under the banner of socialism strengthened the ranks of existing prodemocracy movements on the continent and increased their chances of success.

Furthermore, the demise of communism not only helped expose those right-wing dictators in Africa who based their repressive rule on the premise of containing the spread of communism but made their further existence unjustifiable. The result is that in Africa today both the left-wing and right-wing dictators are being forced by popular pressure to accept a policy of democratization based on pluralism.

The changes in governance and political leadership in Africa previously described are indeed a welcome trend on the continent. Africa may be entering a new era in which its leaders will no longer choose to ignore the voices and the votes of their people and trample on their fundamental human rights. The present situation, if managed properly, may open the way to security and stability, which are indispensable for social and economic development.

Attractive as this trend may be, the vacuum created by the collapse of communism and consequently of Soviet influence in Africa may have damaged future developments in the region. With the socioeconomic inequalities characteristic of the capitalist system, the question arises whether, in the long term, a democratic welfarist model should provide a better, more sustainable solution to Africa's development problems. Put another way, does capitalism need the mitigating influence of the state to bring about humanism and humanness? Without such influence, the spread and continuity of capitalism may again produce the normal crisis of capitalism, which was what led to the emergence of socialism in Africa previously.

An obvious cause of unease in Africa is what is seen as an attempt by outside countries to impose Western democratic models lock, stock, and barrel on African countries as a condition for economic assistance. For democracy to endure, it must be home-induced, home-grown, and home-sustained. Africa has a tradition of some forms of democracy that should not be completely discarded, since a single model may not be applicable to all societies. Moreover, the democratization process might take more time in some countries than in others. For democracy to flourish, all concerned will need to be patient and tolerant and take into account Africa's particular history and culture. The swapping of ideologies is not sufficient to provide relief for Africa; democracy and poverty are strange bedfellows. Conflict resolution and democratic reform will be fragile and inconclusive unless they are matched by resources to accelerate economic growth and enhance human development in Africa.

Although the elimination of apartheid in South Africa, the achievement of self-government in Namibia, and the enthronement of democracy in Malawi and Benin can, in part, be attributed to the demise of the Cold War, the attribution is only somewhat accurate. These positive developments are due to the tenacity of purpose, unwavering commitment, and perseverance of prodemocracy groups in each of these countries, as well as to the military's refusal to unquestionably support autocratic civilian regimes or intervene on its own behalf in political matters.

Although we may talk about the end of the Cold War in the East and the West, for us in Africa the Cold War is not fully over. We are still left holding on to the debris of the war; with little means of support, we have a long, arduous task of reconstruction, rehabilitation, and reconciliation. In addition, we are even blamed and condemned for the ills of the war that have become our lot. The conditions in Angola, Somalia, Mozambique, Zaire, and Liberia, to mention a few, are all part of the legacy of the Cold War era, as is the common practice, until recently, of autocratic African leaders being able to rely on the support of external patrons to indefinitely prolong their rule.

Present socioeconomic indicators underscore the marginalized status to which Africa has been reduced, particularly within the last decade. More than any other factor, the nondemocratic and autocratic nature of most regimes in Africa has undermined the continent's potential and opportunity for sustainable economic development and growth. Africa's global economic prospects do not appear bright under the emerging world order. From the late 1990s to the opening decades of the twenty-first century, the world economy will become more and more competitive, with the emergence of economic blocs and trade zones. The European Union promises to provide opportunities for increased trade between Africa and Europe, the whole of Europe will become a great economic market, and exchanges between East and West will increase considerably.

But the opportunities will not be handed to Africa; to be able to partake in the expanding trade environment, African states must carry out radical reforms in their economies that are in tune with the current politico-economic strategy. Accompanying the new economic order is a new political thinking, the objective of which is the complete dismantling of all authoritarian regimes in Africa. The released energies from the political and economic renewal process on the continent must be channeled into productive forces at all levels in order to revive and sustain the present tottering economy.

To appreciate the magnitude of the challenges that African states face under the emerging world economic system, one must realize that the dynamics of the global economy tend to operate against Africa's development plans. The current political events in Europe provide an example.

The dissolution of Eastern Europe as a socialist bloc, and the attendant radical political transformation that followed, has attracted the attention and the economic interest of the West and has opened the way for massive investment opportunities in those countries, seemingly at the expense of the poorer and needier countries of Africa. It is true that Eastern European countries provide a better investment environment for the West than Africa and that these countries have put forward a host of incentives to attract foreign investors, incentives African states are not in a position to offer. Moreover, the West could justify these massive resource flows to the East on the grounds of the need to rescue Eastern Europe from communist domination.

The marginalization and the precarious socioeconomic conditions of Africa predate recent events in Europe, yet Africa has never enjoyed similar relief packages from the West. Not only is the increase of resource flows to Eastern Europe remarkable and unprecedented, its magnitude rivals that of the Marshall Plan. The establishment of the European Reconstruction and Development Bank (ERDB) for the rapid modernization of Eastern European economies institutionalized and crowned the appropriation of development finance.

For Africa, resource diversion has now become a naked and troublesome necessity. Hitherto, resource flows to Africa came only in trickles. With the recent developments in Europe and overwhelmingly favorable conditions elsewhere, the inevitable question is whether this meager flow will continue. On the economic front, Africa has been identified as the only regional loser in the December 1993 Uruguay Round of the General Agreement on Tariffs and Trade (GATT); in its wake the continent faces a likely increase of imported food prices, loss of preferential advantage, stiff competition in the field of banking and services, and loss of bioproperty rights. According to a September 1993 publication of the OECD/World Bank, net annual losses for Africa will be about $2.6 billion by the year 2000. Meanwhile, within the same period, the leading industrialized countries stand to gain about 64 percent of total annual income gains from GATT, which amounts to $135 billion. What is more, the Multi-Fibre Textile Agreement, which could have enhanced African textile exports, was excluded from the GATT talks.

Since the commencement of the 1990s, African economies have grown by only a miserable 1.5 percent per annum, which is worse than the rate of growth in the 1980s, a period that has been described as a "lost decade." Whereas Africa's share of official development assistance (ODA) fell from 37.1 percent in 1990 to 36.3 percent, the ODA share of Eastern Europe and the former Soviet Union rose from 1.4 percent to over 7 percent. Sub-Saharan African (SSA) debt is simultaneously on the increase: Total SSA debt in 1980 was $84 billion, in 1992 it was $194,264 billion, and in 1993 it was estimated at $199,046 billion, in spite of some African countries' great efforts to service their debt.

The integration of the European Union (EU), embracing the enormous economic potential of united Germany, risks diverting from Africa the attention of big investors from North America, Europe, and Asia. What is more, an enlarged, strong, and integrated Europe could give rise to Eurocentrism and lead to a protectionist Europe, which in terms of trade relations may create problems for the African, Caribbean, and Pacific group (ACP) countries. Even now, the ACP countries face declining trade possibilities as a result of ad hoc preferences granted to products from Eastern European countries irrespective of any guidelines from the Lomé agreements between the EU and the ACP countries. To compete successfully in the European market, the ACP countries, particularly Africa, have to establish democratic regimes and present a certificate of complete free enterprise, as part of a new set of stringent conditions for the Lomé Convention.

Africa stands to lose relative to Eastern Europe in several other ways. Future ODA flows commensurate to the challenges of Africa are unlikely to be provided as Eastern Europe makes increasing claims on the resources of international financial and development institutions. The volume of resources available for rescheduling, reduction, or outright debt forgiveness for African countries will shrink. The best brains in Western government, multinational and medium-sized corporations, and banks will be assigned to programs and projects in Eastern Europe. Political and media attention and concern will be diverted from the Third World, particularly Africa, to Eastern Europe.

Even at the global level, African countries face the threat of economic isolation. The emergence of regional economic blocs in many parts of the world—Europe, North America, Asia Pacific, and the Middle East—may leave Africa isolated in the new global economic configuration. Under the circumstances, self-reliance and rapid physical and economic integration of the African continent are indispensable to its economic survival in the 1990s.

A Framework for Progress

History is replete with the rise and fall of peoples, nations, kingdoms, and empires. What Africa needs is to make conscious efforts to redress the distressing and depressing present situation and outlive its inabilities. New initiatives are needed to achieve effective political and economic restructuring of society. Responsive and effective governance is required to motivate economic growth, promote human development, and revive the international community's dwindling interest in Africa's development efforts. These goals can be achieved only in an atmosphere of peace, security, stability, cooperation, and development.

In search for a meaningful solution to their problems, African states now, fortunately, have a set of interrelated preconditions that, when instituted and institutionalized, would meet the aspirations of their people for responsive governance and development and would also elicit the cooperation and support of the international community.

In May 1991, participants from Africa converged in Kampala, Uganda, for the Conference on Security, Stability, Development and Cooperation in Africa (CSSDCA). The Kampala Document, which was the outcome of those deliberations, stipulated that peace, security, and stability are the preconditions and the basis for development and cooperation in Africa. The security, stability, and development of African states are inseparably linked; the erosion of security and stability is one of the major causes of the continuing crises on the continent and one of its principal impediments to economic growth and human development.

The Kampala Document further noted that peace constitutes the basis of all wholesome human interaction and with peace should go security. Lack of democracy, denial of personal liberty, and abuse of human rights are the causes of insecurity. The concept of security transcends military considerations. On the one hand, it includes conflict prevention, containment, and resolution and derives from common and collective continental security. On the other hand, it embraces all aspects of the society, including economic, political, and social dimensions of the individual, family, community, and local and national life. The security of a nation must be construed in terms of the security of the individual citizen not only to live in peace but also to have access to the basic necessities of life, participate in freedom in the affairs of society, and enjoy fundamental human rights.

The issue of stability is just as important to development; therefore, promoting political and social stability in individual African countries is the key component of the CSSDCA process. Under the stability guidelines, all African states are to be guided by strict adherence to the rule of law, popular participation in governance, respect for human rights, and fundamental freedoms; political organizations should not be based on religious, ethnic, regional, or racial considerations; and there should be clarity in public policymaking and an absence of fundamentalism in religious practice.

For the purpose of economic development, African states are to subscribe to certain fundamental principles under the CSSDCA process. Development based on self-reliance is the only viable foundation for Africa's self-sustaining economic development and growth. One of the major causes of Africa's present economic crisis is its reliance and dependence on commodity production solely for export. The time has come for effective diversification, both horizontally in terms of broadening the production base and vertically in terms of processing and marketing for rapid social and economic transformation.

Popular participation and equal opportunity and access must be promoted and sustained to realize Africa's development objectives and to create a truly people-centered development effort. Domestic partnership in development should be promoted; leaders and citizens should assume responsibilities for various aspects of it; and leaders should provide the vision that guides it.

The Kampala Document also provides a framework for collective action and for cooperation on a continental, regional, and international basis: It specifies cooperation between African states, especially among southern countries and also among northern and southern countries; economic integration of African states in the African Economic Community; joint cooperative relations with other developing and industrialized nations; and supernationality based on the need to devolve certain responsibilities to continental institutions.

The CSSDCA process has thus charted an invaluable course and framework for Africa's development based on self-reliance, effective and responsive governance, regional integration, and international cooperation.

Integration and cooperation are to be guided by some basic common policy measures. If orthodox technical cooperation has not yielded satisfactory results for both donors and recipients, and if projects like the UN Program of Action for Africa's Economic Recovery and Development have made very little impact because of a lack of support for Africa's reform efforts, a new agreement should be drawn up. This agreement should challenge and satisfy both sides through setting targets and objectives and through monitoring results, involving donor agencies and the private sector in the donor countries as well as nongovernmental organizations and the government in the recipient countries.

At the same time, Africa's leaders should try to enhance endogenous institutional capacity, beginning with cooperation in ensuring communal efforts, peace, and security within the locality, the nation, at subregional and regional levels, and to motivate incentives for development and increased assistance.

Conclusion

The debt problem in Africa is not only a financial problem, it is also a developmental and management problem. The solution must be all-embracing, involving debt relief, capacity building, democratization, accountability, and the institution of sustainable, sound policies that will be executed with commitment. The African situation is not a "basket case," rather, it is a "calabash case." That is, instead of considering Africa a lost cause, Africa's leaders should view Africa's predicament as a challenge in the traditional manner and cooperate to find solutions to common problems, drawing assets from the community's calabash, so to speak.

Although the United States and its Western allies can rejoice in the demise of communism and the enthronement of market economy, Africans have become the Cold War's victims, just as Africa was its pawn. The turn of events since the end of the Cold War suggests that Africa has been discarded like banana peels. As extreme as it sounds, this is the reality of the African situation.

At the end of any war, peace is supposed to reign and with it comes the peace dividends. Whatever dividends are available in the post–Cold War global system seem to be passing Africa by. After any war, the processes of reconstruction, rehabilitation, reconciliation, and redevelopment are usually pursued, all of which require enormous resources. In most cases, the magnitude of the resources required far outstrips the resources expended on the war itself.

Africa, with dwindling resources in world trade and a crushing debt, is facing serious reductions of aid and other forms of assistance. To these problems must be added the projected losses from the Uruguay Round of GATT and the continuous losses from intranational conflicts and instability, most of which are direct products of the Cold War. Perhaps it is necessary to ask ourselves if the war has really ended for Africa. If so, how and when will the process of rehabilitation and reconstruction start? If the Cold War has not ended in Africa, then it is incumbent on Africa and the international community to bring about its end by way of the effective and sustained cooperation and collaboration that the CSSDCA process provides.

Although the West may talk of the end of the Cold War, the reality is quite different in Africa. If, by accident or design, another bipolar world emerges, an Africa neglected by the West could well become the soft underbelly for a renewed onslaught.

PART 1

Perspectives on Regional and Global Security Issues

2

The Role of Regional and Global Organizations in Addressing Africa's Security Issues

IBRAHIM A. GAMBARI

There are, at present, conflicts in six African countries—Rwanda, Burundi, Angola, Somalia, Liberia, and Western Sahara—on the active agenda of the UN Security Council, more than any other continent. Furthermore, Sudan and the perennial Togo-Ghana conflicts may be prime candidates for consideration by that world body. This unfortunate situation, along with the deteriorating socioeconomic condition of the continent, poses serious challenges for scholars and policymakers alike. Under present circumstances, what will Africa's role be in a changing world order? Will Africa be able to take charge of its own destiny, or will it remain a tedious subject of international concern? How should we address Africa's security issues? Finally, would the efforts to address and resolve African conflicts detract from the need to address the socioeconomic problems that are the root causes of these conflicts?

We are at the end of an era. Although the contours of a new world order have yet to clearly emerge, the elements of a new world disorder are already appearing. In this context, Africa has the dual capacity to play a role in the definition, design, and defense of a new world order and to be a beneficiary of such an order. In other words, Africa is likely to be both part of the solution and part of the problem of international security. This chapter attempts to discern the new order's direction, its configuration, and its likely implications for Africa.

The Specter of Africa's Marginalization

The specter of Africa being further marginalized on the world's political and economic scene became an issue of debate at the end of the Cold War

29

because Africa feared that world attention was being disproportionately drawn to the newly democratizing states of Eastern Europe at its expense. As a result, Africa thought that unless the international community gave the continent its share of interest, attention, and support, its fate in the post–Cold War era would be worse than it was during the Cold War period.

Thus, except for the international attention drawn to Somalia, superpower interest in Africa's political and economic problems has never been so minimal, and the flow of aid and other resource assistance to Africa from the industrialized countries has never been so paltry. Apparently more preoccupied with the ongoing economic restructuring efforts in Eastern Europe and the Commonwealth of Independent States (CIS), Boutros Boutros-Ghali observed, before he became UN Secretary-General, that virtually no place was left in the post–Cold War era "for the Third World and Africa, except where humanitarian aid is concerned."[1] In contrast to its apparent neglect of Africa, the West showed its level of concern for the East when in April 1991 it announced a $24 billion package of assistance to Russia, in addition to its earlier pledge to the CIS of $80 billion. This generosity also contrasted with the West's neglect to answer Africa's requests for assistance to implement such programs as the UN Program for Action for African Economic Recovery and Development and the New Agenda for African Development. Indeed, the West's annual commitment to the whole of Africa at the end of the 1980s was only $3.4 billion. As Gehbray Berhane, secretary-general of African, Caribbean, and Pacific grouping of signatories to the Lomé Convention, observed, "West Europe is devoting more and more resources to promote not only industry and agriculture in Eastern Europe and the CIS, but also technical assistance and institution building and there is less emphasis on these things for Africa. In general, the West's preoccupation with the problems of Eastern Europe is at the expense of its African relations."[2]

Africa's development prospects are constrained not only by the comparative shortfall in assistance from the West but also by the virtual drying up of assistance, however meager it was, from the former Eastern bloc countries. The situation is made worse now that Russia and other key Eastern European countries, which had always given assistance to their African allies, are in fact exerting pressure on these countries to pay up their debt to them.

The specter of marginalization also has profound implications for Africa's continuing role in the global system. There are real signs that unless African states become democratic, the continent could become even more isolated by the international community. Presently, undemocratic regimes run by dictators during the Cold War era have already either collapsed or hastily begun to prepare to install democratic governments in their countries. The fact that some industrialized countries are now introducing new political conditions to their grants of aid and assistance adds an interesting dimension to the new political processes in Africa and the evolving role that the continent will play in the international system.

The emerging new world order, by de-emphasizing the import of ideology in international relations, has, indeed, produced beneficial results: It facilitated the independence of Namibia in 1990, enhanced the prospects of peace in Angola and Mozambique, and ensured that apartheid in South Africa had become a thing of the past. However, since the end of rivalry between the major powers has brought with it the virtual cessation of their meaningful interest in the continent, Africa's geostrategic and political relevance in the global political system has been undermined. In the Cold War era, Liberia, Ethiopia, and Somalia occupied strategic importance in Africa—Liberia was one of the United States' most important listening posts in the Western Hemisphere; Ethiopia and Somalia alternated as strategic military intelligence–gathering posts for both the Soviet Union and the United States. The power vacuum created after the Cold War accounts partly for the subsequent anarchy and civil war in these countries.

The degree of Africa's current economic and political marginalization can to some extent be gauged by the continent's reinterpretation of sovereignty. In the preceding international order, especially during the decades immediately following Africa's independence, the legacies of centuries of colonialism fostered a rigid and uncompromising attachment to the principle of the sovereign right of nations, not only by African states but even by the erstwhile colonial powers. Presently, however, with the breakdown of law and order in several African states that has led to interventions by multilateral military and humanitarian forces, "the cruel calculus of sovereignty versus misery has changed the way the international community thinks about foreign intervention and the rights of states."[3] Perhaps this could not have been otherwise considering the intervention of the Economic Community of West African States (ECOWAS) Monitoring Group (ECOMOG) in Liberia and of massive U.S. troops in Somalia. It is doubtful that these interventions would have received international support without the change in African policy, which now seems ready to make some qualifications to the principle of the sovereign right of nations. As Fouad Ajami has said, "In the face of an absolutist doctrine of the rights of nations, there is now a tentative right to interfere. Man cannot eat sovereignty, we have learned; the order within nations is just as important as that among them."[4]

Strategies for Enhancing Africa's Global Position

In the aftermath of the Gulf War, it was former U.S. president George Bush who evoked the notion of a new world order, referring to a more civil world where there is expanded respect among the nations for the rule of law. Looking back with some irony at this historic pronouncement, it is clear that the implicit vision of a Pax Americana, as opposed to, say, a Pax Universalis, is at best still a work in progress.

Clearly, we are all in need of a collective and coherently structured new order to manage this increasingly complex world. Initially, the preeminence of the United States was thought to be the natural replacement for the old order, a logical extension of its role as the global policeman; but this has not turned out to be the case. The United States' withdrawal from Somalia in March 1994 and the general redefinition of its role in UN peacekeeping efforts have cast doubts on U.S. political will in the world today.

The competing vision is the Pax Universalis, or the UN vision of a new world order, with a truly functioning collective security system in which international law would be applied impartially to all nations and members would collectively punish acts of aggression. War prevention, settlement of disputes, international peacekeeping, and protection of human rights and basic freedoms would constitute the basic elements of this vision. Unfortunately, the reality is increasingly running at cross-purposes with this overarching vision. Indeed, the fragmentation of some former member states of the UN into increasingly smaller ethnic constituents reinforces the sometimes violent assertions of national sovereignty and interests that we see in parts of Eastern Europe and elsewhere. The immediate challenge is to establish common structures and mechanisms for integrating all concerned parties, to mediate conflicts under uniform rules and agreed sanctions, and, in some cases, to try to put collapsed states back together.

We in Africa prefer the global perspective of a new world order. The UN is, or should be, the organization within which African states can pursue their own agenda, contribute to international peace and security, and defend by peaceful means their own independence and territorial integrity. The end of the Cold War has driven us further into the arms of the UN as a means to escape total marginalization in world politics and international economic relations.

It is to Africa's credit that it has—with the recent exception of Eritrea—more or less managed to preserve its colonially inspired boundaries without breaking into numerous full-blown secessionist wars like those now occurring in much of Eastern Europe. But this fact should not be too loudly applauded, because in roughly thirty years, Africa has experienced some sixty coups d'état and countless coup attempts. Major civil wars have erupted in more than ten countries and quite a few are still heavily raging. Fifteen separate border disputes involving thirty countries developed into military confrontations, and tension still exists on certain borders.

Ten countries have been subjected to external military interventions or direct involvement of external forces in attacks against them. The continent remains a fertile ground for mercenaries and an object of external security manipulations.

Many African countries presently lack the capacity to curb the flow of unauthorized arms into their countries or to deter any infiltration of armed groups across their borders. The majority of African countries simply lack the capacity to deal with any large-scale security crisis, whether domestic or external, without the direct support of foreign military forces. Part of Africa's security problems can be attributed to the ingrained psychology of a generation of rulers who protected their rulership at all costs within the artificial boundaries created by former colonial powers. In Europe, the breakup of the Roman Empire triggered centuries of successive continental and global conflicts involving nationality claims and sharp ideological divisions; this redefined Europe's concept of security as the delineation of defensible and secure borders under shifting security alliances. But Africa's experience has been different. To a large extent, Africa copied the structures of European security without the benefit of similar experiences or clearly defined security needs.

Redefining the Concept of African Security

At the national and continental levels, African security should be considered beyond the bounds of traditional maintenance of military strength to ward off aggression against the state or the expansion of an apparatus of internal security to ensure domestic order. Today, it would be grossly erroneous for African nations to assume that security came solely from military power and secure geographical borders.

Because the physical security of a state is not synonymous with the security of its peoples Africa must find new and creative ways to resolve the conflicts between topography and demography. The answers are sure to be situated within the larger framework of socioeconomic development and not necessarily in the militarism and internal security mechanism that are now the norm. In recent times, Africa has reappraised its security issues, essentially moving away from narrow definitions to broader geopolitical considerations.

Since the 1992 Organization of African Unity (OAU) Summit of African Heads of State and Government in Dakar, Senegal, acknowledged in its communiqué that "there is a link between security, stability, development and cooperation in Africa," there have been many thoughtful and important documents on the subject. One major effort is the Kampala Document, jointly put out by the secretariats of the OAU, the UN Economic Commission for Africa, and the Africa Leadership Forum. The Kampala Document states:

> The concept of security goes beyond military consideration. It embraces all aspects of the society including economic, political and social dimensions of individual, family, community, local and national life. The security of a nation must be construed in terms of the security of the individual citizen to live in peace with access to basic necessities of life while fully participating in the affairs of his/her society in freedom and enjoying all fundamental human rights.[5]

In addition the document offers some useful principles that can form the basis of new ideas of addressing African Security issues:

(a) conflict prevention and containment: greater attention should be paid to measures to prevent or contain crises before they erupt into violent confrontations;

(b) internal and external security for Africa must derive from a framework of common and collective continental security;

(c) African governments must individually and collectively be guided by the principle of good neighborliness and a peaceful resolution of conflicts;

(d) national and continental self-reliance in certain strategic areas covering both military and non-military, including popular participation in national defense, is vital for Africa's security.[6]

To be able to meet these challenges, it is clear that new institutions, mechanisms, and instruments must be put in place both regionally in Africa and globally. In this new thinking, the United Nations should be entrusted with two main tasks: establishing and managing a reliable system of collective and universal security that comprises peacemaking, peacekeeping, and enforcement; and working toward a system of collective economic security, including sustainable growth and development.

This proposed collective security structure will have to monitor developments permanently; preempt, prevent, or contain conflicts; mediate disputes; assure the protection of small and weak states; and deal authoritatively and decisively with aggressors. No longer should international action be taken only when a situation is a threat to the interests of the most powerful nations or their friends and allies.

Developments in the UN are encouraging: Nigeria was elected and served as a nonpermanent member of the Security Council and has signaled its intentions for full and permanent membership whenever the issue comes up for serious consideration by the General Assembly. Africa must struggle to make the Security Council's work more transparent and representative, and, thus, its decisions more legitimate.

On a regional level, the OAU must be charged with the responsibility of putting into place new methods for dealing with old problems. Although the low secession rate of African nations is a sign that most states prefer to maintain their inherited boundaries, serious consideration must be given to redefining Article 11, paragraph 3 of the OAU charter, which says that members solemnly affirm and declare their adherence to "respect the sovereignty and territorial integrity of each State."

An idea worthy of consideration is the creation of a security council, similar to that of the UN, for the OAU. This supraexecutive body would have the authority to make decisions that are binding on member states, especially in continental security matters, and, in tandem with an African High Command, could possibly be a viable mechanism for dealing with African security issues in the next century.

Conclusion

African states, although largely impoverished and beset by all kinds of natural and manmade upheavals, have continued to pursue their respective national and regional interests within the UN. Despite occasional deviations, these nations have remained largely cohesive, an achievement given the small size and perilous financial situation of most African states. Africa's permanent representation in the UN Security Council is under active consideration at the highest political level, that is, at the Summit Conferences of the OAU. It is essential that a continent that accounts for roughly one-third of the UN's membership be permanently represented in the most powerful chamber. Nigeria, along with other like-minded states, is now addressing this issue in a more systematic and formal manner.

Africa is at a crossroads in the emerging new world order. The deideologization of international politics and the consequent rapprochement between the two superpowers are likely to have both positive and negative consequences for Africa, which should work to enhance the positive and minimize the negative factors. Similarly, the democratization and liberalization of the politics of many of the world's regions may have a demonstrative effect, but this is likely to take the form of social upheavals and political instability.

Africa's ability to attract Western capital and development assistance may be hindered, at least in the short run, if the CIS and Russia continue to open up their markets and liberalize their economies. Nevertheless, Africa's abundance of natural resources holds out a small hope for a reversal of this trend in the long run.

All of these factors might have implications for Africa's ability to play a befitting role in the UN, the world's most important multilateral forum.

Good leadership, creative and imaginative policies, and international cooperation can, however, stem Africa's current crises that threaten the continent with political isolation and further socioeconomic marginalization. Ultimately, Africa's fate, and the future of its people, is in Africa's own hands.

That is why the ratification of the treaty establishing the African Economic Community and the OAU Mechanism for Conflict Prevention, Management and Resolution are very important steps in promoting collective self-determination in the economic and security spheres. Their success and the role of subregional organizations such as ECOWAS in conflict resolution in Liberia are likely to encourage the UN and the international community as a whole to supplement and complement Africa's own efforts to address the continent's development and security issues. This would be in line with the prospects of cooperation between regional organizations and the UN in the context of secretary-general Boutros Boutros-Ghali's *Agenda for Peace,* as well as his closely related *Agenda for Development.*

Notes

1. Cited in Tim Wa, "Soviet Demise brings Africa New Challenges," *Africa Recovery,* April 1992, p. 14.

2. Wa, "Soviet Demise," p. 14.

3. Fouad Ajami, "Somalis: The work of order and mercy," *U.S. News and World Report,* December 21, 1992, p. 25.

4. Ajami, "Somalis," p. 25.

5. African Leadership Forum, *The Kampala Document: Towards a Conference on Security, Stability, Development and Cooperation* (New York: African Leadership Forum, 1992), p. 9.

6. African Leadership Forum, *The Kampala Document,* pp. 9–10.

3
The OAU, State Sovereignty, and Regional Security

SOLOMON GOMES

The Organization of African Unity (OAU) was created in 1963 to promote the unity and solidarity of its member states. In order to achieve this objective, the member states pledged to adhere to certain principles and international legal norms, which are outlined in the charter of the organization. In accepting the principles of sovereign equality and noninterference in the internal affairs of other states, the member states have more or less demarcated a common ground for collective action.

The OAU was the result of political compromise between the Casablanca Group, the Monrovia Group, and the Brazzaville Conference. Founded as it was at the height of the Cold War, the OAU adopted those principles that would ensure harmony, cooperation, nonalignment with respect to the Cold War ideological blocs, and, most particularly, the emancipation of all colonial territories in Africa.

The OAU emerged, therefore, as the champion of liberation from colonial and racist rule in Africa and also as an advocate for African cooperation, solidarity, and unity. The international milieu of the 1960s and 1970s affected the OAU's ability to pursue the purposes for which it was founded. As an organization of sovereign states with no enforcement machinery, dominant state or group of states, the OAU could not deter the effects of the Cold War on the continent.

The principles of the charter reflect the preoccupations of Africa at that time, and there is no doubt that the charter needs to be amended, especially in light of the changing circumstances in the international system. As a matter of fact, the Assembly of African Heads of State and Government established a Charter Review Committee in 1979 charged with the task of amending the charter. This committee has not made any progress because it has been hampered by a variety of factors, foremost of which is the political, as opposed to the legal, approach taken by some of its

37

members. The level and quality of representation has transformed this committee into a political discussion group.

In the thirty years of its existence, the OAU has had some successes and failures. Both the liberation of many colonial territories and the establishment of subregional economic groupings in western, eastern, central, southern, and, to some extent, northern Africa can be attributed to the organization.

The OAU has had several failures, ranging from an inability to prevent, manage, and resolve conflict and violence to a tendency to keep silent over some violations of human rights. The causes of these failures can be found in the colonial past of Africa and also in the absence of a strong commitment to democratic government, interstate cooperation, and African unity. Africa's proclivity to depend on the former colonial powers—Britain, France, and Belgium and also the rest of the Western industrialized nations—is an impediment to its self-reliance.

Can a new African political order emerge? What should the OAU do to bring this about? What should the individual African states do? More important, what should the African people do?

Initially, it was colonialism that denied the African people their basic freedoms. An offshoot of nineteenth-century European imperialism, it was oppressive in design and racist in outlook. Colonialism was anchored on the policy of "divide and rule" and on the mistaken belief that the Europeans had a moral mission of civilizing the Africans. As a system of rule, it selected and favored some Africans whom it wanted to become black Europeans, immersing them in European history, literature, philosophy, culture, politics, and, most especially, European social value systems.

The divide and rule policy was the antithesis of the democratic tradition that nineteenth- and twentieth-century Europe enjoyed. It advanced the idea of a distinction between and within colonial territories in the so-called colony areas and the protectorates, and between the European and the African.

The imposition of alien rule manifested itself very early on and resulted in what David B. Abernethy described as a system of multiple relationships of dominance and subordination between the European and African spheres, as well as multiple relationships in the political, economic, social, administrative, cultural, religious, and psychological spheres, especially as they related to urban and rural populations.[1] These relationships and the consequent imbalances that colonialism left behind have affected African development efforts at the national, subregional, and continental levels.

The impact of colonial intervention is still with us in Africa, but it is a legacy that should be discarded because it has never served African interests. It persists because since independence African leadership has not been revolutionary in its outlook; it is caught, as it were, in the crossroads of Western political and social values and African values and between stagnation and revolutionary change.

If there is an emerging new African political order, it must of necessity discard the legacies of European colonial rule, especially those value systems that have negatively affected administrative, political, social, and cultural institutions.

Perspectives on Africa

The end of the Cold War and the changing circumstances in the international system have provided discussions and debate over the priorities that Africa must now pursue. Francis Deng noted:

> In the past Africa was tied into global structures and processes, first by colonial intervention and then by Cold War ideological linkages into a chain of interdependent dependency. Absent those ties, self-reliance, both in the resolution of management of conflicts and in development, is increasingly imperative. However, having been dislodged by their colonial past from the indigenous values and institutions that permit building from within, Africans are left hanging between the local and global systems.[2]

The new perspectives that are being presented on Africa use the colonial experience as a starting point to advance arguments for change and reaction. In his address at the Kampala conference in 1991, Professor Adebayo Adedeji, the former executive secretary of the UN Economic Commission for Africa (UNECA), called for the fundamental elaboration of an African Security Plan. This plan would embrace what he described as "the requirements for a concerted African initiative—regime peace and security, democratization, irreversible recovery and transformation."[3]

At the Kampala Conference on Security, Stability and Development in Africa the former president of Tanzania, Julius Nyerere, stated

> Africa is inextricably a part of the world—a world dominated economically, socially, politically and militarily by the developed nations of Europe and North America. Neither the peoples nor the governments of this continent have measurable influence on what happens in international relations in any sphere—and particularly not in the areas of economics, science and technology, or political relations between other states. Yet, all such changes have immense implications for Africa. . . . Africa must respond to these international and African changes if its peoples are not to find themselves even worse off than now, and even less capable of determining their own future. And they can respond. They can do something to improve their own conditions and their own prospects. The widespread scenes of economic and social impotence is unjustified, albeit understandable in the light of

hopes, efforts, and disappointments of the last twenty years. If its people can do something about the present dire conditions of its people, Africa must do something.[4]

At the same conference, the secretary-general of the OAU, Dr. Salim Ahmed Salim, noted what he termed "the emergence of a new geo-political balance of forces, as well as a new international economic order that could further debilitate and marginalize Africa." Concern for the marginalization of Africa has prompted the OAU, at the level of the Assembly of African Heads of State and Government, to issue a declaration that underlines a new determination to further democratize African society, resolve conflict situations, foster greater subregional cooperation, and integration, and accelerate socioeconomic growth and development. The declaration states in part:

> We realize at the same time that the possibilities of achieving the objectives we have set will be constrained as long as an atmosphere of lasting peace and stability does not prevail in Africa. We therefore renew our determination to work together towards the peaceful and speedy resolution of all conflicts on our continent. The resolution of conflicts will be conducive to the creation of peace and stability thus releasing expenditures on defense and security and direct them as additional resources for socioeconomic development. We are equally determined to make renewed efforts to eradicate the root causes of the refugee problem. It is only through the creation of stable conditions that Africa can fully harness its human and material resources and direct them to development.[5]

National Sovereignty

National sovereignty is an accepted principle of international law that is held sacrosanct by the OAU member states and is also enshrined in the UN charter. "National sovereignty" means that the state has an absolute right to decide on what happens within its recognized borders. Concomitant with it is the principle of noninterference in the internal affairs of the state, a principle that has come under attack, especially in those situations of conflict in which even humanitarian assistance is denied to the victims of violence and war. Both principles are meant to ensure international harmony and thus the maintenance of international peace and security.

The issue of national sovereignty has come under scrutiny in many forums and is being debated with greater frequency. Some people hold the view that the concept needs to be redefined in light of the new global system and the increasing interdependence within it. One advocate of this view is Sir Shridath Kamphal, the former secretary-general of the Commonwealth, who advanced what some may call the "realistic" view. As he put it:

The reality in the developing world is powerlessness. Sovereignty is a tool that is only defensive. Developing nations cannot use sovereignty for their development because they function in a world dominated by power and in that world they are powerless. However, it is important for the developing world to provide intellectual leadership to redefine sovereignty. Industrialised nations will not take this initiative because to them, sovereignty is a tool used to manage the world.[6]

OAU secretary-general Salim argues that there is need to "maintain a balance between national sovereignty and international responsibility," and that "the doctrine of non-intervention precludes the possibility of accountability on the part of states." On redefining national sovereignty, he said, "We should talk about the need for accountability of governments and of their national and international responsibilities. In the process, we shall be redefining sovereignty."[7]

The former head of state of Nigeria, General Olusegun Obasanjo, takes the view that sovereignty should be redefined and efforts should be made at the international level to improve the availability and content of resources and to distribute them more equitably:

An urgent security need is a re-definition of the concept of security and sovereignty. For instance, we must ask why does sovereignty seem to confer absolute immunity on any government who commits genocide and monumental crimes of destruction and elimination of a particular section of its population for political, religious, cultural or social reasons? In an inter-dependent world, is there no minimum standard of decent behavior to be expected and demanded from every government in the interest of common humanity?[8]

What is clear, then, is that African leaders are now willing to reconsider such notions as security, good governance, democracy, development, and state sovereignty.

The OAU is an organization of sovereign states and, not unlike the UN cannot impose its will on its members. The tendency within the OAU "to always seek African solutions to African disputes and conflicts" is the result of the absence of a dominant state or group of states, and it has encouraged the member states to have confidence in their ability to resolve African disputes and conflicts.

Although moral concerns should always underline political considerations and decisions, the reality usually proves otherwise. The problem that the advocates of humanitarian intervention have is how to implement it. National sovereignty opposes demands from outside humanitarian intervention because that would be perceived, rightly or wrongly, as interference. Is there an international will for such intervention? Who should carry out intervention and under what conditions? The answers to these

questions would more than likely determine the acceptance of humanitarian intervention as a principle of action in situations of conflict or famine.
Another issue in Africa that may continue to provoke the evocation of noninterference or national sovereignty is Islamic fundamentalism, which is
on the rise in northern and eastern Africa.

As a regional organization, the OAU is limited in what it can do: For
example, neither the OAU chairman nor the secretary-general is empowered to act unilaterally in situations affecting a member state, and the OAU
cannot become involved in internal conflict without the concurrence and
agreement of the government concerned (in some cases, by both parties in
the conflict, as in Rwanda, Sudan, and Burundi). While the organization
may have a moral responsibility to take initiatives, it does not have a political one. It can intervene only when authorized to do so.

A Window of Opportunity

The end of the Cold War has also signaled a change in the political thinking of the OAU, whose member states have decided that the time has come
for the organization to be proactive. This new disposition has the potential to transform the OAU into a dynamic actor in the effort to bring peace,
stability, and development to the African continent. It encourages the OAU
to become involved with situations of actual and potential conflict and allows for consideration of current concerns over humanitarian intervention
and protection of the victims of conflicts.

The declaration that the Assembly of African Heads of State and Government issued in July 1990 institutes the express manifestation of the new
political disposition and reflects the earlier commitments made but not
widely implemented in four legal and political instruments: the African
Cultural Charter of 1977, the African Charter on Human and People's
Rights of 1981, the African Charter on Popular Participation in Development and Transformation of 1989, and the 1991 African Charter establishing the African Economic Community.

The consequent commitment by the OAU member states to the promotion and protection of human rights and the establishment of democratic political systems is not only politically sound but morally imperative.
The history of Africa has been one of struggle for freedom and for justice.
It is to be expected, therefore, that the OAU would provide the political
and moral leadership to advocate human rights, popular participation in
government, and development.

The challenge facing the African governments is how to transform the
legacies of divisiveness, structural imbalances, and the denial of basic
rights bequeathed by colonial rule. The implementation of the legal and

political instruments that the OAU member states adopted over the years would restore democracy and genuine governance and would also nurture durable security for the individual and for the state at large.

The political responsibilities of the OAU require it to always remind the member states of their obligations and the purpose for which the organization was founded. Its moral responsibilities require it to champion the peaceful settlement of disputes and conflicts both between and within states. The foremost issue that is challenging the OAU in this respect is the rise of Islamic fundamentalism, which threatens the stability of the secular state.

The window that is now open to the OAU provides the opportunity for the desensitization of governments long obsessed with sovereignty and noninterference. However, the OAU must walk the narrow path of objectivity and purpose in dealing with matters previously considered the prerogative of the sovereign.

Islamic Fundamentalism

During the past few years, concerns have been expressed over Islamic fundamentalism and its potential for destabilization in Africa. This new phenomenon makes it difficult, if not impossible, for the OAU to play any role should internal conflict threaten those countries struggling with this religious force. Both the OAU secretary-general and the Council of Ministers addressed this issue in 1992. As the secretary-general put it:

> Religion has had also its own contribution to conflicts though to a much lesser extent. But the resurgence of fundamentalism, Christian and Islamic, threaten to throw the continent into a new form of conflicts. With the exception of Libya, Mauritania, Comoros, and Sudan, all the other African countries have secular governments. Admittedly, there has been a continent-wide effort on the part of all Governments not to precipitate or whip up the latent religious differences. But this does not mean that Africa has, therefore, immunized itself from religious differences. The war in Sudan has religious overtones and we remember the not-so-infrequent confrontations in Northern Nigeria. Religious based differences do in a very real way threaten the security and stability of African countries. It is, therefore, necessary that as an insurance against violence motivated by religious convictions and competitions, African governments should elaborate mechanisms of governance which do not accentuate these differences, but seek national harmony. Based, in part, on unfettered freedom of worship and secure foundations of secular government.[9]

At its fifty-sixth ordinary session in 1992, the OAU Council of Ministers discussed the issue, and views were expressed to the effect that the rise of Islamic fundamentalism is the work of dissidents, extremists, and subversives. It was also suggested that member states should not provide asylum to such groups because they are not bona fide refugees and could endanger interstate relations and threaten intrastate security and stability.

One problem that the OAU secretary-general faces with respect to fundamentalism and its attendant destabilizing effect is how to discern legitimate political opposition groups or movements from dissident, subversive, and extremist ones. Another problem concerns characterization: Is the characterization of any group by a government sufficient grounds for noninvolvement or contact with that group by the OAU? How can the OAU involve itself to defuse a potentially explosive situation when the government concerned is not willing to allow such involvement? Because the OAU secretary-general cannot unilaterally involve himself with any group that finds itself in a situation of conflict without the concurrence of the member state concerned, what are the other ways and means available to him to prevent or manage a possible conflict situation? These are the questions that may keep the issue of national sovereignty and the principle of noninterference continuing inhibiting factors in this post–Cold War period.

Regional Security

The African preoccupation with security is embedded in the OAU charter; military security perceived in terms of an African Defense Force has been a pervasive objective. During the Cold War, this preoccupation was narrow in perspective and definition because it focused only on military security. The end of the Cold War has provided the OAU with the opportunity to assess the issue of security in its wider dimensions. As the 1991 Kampala Conference on Security, Stability, Development and Cooperation in Africa advanced, "Security must be transcendental of orthodox definition and perception of security in military terms. Security must be all-embracing and all-encompassing and ramifying. It must include personal security, food security, economic security and social security."[10]

When security is seen in a larger context that embraces the individual, family, community, and nation, one must look at the programs that have been put in place or contemplated to give meaning to this concept. It is generally accepted that a genuine political democracy provides not only state and individual security but also an atmosphere of tolerance and respect for human rights.

The creation of an enabling political environment across Africa that allows for full participation on the part of the people and accountability on the part of government officials could constitute a fundamental aspect of security at various levels of society. Africa believes that political democracy and economic development should go together and be mutually reinforcing. Africa's instability and insecurity emanate from the legacies of the colonial experience. According to Francis Deng:

> African problems, whether in conflict management or development must be approached from the perspective of their local, regional and national contexts. Politically, the starting point, as in most matters pertaining to Africa, has to be the colonial nation state, which brought together diverse groups that are paradoxically kept separate and unintegrated. Regional ethnic groups were broken up and affiliated with others within the artificial borders of the new states, with colonial masters imposing a superstructure of law in order to maintain relative peace and tranquility.[11]

More important, Deng observes that there is a yearning in Africa for the cultural legitimization of political and economic objectives and strategies and for workable solutions to the problems of the continent.

The Political Agenda

In order to face the challenges of the post–Cold War period, the OAU secretary-general has outlined a political and economic agenda for Africa, which addresses the issues of conflict resolution, refugees, human rights, and democratization. As conflict resolution has become a major priority for the OAU, the secretary-general has made an appeal to the member states on the need to resolve all conflicts in Africa. There is an awareness in Africa today that without such resolution, there will be neither peace nor development. The political agenda thus envisages a proactive OAU that is more involved in the resolution of all conflicts.

Of all the problems facing the African continent, conflict situations have become the most pressing and most demanding; it is therefore necessary that full attention be devoted to them. The appeal made by the secretary-general is thus timely and pertinent. He has called upon the member states to

1. recommit themselves to the principles of the OAU charter, particularly to the settlement of disputes by negotiation, mediation, conciliation, and arbitration;
2. not use the principle of noninterference in the internal affairs of member states as an excuse to exclude the OAU and make it look indifferent;
3. accept the need for institutionalizing confidence-building measures between and among themselves as a major element in the settlement of disputes; and

    4. make use of the permanent institutions established within the OAU,
       including the newly established mechanism for the prevention,
       management and resolution of conflicts.[12]

By asking the member states to recommit themselves to the principles of
the OAU charter, the secretary-general is in fact saying that sovereignty
and the often-invoked principle of noninterference should be secondary to
the imperative need for the OAU to be an effective organization in the promotion of Pan-African unity.

The Economic Agenda

If Africa is the richest continent, why is it so poor, underdeveloped, and
economically weak? The OAU member states have addressed this question
and in the process have acknowledged that the colonial economic legacy is
the primary reason for Africa's underdevelopment. They have also accepted that the policies they adopted in the 1960s, 1970s, and 1980s are responsible for the serious economic situation. In order to understand the
African economic agenda for the Nineties and beyond, one must understand the political and ideological milieu that has influenced Africa's economic strategy since it gained independence in the Sixties.

The Lagos Plan of Action

The end of the 1970s coincided with a meeting held in Monrovia, Liberia,
of African economic experts sponsored by the OAU and UNECA. At this
meeting, a blueprint called the Monrovia Colloquium was outlined for the
development of Africa; the recommendations in that document constituted
the discussion items for the first Economic Summit of African Heads of
State and Government.

    This economic summit, which was held in Lagos, Nigeria, in 1980
was designed to address the obstacles to Africa's development efforts and
what the African governments should do to remove these obstacles. The
Lagos Plan of Action (LPA) emerged from the summit as the plan for
Africa's economic development by the year 2000; its cornerstone is "self-
reliance and self-sustaining development." African self-reliance was pred-
icated upon the readiness of the African governments to accept any and all
assistance that complements the African effort at economic transformation
and development. As an integral part of the international economic system,
Africa was faced with a task: the management of both bilateral economic
ties and multilateral ties with the Bretton Woods institutions—the General
Agreement on Tariffs and Trade, the World Bank, and the International
Monetary Fund.

The Ideological Conflict

The Bretton Woods institutions notwithstanding, African efforts at achieving the objectives outlined in the LPA were hampered, frustrated, and undermined by both internal and external factors. The major external factor concerned the ideological orientations of these institutions vis-à-vis the development strategies that the African states opted for.

Africa's development strategy in the 1980s was in fact a reaction to this ideological victimization. The African states recognized that development had depended excessively on external sources for supply of strategic inputs into the process that generated and sustained the economic growth. Their national markets also depended on external sources for the supply of factor inputs and the production of final goods and services. When the African governments recognized their role in the development of the economy, they collided with the World Bank and with the Western governments that joined the ideological battle against state involvement and control of the economy.

A 1987 editorial in the periodical *Economic Impact* advanced the following argument for less state involvement in the economy: "The Developing countries through strategies that emphasize the free market, can stimulate growth of world trade, the development of an entrepreneurial climate, conditions that attract foreign investment, and policies that reduce government's interference in the national economy."[13]

The administration under U.S. president Ronald Reagan took the lead to argue that increased governmental involvement in the African economy would stifle its growth potential through inefficiency and overregulation of the productive sectors in that economy. The counterargument to the African position focused on the private sector. It read as follows:

> Private enterprises operating in a competitive market have a clear comparative advantage whenever the objective is efficiency in the use of resources, adaptation to variation in local and individual needs or responsiveness to meet new market issues and changed conditions. The superiority of the private market over governmental command and control of large sectors of the economy derives in part from the superiority of the private market over governmental command and control of large and evaluating information, of giving opportunity for the expression of individual tastes and of driving producers to seek the lowest cost methods for transforming raw materials into goods the people want and value.[14]

Paul A. Samuelson, in direct reference to state involvement and control of the African economy, stated:

> Any new nation freed from colonial binding can give itself a socialist constitution and type out a crisp five-year plan. But, so often we know from experience, these good intentions are not worth the paper they are

written on. The mixed economy is mixed. That is its strength: to mobilize
for human ends the mechanism of the market and to police those mechanisms to see that they do not wander too far away from the desired common goals.[15]

The ideological debate over the role of public and private sectors in
the African economy lingered and had an impact on Africa's numerous
calls for international support and assistance. It was clear that the Western
industrial countries and multilateral financial institutions would prevail
eventually because of Africa's dependence upon the Western governments,
despite the pledges to collective self-reliance.

In retrospect, the 1980s taught Africa two lessons: The first was that
the virtues of a free market economy, which stresses the importance of in-
dividualism and economic freedom, is not (given the historic, political,
and socioeconomic legacy of colonial rule) the panacea for Africa's social
and economic problems. The second was that the economic and political
rationale of an increased role for the state in the economy can guarantee
economic growth or development, particularly when the World Bank and
IMF are opposed to it, and especially when past practices proved it to be
unproductive.

The Agenda for Development

The 1990s have found the African states moving to the middle ground, that
is, encouraging the growth of the private sector while giving the state a
role in the economy. This shift to the middle was reflected earlier in
Africa's Priority Programme for Economic Recovery (APPER), which was
submitted to a Special Session of the UN General Assembly in 1986 and
read in part:

> African governments recognize that genuine efforts must be made to im-
> prove the management of the African economies and to rationalize public
> investment and policies, particularly since the public sector will have to
> continue to play an important role in the development of the region. Such
> efforts would require, *inter alia,* improvement of public management of
> the performance of public enterprises; reforming the public services to
> make more development oriented services; greater mobilization of do-
> mestic savings; improvement of financial management, fiscal administra-
> tion and control of public expenditure with a view to promoting the effi-
> cient use of resources and cutting down on wastage and resource
> misallocation; reduction of foreign exchange leakages; better manage-
> ment of foreign debt and external assistance; and reduction of defense ex-
> penditure. The positive role of the private sector is also to be encouraged
> through well defined and consistent policies.[16]

More important than the program was the fact that the African governments admitted that they were partly to blame for the economic policies they adopted.

The mea culpa underscored the reality of inadequate economic structures in postcolonial Africa. The challenge after independence was to make the inherited structures more relevant to the new strategies for African socioeconomic development. This was recognized many years later when economic growth had stagnated and development had stalled in many places. As the African states put it in 1986:

> The African economic crisis is essentially the result of insufficient structural transformation and the economic diversification that are required to move the continent away from inherited colonial economic structures, typified by a vicious interaction between excruciating poverty and abysmally low levels of productivity, in an environment marked by serious infrastructures, most especially the physical capital, research capabilities, technological know-how and human resources development that are indispensable to an integrated and dynamic economy.
>
> Other aggravating indigenous factors include the inadequacy and/or misdirection of human and financial resources; inappropriate economic strategies and policies; poor economic management; inadequacies of the institutional and physical infrastructures; the persistence of social values, attitudes and practices that are not always conducive to development; and, political instability which has manifested itself, *inter alia,* in a large and rapidly growing population of refugees.[17]

The obstacles that the African governments confronted—bias, insufficient structural transformation, and ideological confusion—resulted in misguided policies. The confusion was captured in this illustration by Julius Nyerere:

> We tried to build socialism without socialists! We look at Europe, for example, for democracy, we also like to be democratic. There was private enterprise, and we also like private enterprise. There was something called socialism, especially in Eastern Europe, and we were told, we also wanted to be socialist. I joked with President Neto in Luanda when I saw big posters of Lenin and Marx and Engels in the rooms. And I joked, "Do you eat cassava in here?" He said yes, and I said to late President Samora Machel, "Samora, do you eat cassava in Mozambique?" He said yes. "Have you ever heard of a Marxist-Leninist country which eats cassava?"
>
> The harm they have done to us, because we had to be Marxist-Leninist, we had to be democrats of the British Westminster model or something like that—a lot of stupidity. Yesterday I read something about the movement back to democracy. After slavery, colonialism, before colonialism, we knew the tribes, the kings and so forth. Looking back, the Europeans had their own kings, but we had our own kings. So, how are we able to promote democracy, when they colonized our kings?[18]

Africa remains the only continent that is encouraged to submit economic development programs every five years, including: APPER, which became the UN Program for Action for African Economic Recovery and Development 1985–1990, and the UN New Agenda for African Development.

Despite these programs and the general African commitment to economic reforms, the kind of assistance that Africa expected, especially from the developed economies, has not been forthcoming.

The African states have an opportunity in this post–Cold War period to express both individually and collectively the will to give meaning to self-reliance and self-sustaining development. It is only through this process that African cooperation and unity can truly take off, overcome the pre-occupation with sovereignty, and provide the security that Africa does not now have.

The establishment of democratic political systems in Africa require first and foremost that governments approach the process on a step-by-step basis by establishing the necessary framework, culture, and institutions and providing the needed forum for popular discussion. The free expression of choice must be protected and accountability under the rule of law must also be upheld. One way of removing "the democratic deficit" is to encourage African nongovernmental organizations to become involved in the process of building awareness and educating and informing the people. As the Secretary-General of the UN said in June 1993 at the OAU summit in Cairo, democracy is the missing link between peace and development. The new African political order must therefore be anchored on democratic political systems that safeguard internal as well as international peace and enhance the process of socioeconomic transformation.

The establishment of an OAU mechanism for the prevention, management, and resolution of conflict is the most concrete expression of the African determination to address debilitating conflict situations that nurture instability and destruction. The ability of the OAU to make this mechanism an effective instrument depends on the amount of support that the member states give to it, for it is only in the absence of conflict that subregional cooperation and integration can flourish and bring about relative subregional security.

Conclusion

The powerlessness that Africa represents in the global arena can be changed only when three conditions are met and become self-sustaining: (1) the establishment of genuine democratic political systems; (2) the effective resolution of conflicts; and (3) increased economic, social, cultural, and scientific cooperation at the subregional and regional levels. In fact, these conditions can provide the foundation for security at the national and regional levels. The post–Cold War period presents an opportunity for Africa to take its rightful place in the global system. African governments must provide the needed leadership for the African people to bring about meaningful and lasting change in the continent.

Notes

1. David B. Abernethy, "European Colonialism and the Post-Colonial Crisis in Africa," in Harvey Glickman, ed., *The Crisis and Challenge of African Development* (New York: Greenwood Press, 1988).

2. Francis Deng, "Africa and the New World Disorder: Rethinking Colonial Borders," *Brookings Review*, Spring 1993.

3. Adebayo Adedeji, "Africa in a World in Transition: Laying the Foundation for Security, Stability, Structural Transformation and Co-operation" in Olusegun Obasanjo and F.G.N. Mosha, eds., *Africa: Rise to Challenge* (New York: Africa Leadership Forum, 1993), p. 1.

4. Julius K. Nyerere, "Statement at the Kampala Conference on Security, Stability, and Development in Africa," Kampala, Uganda, May 1991, pp. 254–258.

5. *Declaration of the Assembly of Heads of State and Government of the Organization of African Unity on the Political and Socio-Economic Situation in Africa and the Fundamental Changes Taking Place in the World,* July 1990.

6. Sir Shridath Kamphal, remarks made at a conflict resolution conference, Carter Center, Atlanta, Georgia, May 1993.

7. The statement by Salim Ahmed Salim, secretary-general of the OAU, in Obasanjo and Mosha, eds., *Africa: Rise to Challenge,* pp. 343–346.

8. Obasanjo and Mosha, eds., *Africa: Rise to Challenge.*

9. Salim Ahmed Salim, "Address at the Fifty-Sixth Session of the Council of Ministers," Tunis, Tunisia, 1992.

10. See "The Kampala Document" in Obasanjo and Mosha, eds., *Africa: Rise to Challenge.*

11. Deng, "Africa and the New World Disorder."

12. Salim, in Obasanjo and Mosha, eds., *Africa: Rise to Challenge,* pp. 343–346.

13. *Economic Impact,* No. 57, 1987.

14. Statement of Secretary of State George Schultz at the hearing "Africa: The Crisis of Development and Interdependence," House Subcommittee on Africa, Committee on Foreign Relations, Ninety-Seventh Congress, July 8, 1981.

15. Paul H. Samuelson, "On Development," *Economic Impact,* No. 36, 1981.

16. Africa's submission to the Special Session of the UN General Assembly on Africa's Economic and Social Crisis, Vols. I & II in document OAU/ECM/EXV/ECM1/l/Rev. I, March 1986.

17. Africa's submission to the Special Session.

18. Nyerere, Kampala Forum, p. 256.

4

African Regional Security and Changing Patterns of Relations

I. William Zartman

Proponents of the "Second Independence" are having their revenge in continental Africa today. The political situation is at its most volatile since the colonial departure, security has lost its international connotations, and African states are back to scratch in their efforts to create authoritative institutions of governance that relate to an articulated civil society. Some states, such as Angola and Mozambique, are only just coming out of the continuing crises of the nationalist struggle, which independence has not resolved. Others, such as Zaire, Algeria, Liberia, Somalia, Sierra Leone, and perhaps even Cameroon and Kenya, are seeing their First Independence systems collapse. Still others, such as Congo, Guinea, Zambia, Senegal, and Nigeria, have felt major tremors in the successions to their First Independence systems. These developments effect interstate relations as well. Typical of the condition of security in the first two decades of independence was the judgment that "any African state can have boundary problems if it wants."[1] The current situation is characterized by the judgment that any African state can have an internal conflict whether it wants one (as some do) or not.

The newness of African political systems and the early stage of their political development account for much of the conflict within and among African states. But unlike the earlier decades of independence, non-African states now have much less interest in intervening in African conflicts, either to benefit from them or to calm them. Appeals to outside states for borrowed power fall on deaf ears, and this same deafness is found among African states as well. Who, then, will help Africa manage its endemic conflict and insecurity? The task should fall to regional and subregional organizations of African states themselves, yet the circle of insecurity closes on them, too, since they are manned by the same vulnerable states.

Conflict in Africa, as elsewhere, is a constituent of history.[2] It indicates the importance of issues and it consecrates solutions. Conflict is so prevalent in African development because it is the means by which systems of internal and external relations are founded in the formative stages of new states' history. Conflict concerns real and important stakes: In internal affairs, it establishes and corrects national systems of wielding power; in international relations, it Africanizes a foreign colonial inheritance, particularly boundaries. Once institutions are developed and accepted, conflict can be expected to decrease, but that will come only a decade or more hence. As political attentions turn inward and the restraints of earlier systems of world order—colonial and then Cold War—are lifted, conflict can be expected to increase until Africa feels obliged and empowered to establish its own systems of domestic, regional, and continental order.

Types and Causes of Insecurity

The problems of African states in the 1990s are troublingly similar to those of the 1960s, aggravated by the fact that the social contract of independence has frequently proven inadequate. Few of the fifty-three states are historic entities, and all have had to create and defend new institutions, rules, and practices, often through conflict. In addition to the independence struggles themselves, there have been four underlying sources of conflict: internal consolidations, internal collapse, territorial uncertainties, and structural rivalries.[3]

Political consolidations to determine who is to enjoy the newly won political power and establish the rules for its exercise often pit former factions of the liberation struggle against each other and involve neighboring states offering sanctuary and support. Factions draw on the sources of elite conflict—ethnogeographical, ideological, leadership, and often even generational—and the roots of current conflicts often go back decades.

Thus the rival factions of the Angolan nationalist movement continue their personalized ideological conflict over three decades after the movement's founding and two decades after independence.[4] In Mozambique, a rare case of ethnoregional and ideological splits artificially contrived from the outside have become the basis of the transition to a democratic system.[5] In both democratizing Congo and stagnating Zaire, ethnoregional and leadership conflicts that reach back into the first decade of independence are the basis of struggle for control of a new political system in the 1990s.[6] Rwandan refugees living for two decades in Uganda returned in 1990 to contest the Rwandan government and to face ethnically based and politically motivated slaughter.[7] The southern Sudanese ethnoregional rebellion that broke out in 1955 and was settled by the Addis Ababa Agreement of 1972 broke out again in 1982 when the agreement was abrogated by its architect, Ja'afar Nimeiri. It rages on, into its second decade, torn between the Sudanese Peoples Liberation Movement/Army (SPLM/A), partisans of a revolution in the entire Sudanese political system, and a Sudan Peoples' Liberation Army (United), dissident partisans of outright secession.[8]

These conflicts are not simply feuds between rival leaders or factions or even ethnic groups over power; more important, they are struggles over the structures and practices of government and its beneficiaries. In the near future, the pressure to change nondemocratic regimes and to practice democracy is likely to provide the greatest single cause of conflict among African states, as antiauthoritarian movements and democratic parties find support in neighboring countries.

State collapse results when the internal struggles are so balanced as to produce only losers rather than a clear victor capable of governing the state.[9] The result is a phenomenon deeper than mere rebellion, coup, or riot; it is a situation in which the structure, authority (legitimate power), law, and political order have fallen apart and must be reconstituted. Order and power (but not legitimacy) devolve to local groups and are up for grabs; the state itself as a legitimate, functioning order is gone.

In Congo (Zaire) in 1960–1961, the collapse of the colonial state in the process of transferring to nationalist groups shaped inter-African relations for the next half decade.[10] Subsequent waves of collapse have followed a repeated process of contraction, alienation, and repression by successive regimes until the last one destroys the ability of civil society to rebound and restitute the state. Between 1979 and 1982 in Chad, Uganda, and Ghana, military regimes that had replaced established but poorly functioning civilian regimes of the nationalist generation were in turn replaced by a political vacuum, until in each case only a strongman was able to recreate legitimacy out of raw power.[11] In Chad and Uganda, neighboring African states (and in Chad, non-African states as well) played a significant role in the collapse and eventual replacement of state regimes.

A decade later, Africa is in the midst of yet another round of state collapse. In Somalia, Liberia, Sierra Leone, Angola, and Mozambique, a wide variety of rebellious opposition movements sought to overthrow concentrated, contracting, repressive, inefficient regimes but were thwarted by foreign intervention of various sorts. Although the individual cases differ widely, they all share a similar pattern. The result has been the breakdown of the states into warring factions, with none able to establish itself in authority. In Angola and Mozambique, the factions have worn each other out, and both countries see a better if unequal future in a new political system based on free and fair elections. However, neither exhaustion nor electoral conditions have been reached, despite frequent agreements, in Liberia, Sierra Leone, and Somalia. The strongman solution of the previous decade is rejected in the 1990s, since it is seen as the basis more of the problem than of the solution.

Even in apparently stable states with legitimate regimes, internal conflict has exploded out of a volatile political atmosphere, threatening the established order to its roots. More significantly, this conflict often occurs in the process or aftermath of democratization; hence, the opening up of the system leads to its tearing down. The mass killings in Burundi by both ethnic groups—Tutsis and Hutus—in late 1993, after the army's assassination of the democratically elected president, and the genocide practiced by groups associated with the government in Rwanda in April 1994, after the authoritarian ruler's plane was shot down, are the most fearsome examples, but the similar if lower-scale violence in Congo following similar elections is another case. Race riots in Senegal and Mauritania in 1989 were not related to the democratization process but were coincident with it. In Nigeria, the second transition to democracy, in 1993, was accompanied by such disorder that it caused a sixth military coup and more disorder. These events do not constitute state collapse, but they are steps toward it and major instances of state and personal insecurity.

Territorial insecurity in the first decades of independence came in the form of boundary conflicts and irredenta; in the 1990s, it comes in the form of secessions—regions breaking away from a weak and oppressive state. An example of this trend is Somalia, in the 1960s and 1970s a textbook case of an irredentist state challenging an ill-defined border and in the 1990s a collapsed state split along old colonial lines. African states were born under the Organization of African Unity (OAU) doctrine of *uti possedetis juris,* which declared boundaries inherited from colonial rule to be inviolable.[12] But in some cases, colonial boundaries did not exist (Morocco and Somalia); in others, they were undemarcated and questionable; and in still others, new "African" criteria of geography, ethnic unity, and even history could be evoked to challenge the colonial inheritance. More recently, new situations, notably offshore oil deposits, required new boundaries.

Secession attempts occurred in earlier decades, of course, but they were decreed illegitimate by the OAU doctrine and defeated by force of arms, through international intervention in Katanga (Shaba) in 1960 and by national force in Nigeria (Biafra) in 1970.[13] The doctrine was reversed in 1993 in Eritrea but only apparently so. Two aspects make Eritrea a case admissible by the old rules rather than by their breach: (1) Secession occurred by referendum agreed to by the government of the larger unit, Ethiopia (although that government was helped to power by the national liberation movement of the seceding unit), and (2) secession occurred along colonial lines, conforming to the OAU doctrine (although that division had been abolished under the most recent colonial rule). The important questions, then, are whether Pandora's box has indeed been opened, and if so, what are the new criteria on which to make a stand (and who would establish these criteria)?

The legitimacy of other African cases of secession can be ranked by the closeness of their criteria to the Eritrean case. I will discuss each case in descending order of legitimacy. The declaration of independence of the Republic of Somaliland (the former British Somaliland) in 1992 has already occurred unrecognized and almost unnoticed. Somaliland fits *uti possedetis juris,* having been not only a separate colonial unit—British, as distinct from the Italian trusteeship territory—but actually a separate independent state for four days before joining its formerly Italian neighbor to form Somalia on July 1, 1960.[14] But one poor Somalia is enough, and two are unrecognizable as states, which raises the criterion of viability as an additional measure of legitimacy. Southern Sudan had a separate status under the common colonizer, Britain, before independence.[15] Its case is therefore as good as the states of former French West and Equatorial Africa (AOF/AEF) under *uti possedetis juris* and would fit the first Eritrean condition if Khartoum would agree to secession, as it once appeared to be considering.

Zanzibar is threatening to dissolve its 1963 merger with Tanganyika (Tanzania), reaffirming not only its previous colonial boundary but also its geographic separation by a 40-kilometer channel.[16] In Casamance, the southern appendage of Senegal, the Movement of Democratic Forces in the Casamance, a minority ethnoregional vehicle of Diolas, claims independence as a second Gambia or Guinea-Bissau.[17] The problem is the central government's neglect of this remote region, and the solution lies in Casamance receiving greater benefits from Senegal, not in secession. A similar case is the Algerian, Nigerian, and Malian Sahara, whose independence is also demanded, with more pathos than reality, by the national liberation movement of the Targui nomads. Much more potentially serious is the breakup of Nigeria and Zaire into component state regions. While unlikely under the Abatcha and Mobutu regimes, the possibility of comprehensive secessions in both countries today or in the foreseeable future seems remote. Although the Sudan-AOF/AEF precedent could be invoked, the success of the secessions would doubtless stand on the first Eritrean criterion, acquiescence of a central government created for the purpose and probably without benefit of referendum, as in Somaliland—in a word, a successful Biafra.

Secession depends on force of arms, although its progress is affected by legitimizing considerations during its course. What is remarkable in the 1990s is that none of the aforementioned cases has depended on major foreign involvement. Although the end of Ethiopian sanctuary in 1991 was a serious blow to the SPLM/A, the secessionist movement continues in southern Sudan and elsewhere as African neighbors look on.

Structural rivalries are the apparent exception to the endemic security problems caused by internal conflict. One might think that because states are weak, structural rivalries will diminish boundary disputes, subversion, and aggression. But states are still strong enough and, above all, different enough in their strength to pose problems of regional order.[18]

Structural rivalries arise because new states have not yet worked out expectations about rank and relations among neighbors interacting within a region. Although such rivalries are not the immediate source of conflict, they make smaller disputes more significant. The Western Saharan dispute is a battle between Algeria and Morocco, with Libya also involved, over leadership of the Maghrib.[19] Libya's support for incursions into Tunisia and Niger in 1980 and 1982, into Sudan in 1978 and 1986, and into Chad in 1980 were part of its attempt to dominate Arab Africa, particularly against Egyptian influence.[20] Intervention of West African neighbors in the Liberian civil war is an act in the drama over Nigerian leadership in West Africa and French-speaking states' resistance to it.[21] The Shaba invasions of 1977–1978 and the Angolan civil war are events in the struggle for predominance between Angola and Zaire over the southwest African region. South Africa's incursions into Angola, Zambia, and Zimbabwe and its support for National Union for the Total Independence of Angola and the Mozambican National Resistance (Renamo) under its policy of destabilization (1978–1988) were means of ensuring its predominance in the region as much as means of destroying the foreign bases of the African National Congress.[22] Such rivalries give a large structure to the many smaller conflicts on the continent in the same way that European history was shaped over the past half millennium or that the structural rivalry between the United States and the USSR shaped world history for half a century or more.

External powers have been involved in these rivalries because weak African states sought to borrow power from outside. During the Cold War, conflicts often escalated to the highest level as superpowers supported local efforts to block allies of their superpower rival. The most important support from outside Africa has come from the continuing security role that French-speaking African states expect of their former metropole.[23] When a French-speaking African state with a defense agreement with France faces internal revolt or conflict with a non-French-speaking state, France comes to the aid of its ally. France assumed this role to consolidate postcolonial regimes in the 1960s, but also in Mauritania in 1978, in Chad on repeated occasions until 1990, in Zaire in 1977–1978 and in 1991, in Rwanda since 1990, and in part in Togo-Benin in 1992. When the conflict occurs between French-speaking states, France may seek to manage and mediate the dispute, as it did between Mali and Burkina Faso and between Senegal and Mauritania. Belgium has played a similar role in support of its former colonies, in Zaire in 1977–1978 and 1991 and in Rwanda in 1990, but other European powers, colonial or not, have tended to stay clear of African disputes. There is little in it for them.

With the end of the Cold War, former Communist states have simply dropped off the map and Western states have little interest in any active intervention and therefore in much of a conflict management role. France, Belgium, and the United States are not likely to be involved in any direct intervention in a Zairian collapse, for example, but, even more significantly, neither is Nigeria. In the past, military supplies from external sources provided governments (in Morocco, Chad, Angola, Ethiopia, and others) with an edge over rebels supplied from a competing external sources. Today, Africa, like many other regions, is awash with arms, and competing efforts from foreign governmental arms suppliers have declined with demand.

Management and Resolution of Conflicts

Although the results are not yet in in some important cases such as the Saharan and Sudanese disputes, the fact is that, except for Eritrea, African interstate conflicts have not changed a thing. Although Hissene Habre (1982) and Idris Deby (1990) in Chad, Yoweri Museveni (1986) in Uganda, and Meles Zenawi (1991) in Ethiopia have come to power through warfare, and Samuel Doe (1990) and Mohammed Siad Barre (1991) have been removed from power without clear successors in Liberia and Somalia, respectively, no borders have been altered, no secessions (other than Eritrea) effected, and no power rivalries settled other than by a reinforcement of the status quo. Nor have African states been able to turn their military conflicts into diplomatic successes. Instead, they have fought themselves into stalemates from which third parties have been needed to extricate them.

Collective security (rarely practiced elsewhere in the world) and collective mediation have been useful mechanisms. There is, therefore, much to credit third state efforts at conflict management and much to recommend continuing and institutionalized activities in this direction. But now third parties face a deeper challenge of handling serious internal insecurities in which their help is rebuffed as a interference.

Collective security has been increasingly used as a way to handle conflict. OAU plans for an African Defense Force have yet to come to fruition, and until the early 1990s, its only Inter-African Force (created in Chad in 1981) failed badly for lack of clear purpose, coordination, and money.[24] However, African groups have put together their own collective forces on occasion. A six-state army from the members of the Economic Community of West African States (ECOWAS) has tried to restore peace to Liberia since 1990 and was joined by two East African forces under the OAU in

1994; six allies of Zaire contributed forces to repel insurgents in Shaba in 1977 and 1978; two neighbors sent military forces to Mozambique in 1989–1990 to quell ReNaMo rebels; and three neighbors of Rwanda provided a Neutral Military Observer Group under the OAU in 1993. Neighbors have provided bilateral interventions to ensure the security of African regimes: Zaire intervened in Rwanda in 1990, Guinean troops helped put down riots in Sierra Leone in 1973 and 1979 and in Liberia in 1979 and (along with other ECOWAS members) in 1990, and Senegalese troops defeated a rebellion against the Gambian government in 1981. However, in 1979, Ugandan insurgents supported by Tanzanian troops repelled a Ugandan seizure of Tanzanian territory and, supported by Libyan troops, overthrew the Ugandan government of Idi Amin. This was a unique event in Africa; the closest parallel was the return of Rwandan refugees with Ugandan support in 1993 to overthrow the Rwandan government.

African mediation tends to come from heads of neighboring states and current OAU presidents.[25] Presidents Kenneth Kaunda of Zambia, Daniel arap Moi of Kenya, and Kamazu Banda of Malawi tried mediating the Mozambican civil war, and President Mobutu Sese Seko of Zaire attempted mediation in the Angolan civil war in 1989. Presidents Shehu Shagari of Nigeria and Gnassingbé Eyadéma of Togo successfully mediated a phase of the Chadian conflict in 1979, and a succession of OAU presidents mediated a later phase between 1984 and 1986. The presidents of Zimbabwe, Mozambique and (the new) South Africa mediated to stabilize domestic unrest in Lesotho in 1994. From another region, Saudi Arabia's King Fahd hosted a crucial Algerian and Moroccan summit in 1987 over the Saharan issue. Many other attempts have been made in these and other conflicts, with some successes.

In addition to African mediation and collective defense as means of resolving African conflicts, African states have had recourse to global organizations, notably the UN and the International Court of Justice. Particularly under the leadership of UN Secretary-General Javier Perez de Cuellar and his successor, Boutros Boutros-Ghali, the UN has played an important role of providing the technical arrangements and expertise for carrying out—and even bringing about—the political decision to terminate conflicts. Although it refused to support the OAU in the Chad operation, it relieved the OAU of its burden by preparing a referendum in the Western Sahara in 1987–1991 and provided the peacekeeping and referendum operation through the UN Technical Assistance Group in Namibia in 1989–1990. It provided the mechanism for management of the conflicts in Angola in the late 1980s and 1990s through the Angolan Verification Missions and the mediation mission of the UN representative Blondin Beye, and in Mozambique in the 1990s through its UN Organization in Mozambique (ONUMOZ) mission. Other African disputes—such as the Saharan issue in 1974, offshore territorial disputes between Libya and Tunisia in 1982 and between Guinea-Bissau and Senegal in 1989, boundary disputes between Chad and Libya in 1994 and between Mali and Burkina Faso in 1986—have been taken to the World Court, in some cases for final settlement and in others for opinions that help channel the course of the dispute by setting the parameters for a lasting solution.

In sum, African states have been active in trying a number of collective mechanisms for providing conflict management and security, for both internal and interstate conflicts. These efforts are on the rise but at the same time are seeking an appropriate institutional framework. Although they are frequently ad hoc in nature, their informality requires that they be legitimized by the auspices of a subregional, regional, or global organization.

African Conflict Management Institutions

Three levels of African institutions are available to handle such conflicts in the 1990s, each in a different stage of realization. The OAU is entering its third decade as the continental conflict management forum. In 1991 state representatives and private citizens of Africa convened by the Africa Leadership Forum, in cooperation with the OAU and the UN Economic Commission for Africa (UNECA), adopted the charter of a parallel organization, the Conference on Security, Stability, Development and Cooperation in Africa (CSSDCA), based on the Conference on Security and Cooperation in Europe (CSCE).[26] On the subregional level, a number of institutions already exist or are mooted. The Economic Community of West Africa (CEAO) and ECOWAS, the Inter-Governmental Authority on Drought and Development (IGADD) in East Africa, and the Maghrib Arab Union (UMA) in North Africa have played a role in conflict management. The experience of CSCE has also been used as a model for a proposed Conference for Security and Cooperation in Southern Africa (CSCSA). The remainder of this chapter will make a comparative evaluation of both the process of forming or reforming these institutions and the promise of conflict management that each contains.

The OAU was created in 1963 for the purpose of managing conflict among African states and pursuing conflict against colonial rule and apartheid, the product of an agreement on lowest common denominators between the unionist Casablanca Group and the statist Monrovia Group of African states.[27] For conflict management purposes, the OAU was designed as a collective security system in which the collective efforts of all members are to be focused on any other member that transgressed the rules of the continental system. Once the transgression is repulsed or repaired, all members are again free to form flexible coalitions on other issues. For anticolonial purposes, the OAU was designed as a collective defense system in which the joint efforts of all members are to be focused on predesignated external enemies that transgress the new rules of the world system. Members are committed to basic principles such as "the peaceful settlement of disputes by negotiation, mediation, conciliation and arbitration," and also to the "respect for . . . sovereignty and territorial integrity" and "non-interference in . . . internal affairs" reinforced by "unreserved condemnation . . . of political assassination . . . and subversion" (Article III).

The mechanisms provided for these activities were a separate Commission of Mediation, Conciliation and Arbitration and, ultimately, the Assembly of African Heads of State and Government, the annual summit. The commission was never constituted, essentially because it was impossible to situate its role. It could not be made up of some heads of state without their constituting an inner elite, a notion that was eliminated explicitly by the first principle of the charter, declaring "the sovereign equality of all Member States," and implicitly by the repeated defeat of a proposal for a "Security Council" of selected members who would act for the collectivity in security cases. Furthermore, it could not be made up of independent "wise men"—judges or lesser political figures—because they had no basis on which to dictate policy to sovereign states. That has left only a mediation and conciliation body made up of all heads of state, that is, the annual summit.

The annual summit has indeed acted effectively to manage conflict within its mandate through a number of different and more subtle mechanisms. The ultimate authority remains the summit itself, hamstrung by its inability to offend any member but seeking to act nonetheless in ways that will strengthen principles, using the spotlight of official notice on unprincipled conflict. Resolutions have tended to uphold, deplore, and urge rather than to call for, condemn, and decide. The summit has, however, found other, less institutionalized mechanisms for handling conflict. One is the corridors of the summits, where the presence of heads of state is often used by their colleagues to mediate, conciliate, and provide their good offices. The other is the ad hoc commission, whose members include regional neighbors, friends of both sides, neutrals, and representatives of coalitions, tendencies, and regions. Ad hoc commissions' records have been encouraging—a success rate of one in three cases handled; although success is often only temporary, that is the nature of conflict management —giving the parties time to hesitate, reconsider, and delay.

The OAU summit has been particularly useful in enunciating and upholding principles that define conflicts and legitimize solutions. Although this activity is amorphous and debatable, it has been arguably effective in preventing many conflicts, particularly of irredenta, secession, and domestic interference. By the same token, in the process of upholding some primary principles for its membership, it has hampered its own ability to manage conflict in other ways. Furthermore, these same major principles are under erosive attack in the 1990s. Thus the OAU finds itself in a dilemma: The primary principles that it defends minimally well keep it from moving on to other almost equally primary principles that it cannot implement.

OAU members have repeatedly called for reforms, but the same vicious circle keeps reforms from being in the primary interest of many members. Revival of the Commission of Mediation, Conciliation and Arbitration has been debated and was shelved in the mid-1970s and again in the late 1980s. At the 1991 summit, the OAU secretary-general Salim Ahmed Salim proposed lifting the noninterference prohibition; at the 1992 summit, a Security Council–like bureau was instituted to help the secretary-general provide rapid responses to sudden crises in what is termed the Conflict Management Mechanism; at the 1993 summit, a Conflict Prevention, Management and Resolution section of the Secretariat was added. Like the UN, the OAU represents a consensus on lowest common denominators that makes it impervious to reform attempts until external situations change and make the current lowest denominator no longer common.

The CSSDCA, referred to earlier, was proposed to break out of this stalemate through the pursuit of a parallel reform outside the OAU yet with OAU cosponsorship and the participation of five African heads of state and three prime or foreign ministers. The Kampala Document responded to a resolution of the OAU 1990 summit; it was subsequently discussed in the 1991 and 1992 summits at Abuja, Nigeria, and Dakar, Senegal, and was recommended for adoption by the Council of Ministers in February 1993 for the 1993 summit in Cairo, where it was left in limbo until 1995. The Kampala conference in 1991 was held to reform a regional security organization that could not reform itself from within. Like the OAU charter, the Kampala Declaration, in its "Security Calabash," subscribed to a number of principles on the peaceful resolution of conflict and made specific reference to collective security, but it also added some broader ideas such as conflict prevention and containment, good neighborliness, military self-reliance, and food security. The "Stability Calabash" contains a number of important guidelines for the establishment and maintenance of an open, pluralist polity.

The mechanisms proposed at Kampala also owe something to the OAU but include some innovations. "Africa, under CSSDCA, should revitalize the operational effectiveness of the OAU Commission of Mediation, Conciliation and Arbitration," a curiously opaque formulation. At the same time, an Elders Council for Peace, "pre-eminently comprised of the most distinguished personalities and African elder statesmen," is to be "empowered under the CSSDCA" with discretionary authority "to effect a measure of intervention in national security problems of participating member states" through reconciliation, mediation, or peacekeeping operations.[28] These three subjects are given separate and more detailed treatment as "continental peacekeeping machinery" under CSSDCA. In addition, confidence-building measures such as exchange of military information and joint military activities, a nonaggression pact coupled with a collective defense agreement, the reduction and reporting of military expenses, the creation of an African arms industry, and the introduction of national military service are all proposed. There are no mechanisms offered for enforcing the stability principles.

The effectiveness of the security mechanisms cannot be examined in practical terms, since they are only proposals within the CSSDCA Calabash patch. In principle the ideas are sound and innovative, all useful elements in building a collective security system not only by providing for means of responding to a break of security but also by lowering insecurity and heightening mutual confidence. Individually, however, some of the mechanisms can be examined within the OAU system, where they have been used. The CSSDCA proposal does not indicate how the structural flaws of the Commission of Mediation, Conciliation and Arbitration are to be remedied and its operational effectiveness revitalized, but there may be hope that times have changed and African heads of state are now more open to the good offices of commission members. None of the problems of reform is special to Africa; it takes a peculiar coincidence of members' policy and will to overcome the objections of sovereignty and establish a capacity for preventing violent conflict, and it requires sizeable resources from within or outside the system to support a durable peacekeeping force (PKF) operation.

The greatest novelty of the CSSDCA is the African Peace Council of elder statesmen. Its precedent may be found in the activities of former Nigerian head of state General Olusegun Obasanjo, the animator of the Africa Leadership Forum and the mediator in the Sudanese conflict. Joining Obasanjo in the council are other retired heads of state in good standing, such as Leopold Sedar Senghor, Aristides Pereira, Julius Nyerere, and Kenneth Kaunda. Such figures were not available to augment the OAU system thirty years ago; changed conditions can be attributed to making this proposal possible.

The CSSDCA is a process rather than an institutional structure, although it does call for a permanent secretariat and a summit conference for periodic review purposes every two years. It would thus inevitably be part of or parallel to the OAU system. More precisely, it could be a mechanism for introducing reforms into the OAU system, or—like the Franco-African summits—it can fill in the holes in the unreformed OAU system with its own operations. Although it can ride for a while on African frustrations with OAU weaknesses and on optimism over the new era of democracy and the end of the Cold War, its real test of relevance and effectiveness would come—as it did with CSCE—first, as its repeated messages of human rights and democracy gradually informs the norms of the system, and second, when it is called to deal with a specific conflict.

It is hard to imagine a specific test case for CSSDCA conflict management, but a conceivable opportunity would be a war of succession. Two general scenarios can be envisaged. One would be preemptive, in which the state would go into political receivership, with the African Peace Council overseeing the democratization process; the support of the army would be crucial to this phase. African elders would have to negotiate with the various factional leaders to create an agreement to follow the procedures and principles of the Stability Calabash. Technical and administrative assistance from democratic African states would be required to keep the process on track, until a new legitimate government was elected and installed.

This scenario could easily slip into the second, in which armed rebellion would be the nature of the problem, and the army would be split; the existence or absence of external support (from other African states, the Middle East, Europe, or the United States) for the factions would not be crucial to the scenario. In addition to the actions of the first scenario, the second would require cease-fire negotiations and a PKF, with both financial and operational coordination with the UN. The situation would resemble the Congo crises of the early 1960s, especially the second crisis of 1964, in which the OAU was busy but ineffectual. The genocidal catastrophe in Rwanda in 1994 underscores the need for such a capability, although it also shows the irresponsibility of the U.S. government in withdrawing UN peacekeepers and in not providing the logistic support to ferry willing African troops from nearly a dozen states to the conflict area.[29]

CSSDCA is in suspense at a time of crisis in the OAU system; its original momentum has run out and needs revival, and its author and animator, General Obasanjo, has been subject to repression by the despots of Nigeria. Many of the tasks it outlines are beyond the OAU and therefore appropriate to a new set of institutions. Others, such as conflict management, are tasks the OAU originally claimed and could grow into if it could overcome its structural inhibitions. CSSDCA seeks to abolish these inhibitions by fiat, declaring that democratic stability, security, development, and cooperation are goals that override previous concerns for sovereignty, self-determination, and regime support and previous limitations in financial and military support. Both the effect and the effectiveness of that abolition remain to be put to the test.

Subregional institutions are currently the institutions most utilized for conflict management, and they have an important potential for the future.

Four subregional institutions that have played a major security role—UMA, CEAO, ECOWAS, IGADD—were formed essentially for economic purposes. However, the CEAO, consisting of six French-speaking African states and established in 1973, added an Agreement on Non-Aggression and Defense to its economic cooperation provisions, and the sixteen-member ECOWAS, founded in 1975, provided a nonaggression and mutual defense protocol in 1978 and twelve years later set up a Monitoring Group (ECOMOG) in Liberia.[30] The six-member IGADD, established in 1986 to deal with endemic conditions of the Horn, was required at its first meeting to begin a conflict management process between Ethiopia and Somalia, although it was unable to follow up with conflict resolution before the Somali state fell into ruins; it met again in 1993 to consider the Somali question and in 1994 to send a "mission of last appeal" to Khartoum on the Sudanese conflict.[31] Unlike the others, the UMA, made up of five North African states, was created in 1989 to coordinate internal security efforts, to face the economic challenge of a uniting Europe, and to overcome the conflict that was tearing apart the region of the Western Sahara. In addition, the Economic Community of Central African States has a standing committee of military cooperation, seeking cooperation and openness on military matters. CSCSA, not yet operational, would be a subregional version of CSCE or CSSDCA for southern Africa and a proposed successor to the regional collective security alliance, the Front Line States (FLS), and the parallel economic cooperation agreement, the Southern African Development Community.

Subregional organizations operate as agencies of conflict management through standard mechanisms—summits, secretariats, eventually military committees. Although the UMA has moved to majority decisions except in case of war, the consensus rule generally operates at the various regions' summits and is important for establishing the norms and agreements required for conflict management. Subregional organizations composed of fewer states than continental organizations have greater direct interests in the subregional conflicts and their management. They tend to reflect the structural inequalities of the subregion, whereas continental organizations uphold the notions of equality within their more numerous and widespread membership. The subregional structure also provides greater leverage for mediators from within the region without destroying the consensual basis of norms and restraints that smaller members bring. Yet subregional agencies do, and must, operate within the continental framework; to break away and establish their own norms would exacerbate conflict along the borders between regions.

Subregional organizations have provided Africa with its most striking instances of military cooperation and diplomatic reconciliation. The FLS provided security as well as diplomatic coordination in conflicts in Rhodesia/

Zimbabwe and later in Namibia, Angola, and Mozambique. The CEAO brought the Mali-Burkinabe war of 1986 to resolution.[32] For all its normal difficulties, the ECOMOG experience has been a remarkable case of combined diplomatic and military collaboration; it has gradually overcome uncertainties over its mission, has brought other factions within ECOWAS into supportive diplomacy, and has benefited from the financial commitment from Nigeria of undisclosed proportions. These three elements are the necessary ingredients of any successful security operation, and they have never been present before in any African collaborative operation. Yet ECOMOG has also worsened the conflict, supported various sides, been ineffective in holding confidence and agreements, and been an agent of structural conflicts of rank and rivalry rather than a neutral mechanism of conflict management. On the ground, these factors are damaging, but in the analysis of patterns of regional security, they merely illustrate the problems inherent in the first full-fledged African subregional collective security operation.

Conclusion

What kind of regional order is possible when the larger, formerly strong, active, pivotal states of the region (Nigeria, Algeria, Ethiopia, Zaire, even South Africa) are in disorder and the active intermediate states (Côte d'Ivoire, Cameroon, Kenya, Angola, to name a few) are in deep domestic trouble? In Africa's fourth decade of independence, the underlying security concern is the weakness of the conflict managers in domestic conflicts rather than the prevalence of interstate conflict. At the same time, the OAU, along with subregional organizations, is facing a confrontation of two models of conflict management. One is the established OAU model of ad hoc committees, informal mediation, inhibiting respect for national sovereignty, and a refusal to interfere in internal affairs. The other model favors a new system of more formalized—and hierarchized—procedures, higher-cost operations, and explicit domestic intervention to ensure behavior conforming to higher standards. It is a worthy debate, but in the end it may simply have to await the return of coherent state actors, the fading of domestic instability, and the revival of more traditional interstate security concerns.

Notes

1. I. William Zartman, "The Foreign and Military Politics of African Boundary Problems," in Carl G. Widstrand, ed., *African Boundary Problems* (Uppsala: Scandinavian Africa Institute, 1969), p. 70.

2. See Francis Deng and I. William Zartman, eds., *Conflict Resolution in Africa* (Washington, D.C.: Brookings, 1992).

3. For an earlier analysis, see I. William Zartman, *Ripe for Resolution* (New York: Oxford, 1989), chap. 1.

4. I. William Zartman, ed., *Elusive Peace* (Washington, D.C.: Brookings, 1995).

5. Hilary Anderson, *Mozambique: A War Against the People* (New York: St. Martin's, 1992).

6. Michael Schatzberg, *The Dialectics of Oppression in Zaire* (Bloomington: Indiana University Press, 1988).

7. Rene Lemarchand, *Rwanda and Burundi* (New York: Praeger, 1970).

8. Francis Deng and Prosser Gifford, *Search for Peace and Unity in the Sudan* (Washington, D.C.: Wilson Center, 1987).

9. See I. William Zartman, ed., *Collapsed States: The Disintegration and Restoration of Legitimate Authority* (Boulder, Colo.: Lynne Rienner, 1994).

10. Crawford Young, *Politics in the Congo: Decolonization and Independence* (Princeton, N.J.: Princeton University Press, 1965).

11. Naomi Chazan, *An Anatomy of Ghanaian Politics* (Boulder, Colo.: Westview Press, 1983).

12. See the discussion in I. William Zartman, *International Relations in the New Africa,* 2d ed. (Lanham, Md.: University Presses of America, 1989), chap. 3.

13. Crawford Young, "Self-Determination and the African State System," in Deng and Zartman, eds., *Conflict Resolution in Africa.*

14. Saadia Touval, *Somali Nationalism* (Cambridge: Harvard University Press, 1963).

15. Tim Niblock, *Class and Power in the Sudan* (Binghamton: State University of New York Press, 1986); Dunstan Wai, *The African-Arab Conflict in the Sudan* (New York: Africana, 1981).

16. Michael Lofchie, *Revolution in Zanzibar* (Berkeley: University of California Press, 1965).

17. See *Africa Confidential* 34, 4 (February 19, 1993) and 34, 12 (June 11, 1993), among others.

18. See Kenneth Boulding, *Stable Peace* (Austin: University of Texas Press, 1978), pp. 58–59; Zartman, *Ripe for Resolution,* pp. 15–16.

19. Zartman, *Ripe for Resolution,* chap. 2.

20. Mary Jane Deeb, *Libya's Foreign Policy in North Africa* (Boulder, Colo.: Westview Press, 1990).

21. Margaret Vogt, *The Liberian Crisis and ECOMOG* (Lagos: Gabumo Publishers, 1992); Anthony Williams, "Nigeria in West Africa," in David Myers, ed., *Regional Hegemons* (Boulder, Colo.: Westview Press, 1991).

22. Zartman, *Ripe for Resolution*, chaps. 4 and 5.

23. John Chipman, *French Power in Africa* (Cambridge, U.K.: Basil Blackwell, 1989); Francis McNamara, *France in Black Africa* (Washington, D.C.: National Defense University Press, 1989); Albert Legault, ed., *L'Afrique, enjeu des grandes puissances et despuissances regionales* (Quebec: Centre quebeçois des relations internationales, 1985); Edmond Kwam Kouassi with John White, "Impact of Reduced European Security Roles on African Relations," in I. William Zartman, ed., *Europe and Africa: The Next Phase* (Boulder, Colo.: Lynne Rienner, 1993).

24. Samuel Amoo and I. William Zartman, "Mediation by a Regional Organization: The OAU in Chad," in Jacob Bercovitch and Jeffrey Rubin, eds., *Mediation in International Relations* (Cambridge: St. Martin's, 1992).

25. See I. William Zartman, "Mediation in Africa," in John Harbeson and Donald Rothchild, eds., *Africa in World Politics,* 2d ed. (Boulder, Colo.: Westview, 1994).

26. Olusegun Obasanjo, ed., *The Kampala Document* (New York: Africa Leadership Forum, 1991); Olusegun Obasanjo, "The Need for an African Response," in Zartman, ed., *Europe and Africa*, pp. 179–186.

27. See Zartman, *International Relations in the New Africa;* Yassin El-Ayouty, ed., *The OAU After Ten Years* (New York: Praeger, 1975); Yassin El-Ayouty and I. William Zartman, eds., *The OAU After Twenty Years* (New York: Praeger, 1985); A. O. Amate, *Inside the OAU* (Cambridge, U.K.: St. Martin's, 1986); Ralph Onwuka, Layi Abegunrin, and Dhanjoo Ghista, eds., *African Development* (Lawrenceville, N.J.: Brunswick, 1985); Amadou Sesay, ed., *The OAU After Twenty-five Years* (Cambridge, U.K.: St. Martin's, 1990); Maurice Kamto, Jean-Emmanuel Pondi, and Laurent Zang, eds., *L'OUA: Retrospective et perspectives africaines* (Paris: Economica, 1990).

28. Quotations are from *The Kampala Document,* pp. 11–13.

29. Compare the rapid U.S. response in transporting French troops to Shaba in 1978 or the equally rapid French response in ferrying Moroccan troops to Shaba the previous year; Zartman, *Ripe for Resolution*, pp. 149–156.

30. See Kouassi with White, "Reduced European Security Roles."

31. Zartman, *Ripe for Resolution,* pp. 122–124.

32. Jean-Emmauel Pondi, "Negotiations Between Mali and Burkina Faso," in Jeffrey Rubin and I. William Zartman, eds., *Power and Asymmetry in International Negotiations* (forthcoming).

PART 2

Regional Security and
the End of the Cold War

5

Somalia:
A Regional Security Dilemma

ANNA SIMONS

It is fitting to regard the chaos in Somalia as the internationalization of internal war. Weapons, aid resources, and media coverage have converged from abroad in Somalia; they have all exacerbated the conflict there, principally by prolonging it. The origins of the war are international as well, traceable to colonially manipulated tribalisms and an insufficiently prepared postcolonial series of governments. These problems only intensified during the Cold War as the superpowers sought to keep Somalia out of each other's clutches and as the Somali leadership sought to extract as much as possible from them by exploiting international rivalries. Hence, it is essentially academic to try to figure out whether the dissolution of Somalia was precipitated by the Cold War—and the heightened corruption fostered by foreign aid—or the end of the Cold War, as the aid flow stopped.

The aid flow is certainly central to the drama, as is the timing of Somalia's final disintegration. However, conflict may also be structurally endemic; this being the case, the questions to answer are whether the particulars in Somalia are generalizable and whether what has happened to Somalia can happen elsewhere. These questions make the premise of the internationalization of an internal conflict more difficult. First, I must demonstrate that internationalization may not be the culprit it has been assumed to be. Second, I must also look to Somali social organization for proximate if not determinate causes of conflict.

Indeed, there are two kinds of arguments that can be made about Somalia's dissolution, and both can be linked. First, Somalia as a nation never really did exist.[1] In other words, Somalia is a container of people whose lines were drawn from the outside; in this sense, it is no different from any other African country, despite irredentist rhetoric to the contrary. Second, conflict was bound to erupt in the space that has come to be called Somalia precisely because the state was incapable of either breaking down

Somali social organization or creating a nation out of it once irredentism failed.

Somalia's Internationalization

Despite our tendency to focus on the more recent past to explain the present, Somalia has long been internationalized. Even Richard Burton, the first European to leave a written record about his penetration through Somalia to Harar (in 1854), commented on how likely one was to meet some otherwise indistinguishable-looking nomad in the interior who had actually traveled the world as a sailor.[2] Indeed, his own introduction to Somalis came in Aden—which is where he hired his Somali servants for the journey.[3]

Written accounts in Arabic push Somalia's internationalization much further back than even Burton (who was probably Somalia's best Western ethnographer) realized.[4] It is likely that Somalia was the Land of Punt, that at least some of the incense in the incense trade originated in Somalia, and that Mogadishu served as a service port for ships making their way up the eastern coast of Africa in the tenth century, if not well before.[5]

Even on a more localized scale, Somalia has long been internationalized because of its nomadic population. Two truisms about pastoral nomads also apply to Somalis: The first is that pastoral nomads *are* peripatetic; the second is that they engage in trade—of livestock products for grains—and often this trade is long distance.[6] This means that Somalis have long been engaged in moving across boundaries of linguistics, culture, and modes of production. Also, given nomadism, it is virtually impossible to practice pastoralism *and* recognize any geographical bounds as permanently inviolate (as long as livestock can be maintained in the area).

On a number of levels, then, Somalis have acted, and even thought, internationally for quite some time. However, how Somalis have projected themselves to non-Somalis has changed, which in turn has altered their relationships with their neighbors. This change is due to their containment in, and representation by, the concept of Somalia as a nation-state.

There are at least four specific, significant ways in which Somalia's identity has been given form: First, the establishment of nation-state boundaries between Somalia and Ethiopia, Somalia and Djibouti, and Somalia and Kenya has meant that so-called ethnic Somalis who traverse or live beyond these borders with their herds present a "national" problem for Somalia and an "ethnic" problem for Ethiopia, Kenya, and Djibouti. The problems engendered by the nomadic Somalis have provoked conflict among these states,[7] which in turn has further cemented where the world recognizes Somalia's boundaries to lie and its sovereignty to begin and end.

Second, the establishment of an internationally recognized entity called Somalia has meant that it is included in international world bodies and is automatically treated as a nation by non-Somali entities—other countries, nongovernmental organizations, the International Monetary Fund (IMF), and the World Bank.

Third and concomitant with Somalia's international status has been the elevation of a representative Somali head of state. Most recently this was Mohammed Siad Barre, who busily projected himself across the international stage by inserting himself (and Somalia) into regional and superpower politics, taking advantage of others' latent disputes to garner unprecedented quantities of resources for the Somali state (whose coffers Siad Barre controlled). Again, the more the Somali government was able to present Somalia as a nation like all others, the more trappings of belonging to a nation Somalis were granted, and the more Somalia seemed to cohere. Of course, too, the more resources and prestige the Somali government was able to accrue, the more impact the state had within Somalia—and as long as the state worked, the illusion of nation did not appear so thin.

Fourth, there was yet another international source of support that helped the economy, and thus the state, appear domestically viable. Throughout the 1970s and 1980s, an unprecedented number of Somali laborers migrated to the Gulf states and remitted considerable sums of money home.[8] How these remittances were handled (often under the table) should have undermined state financial structures, but the inability of these structures to work equitably meant that this added flow actually allowed the state to survive, because its people could.

Despite the degrees to which such levels of internationalization gave currency to Somalia, the structural potential for conflict was never entirely dismantled. Indeed, regardless of the overwhelming number of descriptions that cite Somalia (along with Lesotho and Swaziland) as ethnically homogeneous—or as Laitin and Samatar put it, as a *nation* in search of a state—there is nothing ethnically, linguistically, or culturally homogeneous about all of the people occupying Somalia.[9] Such descriptions are nationalist rhetoric designed to make history (by making a Somalia), which in part has been done by reading protonationalism back into the movement led by Sayyid Mohamed Abdille Hasan against first the Ethiopians and then the British and Italians just after the turn of this century. While the Sayyid was clearly a spiritual leader of tremendous vision and a poet of even wider appeal, he did not unite all Somalis; in fact, he split Somali loyalties, some of which remain split today. Nor did he act any less opportunistically in securing himself supporters than his British or Italian foes. Like them, he practiced "divide and conquer" techniques and (not unlike his eventual successor, Siad Barre) skillfully played off both sides (other clans) against his own (allegedly nonclannist) middle.[10]

For scholars to perpetuate this myth about homogeneity (with or without the Sayyid as anchor) is to ignore the realities of the different-looking, different-speaking, different-living peoples who inhabit Somalia. The most glaring differences lie between pastoralists or their descendants and interriverine farmers, who not only have supposedly different physiognomies but speak different languages and practice wholly different sets of customs, doing so with the explicit understanding that their relationship is hierarchical and grounded in myths of origin.[11]

To understand these cultural, ethnic, and linguistic differences, one need only consider Somalia's geography—or its wind patterns and soil types. For instance, northern Somalia directly faces the Gulf, as do its winds at certain times of the year. Central and southern Somalia are positioned quite differently, and neither northern nor central Somalia can support extensive or irrigated agriculture. Only the interriverine region in the southern portion of the country can keep farmers tied directly to the soil. On a smaller scale, soil type and rain patterns determine whether people raise camels or cattle, more sheep than goats, millet or *qat;* whether they move in wide swathes seasonally or stay put; whether they have the mobility and strength to exploit others or must face periodic exploitation themselves; and how and with whom they are socially organized.

Therefore, the rhetoric of a long-standing Somali nationality has only ever been a pleasant, sometimes even soothing, but still costly siren song. Long before any internationalization—before British and Italian, or Ottoman, Ethiopian, and Egyptian intrusions—distinctions existed among Somalis and were such that shared sentiments were pegged not to fixed boundaries but to fixed commonalities.

These sentiments are encoded in clan-family differences, built up through lineages, subclans, and clans. Genealogical history is not just a record of descent and of who is related to whom how many generations ago. Instead, it is a memory of group strengths, group allegiances, and group enmities that, to be remembered historically, means groups must have had a territorial position from which to expand or contract.[12] Indeed, this grounding of genealogical relationship in territory explains why the Hawiye now control Mogadishu, the Isaq the Republic of Somaliland, and the Majertein the northeast—and why none is eager to share control with others. Yet if this linkage is so strong, why hasn't all of the landscape been genealogically redistributed? Why is there still so much fighting? The obvious answer consists of two parts: First, there is fighting where boundaries are contested or are impossible to draw, in other words, where rural-urban or rural-rural migration has mixed people up. And, second, there is the issue of control and what it is over.

In the genealogical relationship to territory looms the specter of segmentary lineage opposition. Encapsulated in "I against my brother, my brother and I against our cousin, our cousins and us against the world," it is the most elegant model political anthropologists have for explaining pastoralist conflict.[13] For generations it has been applied to nomadic peoples both situationally and as situational theory: Nested groups fission and fuse depending on circumstances.[14] For example, segmentary lineage opposition explains why the Hawiye fight the Darood: There are too few genealogical links among the Hawiye, but fighting the Darood keeps them united. Now the Hawiye fight amongst themselves in Mogadishu because not only are there spoils to fight over, but the Darood no longer pose a significant threat there.

Segmentary lineage opposition has long engendered debate in anthropology. Is it a model *of* or a model *for*? And are people really so balanced in their oppositions? For numerous reasons, many anthropologists question the explanatory value of such an equilibrium-driven model.[15] However, these debates about the dynamic or static nature of society may be missing the broader point: The Hawiye exist only in opposition, and then only as a collectivity into which people feel pushed. Otherwise, despite individuals' ties to an area, "Hawiye" has no solidity as a concept, let alone a corporate body: no hierarchy, no offices, no organizational charter. Consequently, its meaning cannot be precisely understood: Is it opposition that generates the Hawiye, or do the Hawiye generate the opposition? Is it defensive action or offensive reaction that calls the Hawiye into being?[16]

Historically this is what we must now examine: at the point where internationalization, timing, geography, and culture converge.

The Aftermath of the Ogaden War

For the sake of brevity, we will concentrate on the last internationalization of an internal conflict in the Horn: the Ogaden War (1977–1978). Although this war has already been well-studied,[17] it is significant to this discussion, because just after Somalia's defeat, the country's dissolution took its greatest leap forward.[18]

Throughout the 1970s into the late 1980s, the Horn of Africa drew significant superpower involvement. In addition to the fact that imperial Ethiopia and Somalia shared a long history of enmity, Ethiopia was invariably considered the greater prize by the superpowers. Thus, as long as Ethiopia under Emperor Haile Selassie was in the U.S. camp (a relationship the United States inherited from the British), Siad Barre had little choice but to try to woo the Soviets to support Somalia. This support lasted until Somalia invaded Ethiopia and was on the verge of wresting away the Ogaden in 1977. At least three different rationales fueled this invasion: First, with the fall of Haile Selassie in 1974 and the resultant turmoil in Ethiopia, the Ogaden looked winnable. Second, successfully wresting away the Ogaden would fulfill Somalis' irredentist dreams. Third, the Soviets had helped build Somalia's armed forces into what many considered to be the most powerful in sub-Saharan Africa.[19]

Somalia was on the verge of victory when Ethiopia's new Marxist government decided to accept the embrace of the USSR and its allies, luring the Soviets away from Somalia, and thus costing Siad Barre the war. Ironically, this loss inadvertently won Somalia what became unprecedented amounts of assistance, as the new Soviet bloc presence in Ethiopia virtually guaranteed a Western (and Arab) response in support of Somalia.[20]

The aid avalanche resulting from Somalia's defeat and the Soviet Union–United States flip-flop over the spoils of the war was one trigger for Somalia's subsequent dissolution. Indeed, it was due to this switch that Somalia traded up—foreign assistance in the form of industry, state farms, and other supervised inputs from the Soviet bloc for money and goods from Western and petro-rich Muslim states. After the Soviets were dismissed from Somalia in 1977, the Arab states essentially stepped in before Western nations began refilling the assistance gap;[21] within the year, aid from UN agencies, the Arab world and the European Community (EC) countries equaled if not surpassed former Soviet contributions,[22] and this was before U.S. interventions. By fiscal year 1982, Somalia was the third-largest recipient of U.S. aid in Africa.[23] In late 1985, the World Bank reported that "the total of official development assistance for Somalia is one of the highest in Africa per head of population."[24]

For at least two reasons beyond sheer dollar value, these Western and Arab resources proved more lucrative than Soviet assistance ever had: They were more liquid and more intrinsically valuable. They were also far easier to siphon off and "misplace," which made them that much more valuable and more controllable by those in authority. In turn, not only did this make authority more coveted, but it also made those who held it more resented.

On the one hand, the assistance that flowed into Mogadishu did so through UN and other nonprofit coffers as Somalia suddenly found itself host to the world's largest number of refugees.[25] On the other hand, there were also unilateral strings attached to much of the aid, as Somalia remained geostrategically significant in Cold War calculations. However, there was a range of self-interested reasons to assist Somalia as well. For instance, the aid industry needed a new locale now that fighting in Cambodia was winding down.[26] In contrast, German government aid came largely as a result of a bargain it struck with the Somali government, which allowed German Special Forces soldiers to rescue a hijacked Lufthansa airliner at Mogadishu's airport. The sudden influx of aid overwhelmed the country's economic institutions, which had been geared to scientific socialism during the previous decade—not capitalism.

At the local level, it was not money and goods only that poured into Mogadishu from the West but also expatriate experts to administer the moneys and projects, and who had to be housed. Those who had access to the kinds of funds with which to build villas for these Westerners were Somali government officials with access to aid money. Thus not only did villas get built with misappropriated funds, they were rented out to foreign governments by these same Somali government officials. In fact, it was being said in Mogadishu in 1989 that because the U.S. government could not openly bribe Somali government ministers (as could other foreign governments), it had to curry favor more surreptitiously—by renting villas for its employees at extravagant rates, which clearly lined the pockets of these important government ministers.

The large amount of aid that poured into Mogadishu and stayed there, or was purposely kept there, was just one more injustice to rankle northern Somalis. Already there were regional and clan tensions as a result of scapegoating and fingerpointing after Somalia's defeat in the Ogaden War; as Siad Barre attempted to variously lay blame, liberalize, and stifle dissension, clannism was suddenly all too easy to read into his every action.[27] In part, it was easy to read because only individuals close to him had access to the aid flow. As criticism grew, Siad Barre tightened control, which fueled further resentment, which led him to rely more and more exclusively on relatives (who were already implicated through corruption), which only further fueled opposition, which eventually grew into war.

However, there is another way to interpret this spiral: As a good Somali, Siad Barre behaved correctly in taking care of kin first and redistributing what he had gained access to either along extended family lines or along other lines that could turn recipients into extended family. Unfortunately, by doing so—by being a good relative and a good Somali—he was bound to be a bad head of state, for two reasons: First, by controlling resources that others sought access to and not redistributing them nationally, Siad Barre not only made a mockery of the idea of "nation" but also ensured individuals' allegiance to family (and lineage and clan). Second, he set an example that made genealogy all too clear a determinant for group self-aggrandizement at the expense of nongroup members.

A full decade after the end of the Ogaden War, a number of militarily successful Somali opposition groups were being supported on Ethiopian soil;[28] indeed, occasionally both Libya and Ethiopia simultaneously supported the same groups. Yet none of these opposition movements ever successfully fused. Their failure is based not just on the fact that they were clan or clan family–based, as is often argued. Rather, regional players consciously kept the Somali opposition splintered enough to be nonthreatening as a supra-Somali force yet still capable of harrying Siad Barre. Indeed, the on-again, off-again relationship between Muammar Qaddafi and Siad Barre clearly matches the on-again, off-again relationship between

Qaddafi and the Somali rebels he was supporting. Nor was it only Qaddafi and Mengistu Haile Mariam who played a regional role in events in Somalia; it is likely that some members of the Saudi royal family also had a regional agenda, and one can only assume that a number of other local leaders were similarly engaged.[29]

Just as regional leaders played cat and mouse with Siad Barre, he busily did the same with them, successively wooing Libya, Saudi Arabia, Kuwait, Iraq, even Israel and South Africa. In fact, shifts in regional politics played a large role in the country's dissolution, as hindsight clearly points a causal arrow from the agreement worked out between Mengistu and Siad Barre in the spring of 1988 to Siad Barre's downfall in 1991.

In particular, two momentous decisions made at this summit between the two Horn of Africa leaders split Somalia open: First, Mengistu agreed to no longer support any Somali opposition movements (in return for Siad Barre's promise not to meddle in Ethiopian affairs). Second, Siad Barre secretly agreed to give up Somalia's irredentist claims to the Ogaden.

What resulted from the first decision was a choice for Somali rebels. Essentially, they were faced with deciding how best to return to Somalia: peacefully or militarily. The Somali National Movement (SNM) the most prominent of the movements, chose the military option. Thus, in late spring of 1988, this predominantly Isaq force launched a stunningly successful offensive against the Somali army in the north; however, the SNM was unable to consolidate its victories before the government retaliated—with destructive force. Civil war, between north and south (the government vs. the Isaq), ensued.[30]

As for the secret agreement on the Ogaden, when this finally became public, it became the thin end of the wedge between Siad Barre and members of his mother's Ogaden clan—whose core territory was the Ogaden. This region had formerly offered Siad Barre considerable numerical strength, particularly since his own clan (the Marehan) was so small and a significant portion of the army was Ogadeni. There was also at least one broader regional implication in Ogadeni-Somali relations: In addition to the Ogaden clan's natural base of support among fellow clan members still in Ethiopia, there were also Ogadeni in Kenya. Indeed, Kenyan president Daniel arap Moi owed his longevity, if not his life, to the head of his Army, who is an Ogadeni.

Meanwhile, the more successes the SNM had—on behalf of northerners, who were predominantly Isaq—the more other clans were galvanized to establish or energize their own movements, and the longer the war in the north progressed, the more this encouraged these other groups (such as the Somali Salvation Democratic Front and, eventually, the Somali Patriotic Movement) to take advantage of the government's preoccupation with the SNM to further their own interests and carve out their own areas of

influence. Much of what subsequently occurred in Somalia, in terms of pe-
ripheries swinging out of government control, was a matter of clans and/or
clan families forming oppositions in order to project newly emergent corporate interests not only offensively but defensively against one another. It
is not coincidental that the Hawiye, who were among the last clan families
to organize, wound up being the most successful. Their success had as
much to do with the position that many Hawiye happened to be in—surrounding Mogadishu—as with their aim to oust Siad Barre and keep
everyone else away from the spoils of the capital, which lay in the heart of
their territory.

However, while all of this was going on within Somalia, there was yet
more going on outside the country. The World Bank, IMF, the EC, the
Club of Paris, bilateral aid agencies (such as the U.S. Agency for International Development and the German Association for Technical Cooperation [GTZ]), and even the UN High Commissioner for Refugees (which
was still supplying vast sums of money for hundreds of thousands of
refugees in Somalia) variously threatened to withdraw support, did withdraw support, cajoled, relented, and returned support to the Somali government depending on how compliantly or defiantly the regime reacted to
structural adjustment demands and other requirements for reform. All of
these actions had repercussions in Somali markets and on Somalis' moods.

At the same time, on the diplomatic front, Somalia was subject to decisions that it could not always influence and that did not always pertain
directly to it. Most significant of these was the new rapprochement between the superpowers, who had decided to cooperate rather than compete
with one another. This had serious implications for the African clients of
the superpowers. For example, one reason Mengistu and Siad Barre were
so willing to negotiate with one another in the spring of 1988 was because
each was being bled dry by rebels and ceaseless conflict; donors were not
forthcoming with reinforcements, funds to pay for more troops, or arms to
equip them. Both Horn of Africa countries had turned into currency black
holes (and strategic redundancies) for their patrons. Thus, by the summer
of 1989—when the United States could no longer ignore Siad Barre's
prosecution of a war against his own civilians or atrocities committed in
the capital—it was all too easy for George Bush and Mikhail Gorbachev to
agree that neither superpower would continue its support of conflict in the
region.

While Siad Barre still had regional powers to draw on for support—
and was fairly openly being armed by Libya as rebel movements broke out
all through Somalia—the West proceeded to scale back, yet the opposition
movements were still unable to unite. In fact, they kept proliferating,
which proved doubly to Siad Barre's advantage—first, because they were
so splintered and, second, because the situation was far too confusing to

outsiders who, while they may have wanted to see Siad Barre ousted, could not figure out who they would want in his stead.

Collapse of the Somali Nation-State

Why, then, did the oppositions suddenly succeed in 1991? On the one hand, it could be that too many pieces had finally spun out of control for Siad Barre and that the Hawiye finally had gained enough control around Mogadishu. On the other hand, such an answer may be too general and too gentle. And it does not consider timing in a broader context.

Essentially, Somalia was lost as soon as Kuwait was. This connection is both regional and international: The countries in the Gulf region have long played a far more important role in Somali affairs than has generally been recognized,[31] and certainly superpower relations have overshadowed and influenced regional relations. Yet no external actors stayed focused on Somalia once Operation Desert Shield began. And while at first glance this lapse in international interest in Somalia does seem to coincide with the end of the Cold War, in fact it was the inception of the Gulf War that created the real vacuum.

The Gulf War marked the first break in the internationalization of Somalia since well before 1960. Because the United States, Saudi Arabia, and the other Gulf nations were directly embroiled in the war, Somalia was rendered insignificant. Or, to restate this with fuller meaning, Somalia (for the first time since its creation) was not the center of anyone's attention but its own.

The fact that Somalia went underrecognized and ceased to exist almost makes my point too easily: There never was a Somali nation or coherence within, just a Somali state (and faith in the coherence of borders) from without.

What, then, of the space that was Somalia in the immediate post–Gulf War era? The response to Somalia's dissolution and its cost in Somali lives eventually led to yet another international effort toward Somalia: Operation Restore Hope. Despite Operation Restore Hope (and in part because of the aid flow it reintroduced into Somalia), Somalis' future remains unclear. Historically, there has been no lasting union in Somalia beyond the level of clan family and that (as the Hawiye case proves—with component Abgal and Habr Gedir engaged in conflict shortly after the "Hawiye" takeover of Mogadishu in 1991) has not yet proved lasting enough. Rather, what peace there has been in Somalia since independence has been provided by outside pressures and wars extending beyond the state's borders.[32] Consequently, it would appear (as it clearly did to the UN in the launching of Operation Restore Hope) that outside mediation was the only hope for Somalis making peace. Indeed, this is how peace is achieved at lower levels of Somali society; a neutral mediator tries to reconcile the two sides to a dispute. But who could possibly play this role for all Somalis? Who would Somalis regard as having unimpeachable credibility? No one.

In part, I write "no one" because the situation in Somalia has always been more complicated and structured than outsiders imagine anarchy to be. In part, though, "no one" also results from realpolitik. Mediation has always demanded two things: neutrality and an interested party. In terms of being committed, the interested party has to be disinterested enough to be able to think from a Somali point of view. But there are multiple Somali points of view. Who has the patience to absorb these countless views? More significantly, is there any party who has not already been too interested? We need only scroll back through the litany of interested parties who have tried to help so far and consider how they have demonstrated their understanding: with money, weapons, food, jobs, promises, threats. From this perspective, it should be small wonder that Somali trust remains so circumscribed and dissolution so obstinate. What hasn't there been to fight over? And who hasn't supplied it?

Notes

1. This is an argument set forth in Anna Simons, *Networks of Dissolution: Somalia Undone* (Boulder, Colo.: Westview Press, 1995).

2. Richard Burton, *First Footsteps in East Africa* (New York: Dover Publications, 1894/1987), p. 103.

3. Burton, *First Footsteps,* p. 103.

4. See Ali Hersi, "The Arab Factor in Somali History: The Origins and Development of Arab Enterprise and Cultural Influence in the Somali Peninsula" (Ph.D. dissertation, UCLA, 1977).

5. See Mordechai Abir, *Ethiopia and the Red Sea: The Rise and Decline of the Solomonic Dynasty and Muslim-European Rivalry in the Region* (London: Frank Cass, 1980); and Ahmed Yusuf Farah, "The Milk of the Boswellia Forests: Frankincense Production Among Pastoral Somali" (Ph.D. dissertation, London School of Economics, 1988).

6. There is an extensive literature on pastoral nomadism, both comparative and specific. For instance, see A. M. Khazanov, *Nomads and the Outside World* (Cambridge: Cambridge University Press, 1984), and Andrew Smith, *Pastoralism in Africa: Origins and Development Ecology* (London: Hurst & Company, 1992), for general principles; and I. M. Lewis, *A Pastoral Democracy* (London: Oxford University Press, 1961), for an examination of northern Somali pastoralism in particular.

7. For instances of Somali-Kenyan border problems dating back to the so-called *shifta* war, see I. M. Lewis, "The problem of the NFD of Kenya," *Race* 5 (1963); John Drysdale, *The Somali Dispute* (London: Pall Mall Press, 1964); Earl of Lytton, *The Stolen Desert* (London: MacDonald, 1966). For examples of Somali-Ethiopian incursions, there are a number of bodies of literature cited in

notes 10 and 17. For relations between Somalia and Djibouti, see Virginia Thompson and Richard Adloff, *Djibouti and the Horn of Africa* (Stanford, Calif.: Stanford University Press, 1968).

8. This has been described by Allan Hoben, *Somalia: A Social and Institutional Profile*, Working Paper SP-1 (African Studies Center, Boston University, 1983), and Vali Jamal, "Somalia: survival in a 'doomed' economy," *International Labor Review* 127,6 (1988).

9. The title of David Laitin and Said Samatar's 1987 book about Somalia is *Somalia: Nation in Search of a State* (Boulder, Colo.: Westview Press, 1987).

10. The Sayyid's techniques and tactics are described in Said Samatar, *Oral Poetry and Somali Nationalism: The Case of Sayyid Mahammad Abdille Hasan* (Cambridge: Cambridge University Press, 1982); Ray Beachey, *The Warrior Mullah: The Horn Aflame 1892–1920* (London: Bellew Publishing, 1990); and Abdi Sheik-Abdi, *Divine Madness: Mohammed Abdulle Hassan (1856–1920)* (London: Zed Books, 1993).

11. Ethnographic descriptions of interriverine peoples that explicitly point to differences between them and camel-herding pastoralist Somalis can be found in I. M. Lewis, "From Nomadism to Cultivation: The Expansion of Political Solidarity in Southern Somalia," in M. Douglas and P. M. Kaberry, eds., *Man in Africa* (London: Tavistock Publications, 1969); Virginia Luling, "The Social Structure of Southern Somali Tribes" (Ph.D. dissertation, University of London, 1971); Lee Cassanelli, *The Shaping of Somali Society: Reconstructing the History of a Pastoral People, 1600–1900* (Philadelphia: University of Pennsylvania Press, 1982); and Bernhard Helander, "The Slaughtered Camel: Coping with Fictitious Descent Among the Hubeer of Southern Somalia" (Ph.D. dissertation, Uppsala University, 1988).

12. Although it seems increasingly clear in the anthropological literature that groups have merged, disappeared, been engulfed, and transformed, the connection between territoriality and genealogy has been ambiguously described (for perhaps the most comprehensive and detailed account of genealogical changes, see Gunther Schlee, *Identities on the Move: Clanship and Pastoralism in Northern Kenya* [Manchester, U.K.: Manchester University Press, 1989]). From Evans-Pritchard's model ethnography on the Nuer (*The Nuer* [New York: Oxford University Press, 1940/1978]) on through more recent works, kinship appears to take precedence as an organizing principle over territory—which is possible principally because nomads are thought to have no lasting connection to any of the areas they occupy. However, ethnographies that overtly privilege kinship nonetheless imply the significance of "belonging" to an area, so that regardless of attempts to downplay territoriality, ethnographic descriptions of people's connections to wells and grazing areas belie anthropologists' own biases. Nomads' ability to possess (and be possessed by) land is perhaps best set forth by Joseph Hobbs, *Bedouin Life in the Egyptian Wilderness* (Austin: University of Texas Press, 1989). Hobbs (a geographer) unabashedly draws the connections between particular Bedouin kinship groups, identity, and territory.

13. E. E. Evans-Pritchard, *The Nuer,* is most often credited for initially modeling segmentary lineage opposition for anthropologists.

14. I. M. Lewis, *A Pastoral Democracy,* and David Marlowe, "Commitment, Contract, Group Boundaries and Conflict," in J. H. Masserman, ed., *Violence and War with Clinical Studies* (New York: Grune & Stratton, 1963), describe the principles of segmentary lineage opposition for Somalis.

15. There is a long literature that addresses precisely this issue. See, for example, Holy Ladislav, *Segmentary Lineage Systems Reconsidered* (Belfast: The

Queen's University of Belfast, 1979); and Lila Abu-Lughod, "Zones of Theory in the Anthropology of the Arab World," *Annual Review of Anthropology* (1989).

16. Marlowe, "Commitment," emphasizes the paramount yet situational nature of conflict for Somalis. Whom conflict should embrace and how it should escalate is determined by the genealogical and contractual relationship of combatants. Between kin of a certain type, a homicide should not be avenged, whereas it must be avenged when the victim and perpetrator are not so related. Consequently, it is conflict that calls forth group responses, which are specific but never identical since (generally) disputants are rarely identically related. Thus disputes seldom call for the same configurations of kin. Consequently, levels of involvement vary such that groups are never permanently in place but are created by situations.

17. In addition to histories of Somalia that cover this period, such as I. M. Lewis, *A Modern History of Somalia: Nation and State in the Horn of Africa* (London: Longman, 1980), and A. I. Samatar, *Socialist Somalia: Rhetoric and Reality* (London: Zed Books, 1988), there are a number of works that address the internationalization of the Ogaden War. These include: Tom Farer, *War Clouds on the Horn of Africa: A Crisis for Detente* (New York: Carnegie Endowment for International Peace, 1976); Robert Gorman, *Political Conflict on the Horn of Africa* (New York: Praeger, 1981); Robert Patman, *The Soviet Union in the Horn of Africa* (Cambridge: Cambridge University Press, 1980); Bereket Habte Selassie, *Conflict and Intervention in the Horn of Africa* (New York: Monthly Review Press, 1980); Marina Ottaway, *Soviet and American Influence in the Horn of Africa* (New York: Praeger, 1982); and George Shepherd, Jr., "Dominance and Conflict on the Horn: Notes of United States–Soviet Rivalry," *Africa Today* 32,3 (1985). Expressly concerning the Ogaden War and its aftermath for Somalis, also see Colin Legum and Bill Lee, "Crisis in the Horn of Africa: International Dimensions of the Somali-Ethiopian Conflict," *Africa Contemporary Record* 10 (1977–1978); David Laitin, "The War in the Ogaden: Implications for Siyaad's Role in Somali History," *The Journal of Modern African Studies* 17,1 (1979); "The Ogaadeen Question and Changes in Somali Identity," in D. Rothchild and V. A. Olorunsola (eds.), *State Versus Ethnic Claims: African Policy Dilemmas* (Boulder, Colo.: Westview Press, 1983); and Harry Ododa, "Somalia's Domestic Politics and Foreign Relations Since the Ogaden War of 1977–78," *Middle Eastern Studies* 21,3 (1985).

18. Simons, *Networks of Dissolution.*

19. *Africa Contemporary Record* 10 (1977–1978), p. B373.

20. Of course, there were all sorts of geostrategic and military considerations as well, with the Soviets attaining Kagnew Naval Air Station in Ethiopia (formerly occupied by the United States) and the Americans securing Soviet-built naval facilities at Berbera. In other words, it was not just the presence of the Soviets in Ethiopia that provoked U.S. interest in Somalia but also the location of both Ethiopia and Somalia along the Red Sea coast and their proximity to the Suez Canal and the Persian Gulf.

21. *African Contemporary Record* 10 (1977–1978), p. B397. Interestingly, the role the Arab states (Saudi Arabia and Libya in particular) played during this period is glossed over in many of the more extensive works about international relations in the Horn, although it is clear from contemporaneous journal accounts (e.g., *African Contemporary Record* and *Indian Ocean Newsletter*) that Saudi Arabia was able to influence a number of Somali government policies, often in tandem with Western anti-Soviet aims but sometimes, too, through its control of purse strings for its own (or larger Arab/Islamic) purposes.

22. *African Contemporary Record* 11 (1978–1979), p. B289.

23. *African Contemporary Record* 14 (1981–1982), p. B265; *Indian Ocean Newsletter*, March 20, 1982.

24. *Indian Ocean Newsletter*, November 30, 1985. However, this issue of *ION* also notes that Somalia's "debt, which stood at $300 million in 1977, doubled in 1980 and more than quadrupled by the end of 1984, when it was estimated to have reached $1.4 billion; this is more than 12 times the total value of the country's exports in 1983, or the equivalent of 90 percent of the gross national product of that year."

25. *African Contemporary Record* 13 (1980–1981), p. B307.

26. Jonathan Tucker, "The Politics of Refugees in Somalia," *Horn of Africa* 5,3 (1982), p. 22.

27. See Laitin, "The War in the Ogaden"; "The Ogaadeen Question and Changes in Somali Identity"; and Abdi Sheik-Abdi, "Ideology and Leadership in Somalia," *Journal of Modern African Studies* 19,1 (1981).

28. Namely, the SNM and the Somali Salvation Democratic Front.

29. A fuller treatment of this can be found in Simons, *Networks of Dissolution.* Sources for this period and the following summary of events leading up to Siad Barre's demise include *Africa Confidential* (1981–1990); *Africa Contemporary Record* (1968/1969–1986/1987); *Africa Diary* (1973–1984); *Africa Events* (1985–1990); *Africa Report* (1982–1989); *Africa Research Bulletin* (1977–1990); and *Indian Ocean Newsletter* (1981–1990). It should also be noted that there is a long history to the Egyptian-Somali relationship. Unraveling this history would help explain some of the animus many Somalis directed at Boutros Boutros-Ghali, whom they regarded not as the UN Secretary-General but first and foremost an Egyptian.

30. For a fuller treatment of SNM policies and practices, see I. M. Lewis's chapter (with G. P. Markis), "The Rise of the Somali National Movement: A Case History in the Politics of Kinship," in I. M. Lewis, *Blood and Bone* (London: Red Sea Press, 1994).

31. See note 21 and note 29 for sources that lead me to conclude this.

32. I refer to both the so-called shifta war with Kenya (1963–1967) and the Ogaden War with Ethiopia (1977–1978).

6

The International Context
of Internal War: Ethiopia/Eritrea

TERRENCE LYONS

Armed conflicts in Ethiopia/Eritrea have had their roots in the contentious processes of state and nation building, the complex search for justice and equity, the difficult challenges of identity and governance, and the competition for scarce resources and sustainable development. The primary issues, actors, and dynamics have been internal. The conflicts, however, have also taken place in a regional and an international context that sometimes significantly shaped the dynamics of the struggles, the resources competing parties brought to bear in pursuit of their objectives, and therefore the prospects for managing, transforming, or resolving specific conflicts. As locally driven conflicts became internationalized and interlinked with both neighboring states and international actors, their nature was inevitably altered.

The Horn of Africa region, consisting of Ethiopia/Eritrea and its immediate neighbors—Somalia, Sudan, Kenya, and Djibouti—has been the site of endemic inter- and intrastate conflict for decades.[1] The many conflicts are interlinked in a regional "security complex," a group of states whose "primary security concerns link together sufficiently closely that their national securities cannot realistically be considered apart from one another."[2] For example, Somali policies to create a "Greater Somalia" state that included ethnic Somalis living in Ethiopia, Kenya, and Djibouti led to a series of conflicts from 1960 until the late 1980s. Ethiopia and Somalia fought a brief border skirmish in 1963–1964 and a major war in the Ogaden in 1977–1978 and supported insurgent groups and proxy forces throughout the period. Sudan provided critical refuge to the Eritrean People's Liberation Front (EPLF), which was seeking independence from Ethiopia in the 1970s and 1980s; Ethiopia, in turn, supported southern Sudanese rebel movements (first the Anya Nya until 1972, then the Sudan People's Liberation Movement and Army [SPLM/A] from 1983–1991).

85

The complex interlinking of these internal and regional conflicts tied each actor's security to the others and created significant obstacles to reducing conflict.

During the Cold War, this regional security complex was complicated further by superpower competition for clients. In the 1960s, the United States provided Emperor Haile Selassie with assistance, and the Soviet Union armed Ethiopia's regional rivals, Somalia and, for a time, Sudan. Following the first Ethiopian revolution, the patron-client relationships switched as the Soviet Union supported the Marxist regime of Mengistu Haile Mariam in Ethiopia and the United States provided assistance to Siad Barre in Somalia and Ja'afar Nimeiri in Sudan. The enduring cleavages between Ethiopia and Somalia, Ethiopia and Sudan, and—to a lesser extent—Somalia and Kenya provided the entry point for external powers into the regional security system. Vulnerable regional leaders sought to "borrow power" by inviting in great powers from beyond the region to reinforce their positions relative to their regional rivals.[3]

In the late 1980s, the internal changes in the Soviet Union unleashed by Mikhail Gorbachev's policies of perestroika led Moscow to disengage itself from Ethiopia; Washington, no longer concerned with Soviet activities in the region and troubled by the undemocratic policies of its clients, followed suit in Sudan, Somalia, and Kenya. At the same time, insurgents in Ethiopia successfully overthrew Mengistu and set up new governments in Addis Ababa and Asmara, developments resulting primarily from Mengistu's alienation of most of the population and only secondarily from the reduced patronage. The United States played a small but significant role in encouraging a less violent transition following Mengistu's defeat.

Regional Dimensions of Conflict in Ethiopia/Eritrea

Internal conflicts nearly always draw in neighboring states in one manner or another.[4] This is particularly true in state systems such as Africa, where regime legitimacy is often under challenge and borders are often porous. As Ayoob puts it, "Fragile polities, by definition, are easily permeable. Therefore, internal issues in Third World societies . . . get transformed into interstate issues quite readily."[5] Modelski similarly states, "Every internal war creates a demand for foreign intervention."[6]

The permeability of borders in the region means that conflict in one state has spillover effects in neighboring territories. One of the most devastating consequences of regional instability has been the massive numbers of refugees and displaced persons it generates. The region's refugee populations are proportionately the highest in the world, with Sudanese fleeing to Ethiopia; Ethiopians and Eritreans, in turn, seeking safety in Sudan,

Somalia, and Djibouti; and Somalis escaping to Ethiopia and Kenya.[7] The inability or unwillingness of regional governments and international organizations to develop long-term policies to repatriate or integrate these vulnerable populations has drained scarce resources and resulted in alienated groups susceptible to manipulation by unscrupulous leaders.

Weapons also move freely from armories in one state to combatants and bandits throughout the region. The Horn of Africa has been the recipient of massive quantities of weapons bought by the various governments in a generally futile search for security or provided by external powers in an equally ineffectual pursuit for influence. According to one estimate, a total of U.S. $7.5 billion in weapons was delivered to Ethiopia, Kenya, Somalia, and Sudan between 1981 and 1987.[8] Many of these weapons have been lost to insurgent groups or have found their way onto the black market. Following the defeat of Mengistu's army in 1991, thousands of desperate Ethiopian soldiers sold their weapons for next to nothing to insurgent groups. Former members of the Afar militia streamed across the border into Djibouti in 1991 with their weapons, helping to spark antigovernment rebellion in that country. Much of the population across the region is armed and caches of weapons in private hands are large. By the early 1990s, the entire region was so awash in arms that international efforts to limit arms shipments to the region will have little effect on the level of fighting for years to come.

The black market in the Horn of Africa has been thoroughly regionalized. Following the destruction of Hargeysa in 1988, the Ethiopian city of Diredawa was filled with inexpensive electronic goods and vehicles sold by Somali refugees cashing in what assets they were able to take with them. Particularly in times of conflict and state collapse, trading in coffee and most notably *chat* (the popular stimulant chewed throughout the region) thrive among Ethiopia, Djibouti, and Somalia through informal channels.[9]

The permeability of borders on the Horn of Africa also applies to political ideas. The literature on Africa generally has focused on the demonstration and diffusion effects of coup d'états and conflicts,[10] but political values other than conflict may also be transmitted across national borders.[11] The series of national conferences leading to democratic reforms in Francophone Africa clearly were connected, as activists in Cameroon, Congo, and elsewhere came to understand the potential of this form of activity from their neighbors in Benin.[12] Political change can snowball across a region as reform in one state carries its message and momentum into neighboring states.[13] The success of the EPLF's quest for independence has sparked new thinking about the viability of secession among southern Sudanese groups and may have encouraged northern Somalis to proclaim the independence of the Republic of Somaliland. Khadiagala has suggested that security may be conceived as a learning process that is as contagious as coups or conflict.[14] Lesson drawing by regional leaders (including insurgent leaders) takes place continuously and policymakers can emulate successful neighbors or seek to avoid the mistakes of failed leaders. Which lessons are most appropriately drawn, however, is often highly contested in conflict situations.[15]

These links among states in the Horn means that conflict in any part of the region has ripple effects on neighboring states. As Zartman points out, the attitude of a neighboring state to an internal conflict "may be either friendly or hostile, but scarcely indifferent."[16] The regional involvement in internal conflict often leads to "conflict triangulation" among the insurgents, home state, and host state. For example, the EPLF received support in the form of safe havens from neighboring Sudan in its struggle against Ethiopia. In response, the vulnerable Ethiopian regime provided sanctuary and sustenance to the insurgent SPLM/A. Zartman's findings suggest that triangulation of a bilateral conflict generally worsens the chances for negotiations and makes conflicts more intractable.[17]

Leaders in both Khartoum and Addis Ababa were threatened by the other's policy of intervening by proxy in a mutually destructive game of tit for tat. Each vulnerable regime could counter subversion by its neighbor by using reciprocal subversion in reply.[18] The weak centers had little power to regulate their borders and the insurgent groups, particularly the EPLF, had a degree of autonomy that made control by their host government difficult. The ability to destabilize one's neighbor, however, did not serve to deter or dampen conflict. Instead, a cycle of spiraling provocation disrupted bilateral relations and encouraged insurgent groups.

Conflicts also become regionalized when the arena in which political competition is played does not correspond to the space of the recognized state.[19] Opposition groups made illegal by authoritarian governments organize in neighboring states, thereby regionalizing conflict. Eritreans organized their liberation struggle from Kassala in Sudan and traveled on Somali passports. The Western Somali Liberation Front attacked Ethiopia in the 1970s from bases in Somalia. The SPLM operated out of Gambella, Ethiopia, until 1991, although its target was Khartoum, and the Somali National Movement had its base in Diredawa until 1989 while it fought the powers in Mogadishu. The domestic realm of a country's politics often transcended the boundaries of the territorial state.[20] This disconnection between the space in which political goals are pursued and the space occupied by the existing states inherently draws neighbors into internal conflicts.

The problem of politics being played outside of formal borders will likely increase in the future. A diversity of competing and potentially antithetical modalities of political organization have been proposed in the Horn of Africa. In Eritrea, the EPLF insists that the former boundaries of the Italian colony are the appropriate framework for the state and succeeded in winning international recognition for this claim. The new government of Ethiopia, dominated by the Ethiopian People's Revolutionary Democratic Front (EPRDF), accepts this principle with regard to Eritrea but has introduced a political system for the rest of the country that relies upon ethnic parties in ethnically defined regions to structure politics. The Oromo Liberation Front (OLF), an important opposition party in Ethiopia, has also accepted Eritrea's independence and wants to have the same option for the Oromo region. In addition, there remain "Greater Ethiopia" nationalists who insist that the only legitimate territorial basis for the country is the historic Ethiopian state that most certainly includes, in their view, Oromia and Eritrea. Regardless of the validity or justness of any of these claims, the potential for rival forms of political legitimacy competing violently for dominance suggests that the struggle for nation building is far from complete in Ethiopia and Eritrea.[21]

Great Power Roles During the Cold War

In addition to the regional context, the broader international environment has altered the dynamics of local struggles in Ethiopia and Eritrea. During the Cold War, each superpower assumed the position of patron to one or more regional clients in the Horn of Africa. The United States and the Soviet Union generally provided military, economic, and diplomatic assistance to regional rivals, thereby reinforcing local division with Cold War competition. Ethiopia, Somalia, and Sudan used external patronage to strengthen their own regime security, refusing advice and ignoring pressures from the superpowers when these influences threatened their own perceptions of security and expelling their patrons when the relationship no longer benefited them.[22]

In late 1963, following Somalia's rejection of Washington's offer of military assistance and the establishment of military relations with Moscow, a major border conflict broke out between Ethiopia and Somalia.[23] The United States initially hesitated in sending support because it feared a regional arms race, but once the Ethiopian government threatened to end the patron-client relationship, Washington responded. Somalia and the Soviet Union had signed a military agreement in 1963, and U.S. interests in the Horn were to maintain its relations with Ethiopia and prevent Moscow from expanding its influence in the region. Countering Soviet moves in Somalia by reassuring Ethiopia—rather than reducing conflict— became the imperative.

The two superpowers did act successfully to prevent local conflicts from escalating into superpower crises, most notably during the dramatic *renversement des alliances* following the 1977–1978 Ogaden War. As Zartman has pointed out, in an ad hoc process of coordination, the United States and the Soviet Union managed to switch clients amid revolution and significant interstate conflict while avoiding one another, like pedestrians passing on a sidewalk.[24] In February 1978, the Ethiopian army advanced across the Ogaden toward the Somali border, raising fears that the Soviet Union and Cuba would use force to create the Pax Sovietica in the Horn, a peace they had failed to establish using diplomacy in March 1977. Washington sought to deter any such consideration by Moscow by threatening to arm Somalia in the event of a Soviet-Ethiopian attack.[25] Secretary of State Cyrus Vance received promises from the Soviet Union that Ethiopia would not invade Somalia.

During the Cold War, the two superpowers played only a marginal role in conflict reduction; the depth of regional divisions provided few opportunities. The patronage provided by the superpowers, particularly the very generous support Moscow provided Somalia until 1977 and Ethiopia thereafter, did not encourage regional leaders to seek negotiated settlements. In principle the superpowers wanted conflict reduction because it lessened demands from clients for ever increasing assistance and because regional conflict always risked escalation into superpower conflict. So long as the Cold War played out across the Horn of Africa, however, Moscow and Washington made maintaining ties to their clients the first priority and conflict reduction a clear second.

External Roles Following the Cold War

The politics of competitive patronage declined in the late 1980s, when the Soviet Union began to signal its desire to disengage from the region. This new Soviet policy "undermined the logic" of old Cold War policies toward Africa and provided the rationale for limited but sometimes important U.S. activities designed to promote conflict resolution.[26]

The involvement by U.S. actors followed a long series of failed efforts to end the civil war. General Aman Michael Andom's efforts in the early days of the Ethiopian revolution and Mengistu's attempts to manage the conflict by constitutional engineering in 1987 did not induce the EPLF to end its struggle.[27] Various external actors tried to initiate talks, including East Germany and Sudan.[28] EPLF officials claim they met Derg representatives no fewer than ten times in various European capitals between 1982 and 1985, all without substantial progress.[29]

All of these talks failed largely because the Soviets seemed to encourage hopes of a military victory by providing substantial amounts of military assistance. Between 1984 and 1988 alone, Ethiopia received an estimated $4.1 billion in military equipment, most of it from the Soviet Union and its Eastern European allies.[30] The EPLF also sought and won external support for its cause in Arab capitals seeking to expand their influence along the Red Sea. The most important supporter was Sudan, which provided vital supply routes and a secure hinterland for the insurgents. The level of military support to the EPLF was less clear: By the late 1980s, most of its equipment had been captured from the Ethiopian military, but some supplies, financing, and diplomatic support came from Saudi Arabia, Iraq, and other Arab sources. Both the government and the insurgents persisted in military operations far beyond the capacity of their local resource bases by extracting resources from the international economy in the form of arms, humanitarian relief, and remittances from overseas workers.[31] The willingness of external sponsors to bankroll the conflict encouraged each party's efforts to win unilaterally rather than compromise with its opponent.

After over a decade of generous military support, the Soviet Union began to reconsider its support for Ethiopia's policies, at least as pursued by Mengistu.[32] During the spring of 1989 the Soviets told Mengistu to reform, seek a nonmilitary "just resolution" in Eritrea, and improve relations with the West.[33] By signaling their intention to limit future assistance, the Soviets forced Ethiopian officials to recognize that unconditional victory through unilateral military escalation was impossible, thereby encouraging Addis Ababa to seek a negotiated solution.

In the context of this new message from Moscow, former U.S. president Jimmy Carter organized talks between Ethiopia and the EPLF in 1989. The talks soon faltered, in part because both parties were not yet convinced that military victory was impossible and in part because the talks began after the bilateral Eritrean conflict had been transformed into a new multilateral struggle for power in Ethiopia with the rise of a militarily successful Tigrean People's Liberation Front (TPLF)/EPRDF insurgency.[34]

U.S. Assistant Secretary of State for African Affairs Herman Cohen followed up the Carter talks by chairing a series of meetings between Ethiopian and Eritrean officials in October 1990 and February 1991.[35] At the same time, the insurgent movements began major new offensives, trying to create conditions that the talks would have to accept. Because the balance of military power between the two parties remained undetermined, neither set of talks made significant process. By May 1991, the EPLF occupied nearly all of Eritrea, the EPRDF insurgency was approaching Addis Ababa, and Mengistu had fled to exile in Zimbabwe. The caretaker government left behind in Addis Ababa and the principal armed opposition movements all asked Washington to reconvene talks in order to develop a cease-fire and a nonviolent transition. Cohen accepted the request and called the principal actors to a meeting in London on May 27, 1991.[36]

By the time the talks commenced, the military facts on the ground made the delegation from Addis Ababa marginal players with little choice but to sue for peace. Cohen publicly "recommended" that the EPRDF enter Addis Ababa and take the lead in forming a transitional government. However, the EPRDF was notified that if it wanted to continue to receive Washington's blessings, it had to deliver on its promises of reform. Cohen said, "You must go democratic if you want the full cooperation to help Ethiopia realize its potential. . . . No democracy, no cooperation."[37] Cohen also bolstered the EPLF's position by stating that the United States "favor[s] an act of self-determination by the people of Eritrea who have never been consulted on their desires."[38]

Cohen's acceptance the EPRDF and EPLF takeovers reflected his belief that U.S. interests in democratization and famine relief for Ethiopia and Eritrea would best be served by working with the forces in control. He realized that he could do nothing to change the military facts on the ground: Mengistu's army was shattered, the EPRDF completely surrounded Addis Ababa, and the EPLF occupied all of Eritrea. Rather than oppose what he could not change, Cohen decided to make a virtue of realpolitik.[39]

Cohen's adept use of diplomacy reduced the potential for violence associated with the collapse of Mengistu's regime and the coming to power of the new leaders in Ethiopia and Eritrea. However, Washington's role in managing the conflict was limited; the outcome of the military struggle had been determined on the ground before the London talks began. As in the Ogaden War, the United States sanctified, legitimated, and thereby made cleaner and less violent an ending that it did not cause and could not change.

Since the London talks, the international community, led by the United States, has encouraged additional efforts at conflict resolution to consolidate the settlement and begin democratization and regional cooperation. Following the July 1991 National Conference in Ethiopia and the formation of the EPRDF-led transitional government, armed conflict broke out between the EPRDF and the OLF. The fighting threatened to derail the transition and throw Ethiopia back into full-scale civil war until talks cochaired by the Provisional Government of Eritrea (which maintained strong ties to both groups) and the United States in February, April, and May 1992 resulted in a cease-fire and an encampment of forces. Washington assisted and sent observer delegations to the June 1992 regional elections in Ethiopia and the April 1993 referendum in Eritrea.[40] In February 1994, a number of Ethiopian opposition groups met with Jimmy Carter in Atlanta to explore the possibility of a new round of talks sponsored by a nongovernment organization. The transitional government in Addis Ababa, however, declined Carter's offer to mediate these new talks.[41]

Internationalization and
Conflict Management in the Future

In the mid-1990s, both the regional environment and the international framework are changing rapidly, with implications for conflict management in
Ethiopia and Eritrea. The collapse of the state in Somalia and Sudan has
generated tremendous spillover effects that threaten to swamp both Ethiopia
and Eritrea. The international community has offered financial assistance,
particularly in response to humanitarian emergencies, but otherwise looks to
regional organizations to take the lead in conflict management.

In the longer term, Ethiopia and Eritrea in particular and the Horn of
Africa in general will break the tragic cycle of conflict only when a new,
more just political order is constructed, accepted as legitimate, and institutionalized. The creation of new forms of governance needs to take place
on multiple levels and involve many diverse actors in order to address the
crises. Although some legitimate authority and responsibility will continue
to reside at the old level of the state, new structures or regimes must be
created on the local (provincial), subregional (Horn of Africa), continental,
and global levels. An increased capacity to govern and coordinate on each
of these levels will both check state power and prevent the overburdening
of the state, thereby discouraging the state from either becoming oppressive or collapsing. One issue area may require more management from the
local level, whereas another may demand more regional coordination;
nearly all, however, will have implications and consequences for each of
these multiple sites of decisionmaking and authority. Key questions in the
coming years will be how these different levels interrelate and cooperate,
who will participate and in what manner, and how each level will be ac-
countable to the people who are subject to its decisions.[42]

A number of questions relating to the architecture of a new international order will have implications for continued conflict management in
Ethiopia and Eritrea. Agreements to limit and regulate international arms
transfers will not remove the underlying conflict issues but may reduce violence and prevent leaders from becoming tempted by runaway means to
risk conflicts. New guidelines that redefine the role of the international
community, especially international organizations such as the UN, in responding and preventing humanitarian disasters when sovereignty is at
issue will help reduce the degree to which the politicization of humanitarian relief has hampered efforts in the past.[43] In the early 1990s, the UN and
other international actors widened their consideration of "humanitarian intervention" in response to the crises in Somalia and Yugoslavia. The policies instituted by international financial institutions such as the World
Bank and the International Monetary Fund will have an increasing impact
on impoverished states like Ethiopia and Eritrea that may lack the leverage

to resist conditionalities. Nonstate international actors, ranging from Amnesty International, Citibank, scientific organizations, Oxfam, and Cable News Network to the Catholic church, influence different issues globally and will be critical components in the still evolving international order.

In addition, the regional level will be an important arena for decision-making and the management of the challenges facing the peoples of Ethiopia and Eritrea in the coming decades. Regional cooperation has been derailed in the past because state interests, priorities, and sovereignty have conflicted with regional regimes, gains, and cooperation.[44] In the Horn of Africa region, states competed on a nearly continuous basis and recognized few norms that might have limited conflict. Even the identity and legitimacy of actors was in dispute; as Harbeson has stated, "The international politics of the Horn of Africa has largely been a struggle of competing actors to establish just such settled identities."[45] Political accountability, extremely limited in the national arena, was nearly nonexistent for regional organizations, which often served more as private clubs of authoritarian leaders devoted to the preservation of their regimes than representative institutions designed to foster peace, democracy, and equitable development.

The collapse of the old orders in Ethiopia/Eritrea and Somalia and the challenge to old forms of governance in Sudan, Djibouti, and Kenya may provide a window of opportunity for the construction of a new, more broadly defined, inclusive sense of regional identity that will support greater regional cooperation. Giving meaning and institutional form to regional identity, however, is a difficult and long-term process.[46] Many observers have enumerated the mutual gains of cooperation, but fewer have analyzed the structural hurdles to obtaining these benefits. Common problems do not inevitably lead to regional cooperation.

Potential regional relations in the Horn of Africa in the future fall along a continuum from conflict to cooperation.[47] The implications for Ethiopia and Eritrea are large: An openly conflictual relationship will sap already scarce resources, increase insecurity, and further prevent economic or political development; a more cooperative region may provide the margin of security and peace dividends necessary to start the reconstruction of the two states. Regional political leaders preoccupied with the struggle to gain power in a specific territory need to consider the implications of different forms of cooperation for the medium to long term.

The current collapse of the state in Somalia and potentially in Ethiopia/Eritrea, Sudan, and Djibouti may create an anarchic subregional environment that will not facilitate resolution of the material and security problems of the Horn. If powerful centrifugal forces lead these countries to collapse into small microstates controlled by independent warlords, prospects for security and development will halt. The potential for a collapse into a Hobbesian world where authority is exclusively based on military might should give competing political movements cause to reflect.

An alternative model based on a reassertion of central authority by the governments and growing regional cooperation among new heads of state was seen in the "humanitarian summit" held in Addis Ababa in April 1992.[48] The participation of the Provisional Government of Eritrea in this meeting indicated that this model can accommodate the addition of at least certain types of new states, but, for obvious reasons, Somalia could not attend and the SPLM (a critical actor on humanitarian issues) was not invited. A regional order based on heads of state meeting to coordinate their policies and to cooperate on common problems will succeed only if all governments are representative and all significant actors are able to participate.

Similar heads-of-state meetings have taken place under the auspices of the Inter-Governmental Authority on Drought and Development (IGADD), which began as a functional organization, funded largely by the UN, responsible for coordinating regional policies on resource and development issues.[49] Over time, however, broader political and security questions have arisen during the periodic summits. IGADD took the lead in efforts to resolve the Sudanese conflict, holding five meetings in 1994. Despite the lack of progress and the intransigence of the regime in Khartoum, the committee remained engaged because regional leaders recognized that the continuing conflict posed a threat to them.[50]

Other continent-wide organizations, such as the Organization of African Unity (OAU) and the Conference on Security, Stability, Development and Cooperation in Africa (CSSDCA), may play a larger role in shaping regional relations in the future.[51] The CSSDCA proposes a laudable series of norms to advance security and development and calls for greater participation by nongovernment groups. The plan also recognizes sovereignty and "the rights inherent in the territorial integrity and political independence of all African states" in its General Principles.[52] The fundamental conflict between sovereignty and new regional norms therefore remains.

In addition, the relationship between geographically focused organizations such as IGADD and more inclusive, continental institutions such as the OAU and CSSDCA remains vague and open to question. Coordination among such organizations so that each one does what it can do best will only develop with discussion and experience over time. In the end, however, subregional organizations such as IGADD and continental organizations such as the OAU and CSSDCA are limited in their impact by the nature of their membership. Organizations composed of states will only be as representative and responsive as their components.

A final, more speculative category that deserves greater consideration is the issue of how regional cooperation may be facilitated by creative new relationships based on redefining sovereignty, the basis of citizenship, the meaning of borders, and other legal abstractions that have been used by political leaders to control their territories. In the Horn of Africa, as in the former Soviet Union and Yugoslavia, the demise of old structures has left analysts scrambling to develop new international norms that reflect the reality on the ground and may be used to reduce conflict. For the Horn of Africa to develop into a less conflictual subregion, original and more flexible applications of old principles may be necessary.

Notes

1. Terrence Lyons, "The Horn of Africa Regional Politics: A Hobbesian World," in Howard Wriggins, ed., *The Dynamics of Regional Politics* (New York: Columbia University Press, 1992).

2. Barry Buzan, *People, States, and Fear: The National Security Problem in International Relations* (Chapel Hill: University of North Carolina Press, 1983), p. 106; Karl W. Deutsch et al., *Political Community and the North Atlantic Area: International Organization in the Light of Historical Experience* (Princeton, N.J.: Princeton University Press, 1957); Raimo Väyrynen, "Regional Conflict Formations: An Intractable Problem of International Relations," *Journal of Peace Research* 21,4 (1984), pp. 337, 344–347.

3. Terrence Lyons, "Great Powers and Conflict Reduction in the Horn of Africa," in I. William Zartman, ed., *Cooperative Security: Reducing Third World Wars* (Syracuse, N.Y.: Syracuse University Press, 1995).

4. Ted Robert Gurr, "The Internationalization of Protracted Communal Conflicts Since 1945: Which Groups, Where, and How," in Manus I. Midlarsky, ed., *The Internationalization of Communal Strife* (New York: Routledge, 1992).

5. Mohammed Ayoob, "Regional Security and the Third World," in Mohammed Ayoob, ed., *Regional Security in the Third World: Case Studies from Southeast Asia and the Middle East* (Boulder, Colo.: Westview Press, 1986), p. 14; see also Thomas Ohlson, Stephen John Stedman, and Robert Davies, *The New Is Not Yet Born: Conflict Resolution in Southern Africa* (Washington, D.C.: Brookings, 1994).

6. George Modelski, "The International Relations of Internal War," in James N. Rosenau, ed., *International Aspects of Civil Strife* (Princeton, N.J.: Princeton University Press, 1964), p. 20.

7. U.S. Committee for Refugees, *World Refugee Survey, 1993* (Washington, D.C.: U.S. Committee for Refugees, 1993); Hiram Ruiz, *Beyond the Headlines: Refugees in the Horn* (Washington, D.C.: U.S. Committee for Refugees, 1988).

8. Paul B. Henze, *The Horn of Africa: From War to Peace* (New York: St. Martin's Press, 1991), p. 119.

9. Christopher Clapham, *Transformation and Continuity in Revolutionary Ethiopia* (Cambridge: Cambridge University Press, 1988), pp. 185–186; Christopher Clapham, "The Political Economy of Conflict in the Horn of Africa," *Survival* 32,5 (September/October 1990), pp. 403–419.

10. Richard P. Y. Li and William Thompson, "The 'Coup Contagion' Hypothesis," *Journal of Conflict Resolution* 19,1 (March 1975), pp. 63–87; James M. Lutz, "The Diffusion of Political Phenomena in Sub-Saharan Africa," *Journal of Political and Military Sociology* 17,1 (Spring 1989), pp. 93–114.

11. Stuart Hill and Donald Rothchild, "The Contagion of Political Conflict in Africa and the World," *Journal of Conflict Resolution* 30,4 (September 1987), pp. 716–735.

12. I. William Zartman, "Introduction," in I. William Zartman, ed., *Conflict Resolution as Governance in West Africa* (Washington, D.C.: Brookings, 1996).

13. Samuel P. Huntington, *The Third Wave: Democratization in the Late Twentieth Century* (Norman: University of Oklahoma Press, 1991), pp. 100–106.

14. Gilbert M. Khadiagala, "Security in Southern Africa: Cross-National Learning," *The Jerusalem Journal of International Relations* 14,3 (1992), pp. 82–97.

15. Richard Rose, "What Is Lesson-Drawing?" *Journal of Public Policy* 11,1 (January–March 1991), pp. 3–30; David Brian Robertson, "Political Conflict and Lesson-Drawing," *Journal of Public Policy* 11,1 (January–March 1991), pp. 55–78.

16. I. William Zartman, "Internationalization of Communal Strife: Temptations and Opportunities of Triangulation," in Midlarsky, ed., *Communal Strife,* p. 27.

17. Zartman, "Temptations and Opportunities," p. 40.

18. Lyons, "The Horn of Africa Regional Politics," p. 180.

19. I. William Zartman, *Ripe for Resolution: Conflict and Intervention in Africa* (New York: Oxford University Press, 1985), pp. 118–119.

20. William Cyrus Reed, "The New International Order: State, Society, and African International Relations" (Paper prepared for a conference on "The End of the Cold War and the New African Political Order," University of California, Los Angeles, February 17–19, 1994), p. 4.

21. Marina Ottaway, "Nationalism Unbound: The Horn of Africa Revisited," *SAIS Review* 12,2 (Summer–Fall 1992), pp. 111–128.

22. Jeffrey A. Lefebvre, *Arms for the Horn: U.S. Security Policy in Ethiopia and Somalia, 1953–1991* (Pittsburgh: University of Pittsburgh Press, 1991).

23. See Ted Gurr, "Tensions in the Horn of Africa," in Feliks Gross, *World Politics and Tension Areas* (New York: New York University Press, 1966), pp. 316–334.

24. I. William Zartman, "Superpower Cooperation in Northeast and Northwest Africa," in Roger Kanet and Edward Kolodziej, eds., *The Cold War as Cooperation* (Baltimore: Johns Hopkins University Press, 1991).

25. Larry C. Napper, "The Ogaden War: Some Implications for Crisis Prevention," in Alexander L. George, ed., *Managing U.S.-Soviet Rivalry: Problems of Crisis Prevention* (Boulder, Colo.: Westview Press, 1983), p. 234.

26. Michael Chege, "Remembering Africa," *Foreign Affairs* 71,1 (1991/1992), p. 146.

27. Edmond J. Keller, "Constitutionalism and the National Question in Africa: The Case of Eritrea," in Marina Ottaway, ed., *The Political Economy of Ethiopia* (New York: Praeger, 1990), p. 104.

28. I. William Zartman, *African Insurgencies: Negotiations and Mediation* (U.S. Department of States, Bureau of Intelligence and Research, Intelligence Research Report No. 206, June 1, 1989), pp. 8–10.

29. See the interview with EPLF general-secretary Issayas Afwerki, "EPLF Chief: War to Continue; No More Talks," *Le Monde*, November 23, 1988, translated in Foreign Broadcast Information Service, *Daily Report, Sub-Saharan Africa* (hereafter *FBIS-AFR*), November 29, 1988, p. 3.

30. U.S. Arms Control and Disarmament Agency, *World Military Expenditures and Arms Transfers 1989* (Washington, D.C.: Department of Defense, 1990), p. 115.

31. See the excellent discussion in Christopher Clapham, "The Political Economy of Conflict in the Horn of Africa," *Survival* 32,5 (September/October 1990), pp. 403–420.

32. Mark Webber, "Soviet Policy in Sub-Saharan Africa: The Final Phase," *Journal of Modern African Studies* 30,1 (1992), pp. 12–14.

33. "USSR Government Issues Statement on Ethiopia," *Pravda*, June 14, 1989, translated in *FBIS, Daily Report on the Soviet Union*, June 14, 1989, p. 13. See also "Ethiopia: Dark Days for Mengistu," *African Confidential* 30,4 (February 17, 1989). Soviet officials also opened channels with the EPLF. See "Soviet Union Holds Discussions with Rebels," *Indian Ocean Newsletter*, July 22, 1989.

34. Marina Ottaway, "Eritrea and Ethiopia: Negotiations in a Transitional Conflict," in I. William Zartman, ed., *Elusive Peace: Negotiating an End to Civil Wars* (Washington, D.C.: Brookings, 1995).

35. Eritrean People's Liberation Front, "Report on the Deliberations of the Exploratory Talks for Peace Negotiations in Washington, D.C.," February 1991. This document contains the EPLF transcript of the talks. See also Jennifer Parmelee, "Ethiopia and Eritrean Rebels to Open Peace Talks Today," *Washington Post*, February 19, 1991, p. A6; Clifford Krauss, "Conflicting Peace Plans Offered in Ethiopian Strife," *New York Times*, February 24, 1991, p. A11.

36. For more details on these talks, see Terrence Lyons, "The Transition in Ethiopia," *CSIS Africa Notes*, no. 127 (August 27, 1991).

37. Transcript of Press Conference of Assistant Secretary Herman Cohen and Rudy Boschwitz, London, May 23, 1991.

38. Press Conference of Cohen and Boschwitz.

39. Michael Binyon, "West Acts as Midwife at Birth of New Leadership," *Times* (London), May 29, 1991, p. 9.

40. National Democratic Institute, *An Evaluation of the June 21, 1992 Elections in Ethiopia* (Washington, D.C.: NDI, 1992); the African-American Institute, *Eritrea: A Report on the Referendum on Independence* (Washington, D.C.: AAI, 1994).

41. *News from the Carter Center*, "Carter Center Statement on Ethiopia Negotiations," March 23, 1994.

42. Terrence Lyons, "Crises on Multiple Levels: Somalia and the Horn of Africa," in Ahmed I. Samatar, ed., *The Somali Challenge: From Catastrophe to Renewal?* (Boulder, Colo.: Lynne Rienner, 1994).

43. Francis M. Deng and Larry Minear, *The Challenges of Famine Relief: Emergency Operations in the Sudan* (Washington, D.C.: Brookings, 1992).

44. Stephen John Stedman, "Conflict and Conflict Resolution in Africa: A Conceptual Framework," in Francis M. Deng and I. William Zartman, eds., *Conflict Resolution in Africa* (Washington, D.C.: Brookings, 1991), pp. 337–381.

45. John W. Harbeson, "The International Politics of Identity in the Horn of Africa," in John W. Harbeson and Donald Rothchild, eds., *Africa in World Politics* (Boulder, Colo.: Westview Press, 1991), p. 120. See also Lyons, "The Horn of Africa Regional Politics."

46. For a recent account on the complexities of a European identity, see Anthony D. Smith, "National Identity and the Idea of European Unity," *International Affairs* 68,1 (1992), pp. 55–76.

47. Stedman, "Conflict and Conflict Resolution," p. 378.

48. "Horn of Africa Humanitarian Summit Opens 8 Apr," Addis Ababa, Voice of Ethiopia Network in Amharic, translated in *FBIS-Africa*, April 10, 1992, p. 1.

49. Ali Ahmed Saleem, "An Introduction to IGADD," in Martin Doornbos, Lionel Cliffe, Abdel Ghaffar M. Ahmed, and John Markakis, eds., *Beyond Conflict in the Horn: Prospects for Peace, Recovery, and Development in Ethiopia, Somalia, Eritrea, and Sudan* (The Hague: Institute of Social Studies, 1992), pp. 114–115; Reidulf K. Molvaer, "Environmental Cooperation in the Horn of Africa: A UNEP Perspective," *Bulletin of Peace Proposals* 21,2 (1990), p. 142.

50. Francis M. Deng, "Mediating the Sudanese Conflict: A Challenge for the IGADD," *CSIS Africa Notes,* no. 169 (February 1995).

51. On the potential for the OAU to manage conflicts, see Samuel G. Amoo, *The OAU and African Conflicts: Past Successes, Present Paralysis and Future Perspectives* (Fairfax, Va.: George Mason University Institute of Conflict Analysis and Resolution, May 1992).

52. African Leadership Forum, *The Kampala Document: Towards a Conference on Security, Stability, Development and Cooperation in Africa* (Kampala, Uganda, May 19–22, 1991).

7

Civil War and Identity in Sudan's Foreign Policy

FRANCIS M. DENG AND KHALID M. MEDANI

Sudan's external relations have been pivotally influenced if not totally determined by the nation's civil war that has raged intermittently for nearly four decades. It is ironic that this internecine conflict is the result of the country's greatest promise as a microcosm of Africa and a bridge or crossroads between the continent and the Middle East. The racial, ethnic, cultural, and religious diversities in Sudan's composition are most often described as falling into north and south. The north, two-thirds of the country in land and population, is inhabited by indigenous ethnic groups, the dominant among whom intermarried with incoming Arab traders and over centuries produced a genetically mixed African-Arab racial and cultural hybrid. The resulting racial characteristics are very similar to those of the African groups in the continent below the Sahara: Ethiopia, Eritrea, Djibouti, and Somalia in the east; Chad, Niger, and Mali in the center; and Senegal to the west. Indeed, the Arabic phrase *Bilad El Sudan,* from which Sudan derives its name, means "Land of the Blacks" and refers to all these sub-Saharan territories.

However, unlike the people in these countries, who identify themselves as Africans, the northern Sudanese see themselves as Arabs and deny the strongly African element in their skin color, physical features, and cultural elements, even in the practice of Islam. Having been permitted by Islam and the assimilationist Arab culture to pass into the supposedly superior Arab-Islamic identity, northern Sudanese "Arabs" vehemently resist any attempt by the non-Arab population to identify the country with black Africa.

There are, however, non-Arab communities in the north that, though large compared with the Arabized tribes, have been partially assimilated by their conversion to Islam and their adoption of Arabic as the language of communication with other groups. Since Islam, Arabic, and the racial

100

and ethnic concepts of Arabism are viewed in Sudan as closely inter-twined, these groups have been virtually adopted into Arabism and sup-posedly redeemed from the degrading status of their black African origin.

While the north was undergoing Arabization and Islamization, the south, where the African identity has predominated, remained isolated, protected by natural barriers and the resistance of the Nilotic warrior tribes, primarily Dinka, Nuer, and Shilluk. This isolation was punctuated, however, with the violent incursions by waves of adventurous invaders from the north in search of slaves, ivory, and gold. The Nile was the link with their victims and their eventual redeemers.

This dichotomy has been reinforced by the legacy of colonial rule, the independence movement that it triggered, and the flawed policies of nation building. Indeed, Sudan's failure to establish a unifying concept of self-identification has played a large role in determining its interaction with the outside world. While demographic and geographic realities have made the internationalization of the war inevitable in some respects, this has largely been a result of the seemingly intractable cleavage between a politically dominant Arabized/Muslim north and an increasingly marginalized African and Christian-influenced south.

It is this "war of visions," triggered by the complex challenges of eq-uity, justice, and competition for scarce resources, that determines Sudan's relations in African and Arab circles and in the international community at large. John Garang de Mabior, leader of the Sudan People's Liberation Movement (SPLM), summarized this dilemma:

> Our major problem is that Sudan has been looking and is still looking for its soul; for its true identity. Failing to find it [northern] Sudanese take refuge in Arabism; failing this they find refuge in Islam as a uniting fac-tor. Others [i.e., southerners] get frustrated as they fail to see how they could become Arabs when their Creator thought otherwise. And they take refuge in separation. In all this there is a lot of mystification and distor-tion to suit the various sectarian interests. . . . there is no sharpness in our identity. . . . we need to throw away this sectarianism and look deep in-side our country.[1]

With this challenge in mind, we will explore the roots of the civil war in the evolution of opposing political identities, the manner in which they have violently clashed, and occasions when they have arrived at some form of mutual accommodation. These dynamics suggest that the compo-nents fueling the coercive power of the politics of identity are shifting and ambiguous and, as such, are susceptible to the push and tug of external surroundings, particularly at the elite level. That is not to say that popu-lar, as opposed to elite, perceptions of Arab-African differences in Sudan do not lead to contentious behavior that may eventually cement cleavages, but only to stress that decisionmaking at the center shoulders most of the responsibility for exacerbating suspicions and escalating conflicts.

Because of the connection between the internal and external dimensions, the posture of international actors organizations is salient to the prospects of conflict or exacerbation. Consequently, it is just as important to understand the motivation of external involvement in the conflict as it is to explore the tendency of the warring parties to seek to strengthen their positions by looking beyond the nation's borders for material and nonmaterial assistance.

If the Arab/Muslim north has traditionally looked to the Arab world and the south to its African neighbors for legitimacy and advantage, what has motivated actors exogenous to the conflict to welcome or resist intervention? Does this behavior stem from geostrategic, economic, or ideological considerations—that is, "instrumental" reasons—or is it imbued with "affective" reasons, such as racial-cultural affinity and humanitarian considerations?[2] Clearly, domestic and external actors to the conflict in Sudan have exhibited both patterns. Nevertheless, this path of inquiry may serve to illuminate the character, reliability, and longevity of external involvement and, in so doing, shed some light on much-needed remedial policies to the conflict and circles of actual and potential influence.

The cycle of violence in Sudan can be summarized in the dynamics of identification, confrontation, reconciliation, disaffection, and alienation. At independence in 1956, Sudan was burdened with a legacy of colonial rule that helped fashion contrasting visions for the nation that set the stage for civil war. External involvement during this period, most notably British colonial policies, played an important role in exacerbating the cleavage between north and south.

In retrospect the confrontation that erupted violently on the eve of independence was inevitable. During the first phase of the civil war (1955–1972), northern politicians quickly monopolized political and economic power and sought to mold the nascent state into what they imagined to be its natural Arab/Muslim image. In reaction, the southern insurgents called for a complete break from the north. Yet their strident calls for secession earned them little support from the newly independent African countries, all of which faced the daunting task of building nation-states out of multiethnic and, in many cases, multireligious populations. In the north, the external dimension of the conflict was driven by Arab-centered concerns. By injecting themselves in the politics of the Middle East and siding with the Arab world on the highly contentious Arab-Israeli issue, northern politicians were rewarded with support from the Arab world, albeit not from the United States, which saw Sudan's radical Arab posture as antithetical to its geostrategic interests. The southern insurgents received military support from Israel during this period as a result of Khartoum's alliance with the Jewish state's Arab foes.

In the end, however, the north's continued attempts to find a military solution to the conflict at the expense of working toward a genuine compromise on the issue of national identity proved fatal. Reconciliation did come in 1972 but only after a new introspective vision for the nation that recognized Sudan's cultural diversity and managed to bridge the ethnic and religious divisions in the country. Ja'afar Nimeiri, who took over power through a military coup in 1969, recognized Sudan's dual Arab and African identity with the signing of the 1972 Addis Ababa Agreement brokered by Ethiopia's emperor Haile Selassie. Not coincidentally, this period saw Sudan for the first time pursuing a balanced foreign policy based on the promotion of a pragmatic and internally derived concept of "unity in diversity."

But by the early 1980s, domestic political and economic problems caused Nimeiri to look abroad for salvation and to the Sudanese Islamists at home for legitimacy. Nimeiri moved closer to Egypt, the oil-rich Arab countries, and the United States, which, out of its apprehension over Muammar Qaddafi in Libya and the Marxist regime in Ethiopia, provided him with more assistance than any other leader in sub-Saharan Africa. In the meantime, the south's disaffection with Nimeiri's policies increased. In 1983 the Sudan People's Liberation Army (SPLA), led by Garang, rebelled, ushering in the latest phase of the civil war. For a time, until the overthrow of Ethiopia's strongman Mengistu Haile Mariam in 1990, the SPLA found refuge and received support from neighboring Ethiopia. Sudan's hostile relations with Libya and Ethiopia were closely linked to the civil war: Libya had backed a coup attempt against Nimeiri in 1976, and Sudan and Ethiopia suspected each other of supporting antigovernment insurgents.

In 1985 Nimeiri was toppled by a popular uprising primarily as a result of his bankrupt economic policies and his failure to bring an end to the civil war. His support of the Islamist agenda, particularly Islamic (shari'a) law, in his final years proved instrumental in the rise to power of the National Islamic Front (NIF) following the military coup of 1989. Subsequently, the regime in Khartoum has pursued domestic and foreign policies grounded in an ideology of Islamic revivalism, alienating it from both the south and the international community as never before. Predictably, the result has been a widening of the historical split between the north and south, an increase in civil violence, and the West's isolation of the regime in Khartoum in a manner that has compelled the latter to seek an alliance with Iran, to the alarm of the United States as well as the majority of Arab states. Moreover, the heightened polarization between north and south has made the task of international mediation leading to the resolution of the conflict more arduous than at any time in Sudan's postindependence history.

Identification

In his discussion of the problems inherent in studies of nationalism and nation building, Ernest Gellner wrote that "nations as a natural, God-given way of classifying men, as an inherent . . . political destiny, are a myth; nationalism, which sometimes takes pre-existing cultures and turns them into nations, sometimes invents them, and often obliterates pre-existing cultures: that is a reality."[3] Although there is considerable controversy over the extent to which the causes of the present conflict in Sudan are internally or externally generated, there is no question that the very creation of the Sudanese nation was a foreign, and essentially opportunistic, enterprise of social engineering. The Europeans who drew up the borders of modern Sudan in the late nineteenth and early twentieth centuries took into account mainly European geopolitical interests rather than the ethnic, religious, and socioeconomic configurations that have proved so tragically hard to manage within a congruent political and national unit.

The effects of foreign rule in Sudan (1898–1956) can be seen in the country's present crisis of nation building; the decolonizing, anti-imperialist movement that mobilized against this foreign rule neglected to address the very real domestic problems of social injustice, economic disparities, and the capture of the newly independent state by a privileged Arabized elite. The early northern Sudanese nationalists, in their quest for a coherent national identity, saw colonial rule as on artificial interruption to Sudanese nation building. While they spoke rhetorically of their past as an amalgam of Arab/Muslim and African cultures, in practice they looked increasingly northward instead of inward in asserting their identity.[4] This inevitably led to an elitism of the intelligentsia rooted in the largely fictitious notion of a homogeneous Arab and Islamic identity. No wonder, then, that exuberant calls for Arab nationalism became increasingly inert once its role as a potent symbol of protest to the status quo outlived its usefulness. Ultimately, it was replaced with a discourse of Islamic revivalism that offered to a new generation of middle-class elites an even more complete, inclusive, and extravagant worldview.

Political elites' passion for and identification with Arabic language and, later, Islamic culture eclipsed the influence of other indigenous or African cultures. Instead of fostering a Sudanese society and culture that recognized its ethnic, racial, and religious diversity, as well as its historical injustices, these elites nurtured the strident internationalist movement for Pan-Arabism and Pan-Islamism.

Just as northern Sudanese were inventing their identity in opposition to British and, to a lesser degree, Egyptian rule, an adversarial "Africanist" identity composed of traditional beliefs and Christianity coalesced in the educated southern elite. At the popular level, fears of the return of Arab slavery induced in the south a heightened sense of cultural assertiveness that looked to sub-Saharan Africa for reinforcement and refuge.

Much of Sudan's foreign relations since independence, particularly with African and Arab states, reflected this tendency to look to externally based systems as models in the pursuit of identities at the exclusion of knowing about others within the borders of the nation or critically thinking about the national program. A significant exception to this pattern occurred during the period of the Addis Ababa Agreement (1972–1983), when north and south and their respective agendas came close together. For the first time, Sudan was quite effective at playing its postulated role as a bridge or a mediator between Africa and the Middle East and became a dynamic force for moderation and even conciliation.

Confrontation

The first phase of Sudan's civil war witnessed the loudest cries for secession in Sudan's history. The northern politicians who took over from the British colonial authorities at independence, headed by Prime Minister Ismail El Azhari, inspired as they were by the divisive notion of Arabism, pursued a discriminatory policy of power sharing and civil service appointments. This policy largely excluded southerners, which generated discontent and planted the seeds of conflict. Combined with the fact that Khartoum used its monopoly of the state to dominate and Arabize every aspect of national life, this "Sudanization" program caused many southerners to believe that independence meant nothing more than the replacement of the British colonial administration by a northern Sudanese version of foreign rule. This belief was the primary cause of the 1955 mutiny at the Torit Garrison, which signaled the war to come.

When General Ibrahim Abboud seized the reigns of power through a military coup in 1958, he further alienated southerners by pursuing a policy of forced Arabization and Islamization in the south and adopting the Foreign Missionary Societies Act of 1962, which restricted the operation of Christian churches and missionary schools and expelled them entirely in 1964. By 1961, full-fledged war broke out, with many southerners demanding the separation of the south as an independent state. Despite attempts at negotiations between the two warring parties (most notably the Round Table Conference of 1965), no compromise was reached until after Ja'afar Nimeiri assumed power in May 1969. The Addis Ababa Agreement between the Nimeiri regime and the Southern Sudan Liberation Movement (SSLM), which the regime respected for eleven years, was reached after a military stalemate and was arranged through the good offices of the World Council of Churches and Haile Selassie. The accords of 1972 established the south as one large region with substantial internal self-rule and provided the absorption of the Anya Nya—the military arm of the SSLM—into the regular armed forces with the understanding that they would serve in the south.

Despite the multiplicity of borders dividing the northern and southern Sudanese along racial, religious, ethno-linguistic and socioeconomic lines, the first phase of civil war attracted much less material and diplomatic support from the outside world than it did in later years. Moreover, the absence of a serious clash of interests between the two superpowers engendered little incentive on their part to involve themselves actively in the civil war.

The secessionist inclination of the southern insurgents constrained not only international actors but prospective regional actors as well. Uganda, motivated by a level of ethnic affinity, and Ethiopia, which was experiencing ideological differences with the radical Arab line of Khartoum, hosted refugees from the south and allowed the Anya Nya rebel fighters a measure of access to their territory. Both countries, however, were inhibited from further involvement by the idealism that guided international relations of postindependence Africa in the late 1950s and 1960s and by the multiethnic character of their own nations. The prevalent Pan-Africanist philosophy emphasized the unity and brotherhood of all Africans, Arabs included, and African leaders held fast to the principle of the sacrosanctity of the existing African boundaries borrowed from their former colonizers. Indeed, in 1966, the Ugandan minister of state for foreign affairs implicitly emphasized these principles over issues of identity when he explained his country's policy with regard to the civil war in Sudan: "Uganda would not be influenced in the least by the fact that the North was Muslim while the South was Christian. Nor would they be influenced by the feeling that the Southerners are black and the others are mere Arabs who should be rounded up."[5]

Another reason behind the lack of intervention in the Sudanese civil war was the failure of the SSLM to mobilize African support, which stemmed from its inability to publicize the southern cause and establish a viable administration that would convince outsiders of their inevitable victory.

By virtue of its claim to being an Arab country, Sudan found itself embroiled in the very difficult policies of the Middle East and the collective Arab stand against Israel. Consequently, Israel supported the Anya Nya by supplying a significant amount of weapons and training out of Uganda and

Ethiopia in an effort to sap the strength of an enemy "Arab" country. But this assistance was vulnerable to restraints emanating from the international system. Although Israel gave southerners assistance, particularly in the last three years of the conflict, it consistently denied such aid and did not go so far as to endorse the southern Sudanese right to self-determination.

The ruling Arab/Islamic elite were much more successful in eliciting support from their Arab connections. They moved closer to Egypt, which in turn aided the Sudanese air force and encouraged other Arab countries to provide it with material and financial assistance to prosecute the war in the south. But despite the boast of Mohammed Ahmed Mahjoub (the prime minister of Sudan at the height of the civil war in the 1960s) that his government received "arms, ammunition and funds" from the United Arab Emirates, Algeria, and Saudi Arabia, foreign policy did not play as important a role in the conflict at this time as it did after 1969.[6]

Khartoum's staunch support of the Arab cause vis-à-vis the Arab–Israeli conflict affected its position globally. Its severing of relations with the United States following the 1967 war, combined with its radical Arab nationalist orientation, distanced it from the West and qualified it for support from the Soviet Union. Khartoum relied on Soviet advisers, pilots, ground crews, and weaponry toward the end of the civil war. The United States seemed content at the time to cultivate close relations with neighboring Ethiopia, which hosted U.S. bases.

Ibrahim Abboud's insistence in pursuing a military solution with respect to the south and his failure to solve the "southern problem" led to his downfall in 1964. Although succeeding governments dominated by the traditional sectarian parties put forward proposals to resolve the conflict, as in the first years following independence, they continued to squabble among themselves and pursued a military option with respect to the south. In terms of foreign policy, the sectarian parties, which have dominated civilian politics, operated in a predictable fashion based on their particular historical experiences: The Umma party retained its hostility toward Egypt that dated back to the original Mahdist revolt in the late nineteenth century, and the Khatmiyya-backed National Unionist Party (later the DUP) continued to promote its traditional political and financial links with Cairo.

Reconciliation

Nimeiri's military takeover in May 1969 shifted internal and external alignments in a manner that facilitated an interlude of peace. Following the aborted Communist coup of 1971, Nimeiri became disenchanted and distrustful of his previous supporters, who were inclined toward the radical

Arab hard line. As a result, Sudanese foreign policy took a turn to the right under the new foreign minister, Mansour Khalid. This period witnessed a shift in identity politics that reversed, at least for a time, certain perceptions about Sudanese political culture at the periphery. Khalid articulated the new mood of the period in foreign policy terms:

> For an independent foreign policy to be formulated and have credibility, it would have to be preceded by broad-based home measures designed to foster solidarity within the Sudan, so that the nation could first identify with itself before it could relate to the outside world: the problems of Sudan go beyond its geographic boundaries. Without this there will never be a national consensus on foreign policy and Sudan's foreign policy will always remain an extension of the policies of others.[7]

This new introspective vision emphasized national unity not only as a goal but as a reality and development as a strategy of nation building that preoccupied the nation and effectively substituted the war mentality. The effect was to push Khartoum toward a pragmatic approach and away from the radical Arab camp. For political and financial reasons, Sudan cultivated close relations with Saudi Arabia, the Gulf states, and some of the Arab conservatives. Nimeiri also achieved good relations with his African neighbors and other states on the continent. He worked diligently through the Organization of African Unity (OAU) to promote Sudan's image as a bridge between Africa and the Arab world and engaged in formal and informal contacts with neighboring African states to achieve good relations, acquire greater legitimacy for his regime, and achieve a solution to the conflict in the South.

After purging leftist and sectarian elements, Nimeiri realized that he needed support from southern Sudan and aid from the United States now that he had turned away from the Soviet Union. In March 1971, he reached an agreement with Ethiopia to cease aiding each other's secessionist movements, an accord motivated out of mutual fears that the Anya Nya and Eritrean liberation movements had grown strong enough to internationalize their campaigns and destabilize each other's regimes. Later that year, the Anya Nya lost their second major supply route from Uganda after Nimeiri signed an accord agreeing to terminate support for the forces of Milton Obote, who was overthrown by Idi Amin in 1971, if Amin would curtail external access to the Anya Nya from his borders. The termination of Ethiopian and Ugandan support for southern forces were the key external factors that influenced the southern politicians to reach an agreement with Nimeiri in Addis Ababa in 1972. Another important factor was the mediating role of the World Council of Churches and its African affiliate, the All Africa Conference of Churches, which had the confidence of most southerners. However, while the external atmosphere promoted negotiations and facilitated arbitration, the reality on the ground was the primary factor that ensured a successful outcome. Given the relatively strong position of the rebels, and particularly their unification under the leadership of Joseph Lagu by 1969, the rebels' political interests had to be taken seriously by Khartoum. The accord met the core demands of the rebels by granting them self-rule in a united south provided they abandon the call for secession.

The Addis Ababa Agreement bridged the ethno-linguistic and religious cleavages in the country, the first such agreement in Sudan's modern history. It toned down Sudan's involvement in the quest for Arab unity because there was now a vocal and active segment of Sudanese politics that had strong, negative views on the subject—the southern Sudanese. Similarly, it demonstrated to Muslims in Sudan and the Islamic world at large that they would not compromise their cultural and religious identity if they desisted from stipulating an official state religion or a monolithic notion of Arabism and allowed tolerance to override sectarianism. To the contrary, the agreement legitimized Sudan's dual identity as both African and Arab, and it helped Sudan achieve extraordinarily good relations with other African countries, which saw in Sudan a model of "unity in diversity."

Disaffection

Although the achievement of peace and unity initially seemed to transform the relations between the north and the south, it became increasingly evident that Nimeiri wanted to utilize certain southern Sudan ethnic groups whose support he could win as a countervailing force against regional separatists in Mearea and to promote his African heritage in order to gain legitimacy abroad. The turning point came in 1976, when an aborted coup led by traditional sectarian elements backed by Libya left Nimeiri shaken and insecure. Within a year of the coup attempt, his policy shifted away from an emphasis on economic development and national unity to an obsession with his own survival. He purged all vestiges of power outside the presidency and insisted on complete personal authority. As a result, his reconciliation efforts with Umma party leader Sadiq al-Mahdi and other northern political forces in 1979 failed, and with little regard for the historical grievances of the south, he decided to co-opt the increasingly influential Muslim Brotherhood for political legitimacy. Nimeiri assumed that either the south would remain grateful and loyal or it had become too divided to mount a renewed resistance. He was mistaken, for the south reacted more violently than it had in the first war.

The ensuing collapse of unity and resurgent internal divisions played havoc with Sudan's external relations at a time when regional developments within the contentious politics of the Cold War caused the superpowers to intervene. Following the coup of 1974 that toppled Haile Selassie, Ethiopia's relations with the United States deteriorated considerably, especially after Mengistu's assumption of power. Ethiopia thus emerged as a serious threat to U.S. interests with respect to Egypt, the Gulf, and the Red Sea. Nimeiri's support for the Camp David Accords between Egypt and Israel, which was significantly influenced by the favorable impact the Addis Ababa accords had on the country's image abroad, reinforced the cordial relations between Sudan and the United States. Nimeiri strengthened his military and political ties to the United States by allowing the United States to use Sudan as a base from which to contain Soviet and Libyan influences in the region. By the early 1980s, Khartoum received the most military and economic aid in all of sub-Saharan Africa.[8]

However, these ties engendered hostility from Libya and Ethiopia, which formed a tripartite alliance with Marxist South Yemen in 1981 that compounded Nimeiri's regional insecurity. Short of cash, Nimeiri also cultivated relations with the oil-rich Arab nations and received almost $3 billion from them by the early 1980s, and he acquired a large number of loans from bilateral and multilateral donors. But by the time Nimeiri was ousted by a popular uprising sparked by a severe International Monetary Fund austerity program, Sudan was crippled by a $9 billion debt because of misguided, overly ambitious development projects and rampant corruption.

Nimeiri's abrogation of the Addis Ababa Agreement was motivated by several factors: First, he saw the liberal democracy in the south as antithetical to the authoritarian presidential system that prevailed in the north. Second, he saw the south become increasingly self-assertive in its demands against the central government, especially in economic matters. And third, Nimeiri hoped to take advantage of oil discovered in the south in 1979. Moreover, his domestic weakness resulted in his instituting Shari'a law in 1983 in a thinly disguised effort to win the favor of Sudanese Islamists, the only group in the north still supporting him. These measures triggered an armed rebellion in the south that quickly led to the resumption of civil war. Libya's Qaddafi—angered over Nimeiri's refusal to break with Egypt after Camp David—and Soviet-backed Ethiopia immediately supported the SPLM, drawing the concern of the United States. Although the United States criticized the Nimeiri regime for its policy vis-à-vis the south on humanitarian grounds, it increased assistance to Nimeiri out of fear that his overthrow would lead to a government hostile to U.S. and Egyptian interests. This policy was integral to the United States' "encirclement" strategy toward Soviet client Ethiopia.

As internal divisions between north and south became sharply polarized, both sides sought outside support in a race to acquire military advantage. For the SPLA, the military wing of the SPLM, Ethiopia was by far the most critical ally. Convinced that Nimeiri was supporting Eritrean secessionists and the antiregime forces of the Tigray and Oromo peoples, Mengistu allowed the SPLA to use his country as its main political and military base and as a sanctuary for hundreds of thousands of southern Sudanese refugees. In addition to providing direct military and logistical support, Mengistu facilitated SPLA contacts with Libya, Cuba, and later Israel.

After Nimeiri's downfall, the parliamentary government headed by Sadiq al-Mahdi, which was elected following a one-year interim period, was left with the internal and external problems of the Nimeiri regime. The fragile nature of the coalition government acted as a check against any dramatic realignment. Although al-Mahdi spoke rhetorically of pursuing a more balanced approach in foreign relations, the continuation of the war and its drain on the economy meant that he continued to look to the United States for support. The Unionists continued to look to Egypt to forge political advantage. Meanwhile, Egypt kept a vigilant eye on its water interests in Sudan and the regional ambitions of Qaddafi in Libya. The most important new development that would have dramatic repercussions was the NIF's cultivation of relations with Iran and the Arab Gulf states. These slates in particular supplied significant financing that the NIF, facilitated by its business acumen and the general political ambiguity of the time, used to build a broader political base.

Meanwhile, Ethiopia's hosting of SPLA bases and direct military support to the rebel forces helped SPLA win unprecedented successes in the battlefield and forced Khartoum to the negotiating table. Ethiopia, and to a lesser extent Egypt, facilitated meetings between the SPLM and northern politicians, most notably the Koka Dam Conference in March 1986 and the DUP-SPLM talks in November 1988 held in Addis Ababa. The latter conference appeared especially promising in that it called for, for the first time, the freezing of shari'a law and an immediate ceasefire. But by this time the NIF had gained considerable political prominence, particularly in the armed forces, and it helped instigate the coup d'état of June 30, 1989. Once again, Sudan's predicament of identity was to alter its relations with the outside world, this time reflected by an increasingly divisive Islamist ideology.

Alienation

Khartoum's abysmal human rights record and its fateful decision to support Saddam Hussein during the 1991 Gulf War cemented its regional and international isolation and pushed the regime even more dramatically toward the Islamic Republic of Iran for political, economic, and military salvation. The alliance between Iran and Sudan, closely nurtured in the period following Iranian president Ali Hashemi Rafsanjani's visit to Khartoum in

December 1992, sent shudders through the Arab world and beyond and sparked concern that Iran might attempt to use Sudan as a springboard to promote political Islam in Egypt and across North Africa.

In reality, the Khartoum-Tehran venture was induced perhaps more by pragmatism than by ideological or religious affinity. Denied financial assistance from their old benefactors in the Gulf and repeatedly spurned by the IMF on requests for fresh loans, the Sudanese fundamentalists hoped to consolidate their rule and further their agenda by acquiring commercial and military support from Iran. Iran, however, wanted to use Sudan not so much to encourage Islamic governments in sub-Saharan Africa but to pursue its well-known regional ambitions and politically outmaneuver its key adversaries in the region, Egypt and Saudi Arabia. Moreover, the fact that Rafsanjani's visit to Sudan was preceded by a major conference in October 1991 in which the participants agreed to promote the Islamic revolution and to undermine the U.S.-sponsored Middle East peace indicates that, far from sharing a natural religious affinity with Sudan, Iran is concerned primarily with its search for greater influence in the Middle East. The Bashir regime's policy of maintaining close relations with both Iraq and Iran demonstrates the fluidity and opportunism of officials in Khartoum.

Egypt, the most influential of Sudan's neighbors, has become increasingly alarmed by the NIF regime's alliance with Iran and has charged Khartoum with supplying arms to and training Islamic militants within its borders; Algeria and Tunisia have made similar charges. Egypt's deteriorating relations with Sudan, compounded by its internal concerns over Islamic militants, have rekindled a dispute over Halaib, a remote triangular area bordering on the Red Sea, which was last contested in 1958. A series of talks to resolve the dispute held in 1993 failed to resolve the conflict. In fact, tensions between the two neighbors continue to mount. In early 1994, Sudan took over a joint Egyptian-Sudanese university in Khartoum and a few months later occupied some thirty houses belonging to members of an Egyptian irrigation project, reportedly in retaliation for Egypt's alleged media campaign against Sudan and its lack of seriousness about settling bilateral disputes.[9]

Sudan's relations with its traditional benefactors in the Gulf (Saudi Arabia, United Arab Emirates, and Kuwait) have cooled considerably following Sudan's support of Saddam Hussein, and although Sudan, out of economic desperation, has sought to improve relations, its efforts have met with no response.[10] Moreover, the fact that the Gulf nations are experiencing a recession has dimmed the likelihood of significant assistance in the foreseeable future. As a consequence, Sudan has turned once again to the more radical Arab/Muslim camp for sanctuary, as it did thirty years before. Khartoum has found itself drawing even closer to Iran, Iraq, Libya, and the Palestine Liberation Organization to the concern of Cairo and Washington.

Recently, Arab countries, particularly those in the Gulf, have increased pressure on Khartoum because of its support for North Yemen against South Yemen in the ongoing civil war.

Furthermore Sudan's image on the international scene has never been worse. While Sudanese Islamists have effectively admitted that they need Western capital and investment to develop, Western countries and international organizations have responded by passing a slew of condemning resolutions against the regime and have repeatedly taken Khartoum to task for its alliance with Iran. No longer concerned with Cold War politics as such, the United States (previously Sudan's biggest aid donor) has retained its interest in the strategic value of the Middle East and the problem of international terrorism. In particular, the United States has expressed grave concern that Sudan might emerge as a new Lebanon from which militant groups can launch terrorist operations. In 1993, it went a step further by adding Sudan to its list of states that sponsor terrorism and played an influential role in prodding the IMF to consider suspending Sudan's membership in its programs. By February 1994, Sudan's arrears to the IMF exceeded $1.4 billion, and Sudan became only the second country in Africa, after Zaire, to be threatened with expulsion from the IMF.

Hassan Turabi, the regime's religious and intellectual leader, and his supporters have pledged to "spread the Islamic revival through the Arab and African worlds,"[11] but this movement is no more than a reflection of the extremist policies implemented internally; the disastrous effects of these policies on the peace, unity, and stability of the country far outweigh any regional or international threat. Indeed, one of Iran's chief contributions has been to assist in establishing a ubiquitous security apparatus in Sudan whose operations have exacerbated already sharp cleavages and have led to the worsening humanitarian crisis. Iranian military assistance has enabled Sudan to purchase the Chinese weaponry (estimated at $200 million) that it has used with devastating effect against the South, in violent suppressions of rebellions in northern urban areas, and in the pacification of the western province of Darfur. In the central portion of the country, assistance from Iran has enabled Khartoum to carry out an "ethnic cleansing" against the Muslims of the Nuba mountains involving widespread arrests, killings, and the forced relocation of hundreds of thousands from their fertile—and much coveted—ancestral lands.[12] There are indications that financial transfers from Iran are becoming limited. Recent overtures by the Bashir regime to Tehran for more credit transfers have not gained more than an agreement to expand air and sea transportation routes between the two nations.

Although regional factors have played a role in Khartoum's military successes over the past two years, internal dynamics have been more consequential. More specifically, the SPLA's loss of its strategic bases in

Ethiopia following Mengistu's ouster and the split within SPLA ranks enabled Khartoum to impose punishing blows on the southern population in 1992 and 1994. The SPLA has gained access to Kenya and Uganda in its effort to reestablish reliable conduits for military and relief supplies; however, internal divisions have precluded it from attaining a modicum of the military power it enjoyed in the late 1980s.

Increasing internal opposition to the regime has caused it to veer ever more sharply in the Islamist direction, which has raised the alarm of its Horn neighbors. Unable to engender popularity from within for their particular vision, the NIF elite has demonstrated a preoccupation with Muslim constituencies abroad, as if by converting them it could affirm its own Islamic identity. In January 1995 President Issayas Afwerke of newly independent Eritrea harshly criticized the NIF-backed regime for attempting to use Eritrean refugees in Sudan to promote its agenda of Islamic fundamentalism in Eritrea. A month later, Ethiopia followed suit, charging Khartoum with backing extremist groups to undermine the regime in Addis Ababa.

Meanwhile, Khartoum's singular identification with the Muslim world has brought about a renewed interest in the plight of the Christian and animist southern Sudanese. In 1993, an unprecedented visit to Khartoum by Pope John Paul II demonstrated the Catholic world's concern and, in the process, signified just how much religious and cultural divisions in Sudan have deepened in recent years. In January 1994, the archbishop of Canterbury, Dr. George Carey, accepted an invitation from the Episcopal (Anglican) Church of Sudan to visit Christian communities in the north and south of the country. However, upon learning that Khartoum wanted to restrict his itinerary Carey canceled his visit to the north and journeyed only to rebel-held areas in southern Sudan. Khartoum responded by expelling the British ambassador to Sudan; the British government retaliated by expelling the Sudanese ambassador in London a few days later.

Conclusion

In this chapter we have tried to explain how Sudan's physical location and internal configuration have determined the external alignments of the parties and political factions in the civil war. The dominant north has been the principal beneficiary, with its powerful and rich Arab/Muslim connections in the region and worldwide. Except for the brief period of Mengistu's support for the SPLM/SPLA, the South has received mostly sympathy from sub-Saharan Africa and humanitarian assistance from the West and Christian organizations worldwide. The internal polarization and its external connections have now crystallized in the confrontation between the

Islamic extremists of the ruling NIF military junta and the SPLM/SPLA, which avows secularism, and democratic pluralism, and, more recently, the right of self-determination for the people of the south and other marginalized, non-Arab areas of the north.

Although the external dimension has been vital, the politics of identity and its manifestation in the conflict are domestically rooted. The north has had leverage over the south in both internal power equations and external reinforcement, but the disparity between the two has not been decisive in favor of the north; neither party has been able to exact a decisive victory. The recent support from Iran and Iraq has strengthened Khartoum to an unprecedented degree, it is still generally recognized that the war is not winnable and that both sides may eventually have to compromise at the negotiating table.

Given the history of the political musical chairs in Sudan, it is likely that the present Islamist agenda, like the exclusive ideologies and political agendas before it, will in the long run be unable to resolve the crisis of national identity behind the war or deliver tangible economic and social goods. Its exclusivist vision will be discredited and its proponents will lose political legitimacy and give way to another generation of leaders. The critical questions, then, will be the character of the identity that this new elite will assume and the role the external world will play in helping to fashion an identity that will reflect the racial, cultural, and religious disposition of all Sudanese. Can external actors play a constructive role by helping the weaker side of the conflict or should all outside forces be discouraged from involvement to allow the country to be managed exclusively by the Sudanese themselves? Assuming the inevitability of external connections, will the assistance currently forthcoming from Iran significantly influence the outcome? Will Khartoum be able to refurbish its image in the Arab world and pursue its historical agenda of Arabism in the north as well as the south, or have events in the Middle East now moved irrevocably away from dreams of Arab Unity and Pan-Islamism toward more pragmatic and internalized matters?

In the African sphere, the mood of the times has changed. Although most African leaders continue to cling to principles of territorial sacrosanctity and nonintervention, "secession," as one influential African journalist recently put it, "is no longer a dirty word" in the continent.[13] But Sudan, by cutting through the thick fog of misunderstanding, hatred, and demonization, could still serve as a potent symbol of a continent where religions have to stand side by side and living history is still open to a new, creative, and above all unforced and noncoercive imagination. The question is whether a leadership capable of that imagination will come forth to redeem the nation in time or whether the forces of disintegration will prevail.

Meanwhile, external efforts are being exerted through various channels, and there are signs of hope. Although the attempted OAU mediation (sponsored by Nigeria in 1991) was stalled because of the disarray in the southern movement and Khartoum's intransigence (particularly on the issue of shari'a), in October 1993 the two rival southern factions signed the Washington Declaration under the auspices of U.S. Congressman Harry Johnson of the House Africa Subcommittee. The two factions, led by John Garang de Mabior and Riek Mashar agreed in principle on the right to self-determination, an immediate cessation of hostilities, and a resolution of their differences through "peaceful means."

Moreover, in January 1994 the Inter-Governmental Authority on Drought and Development (IGADD), a forum grouping six Horn countries, continued southern reconciliation efforts by drawing the splintered factions closer together, at least on the major issues of the north-south conflict if not on the more contentious issues relating to leadership. If unity is restored, it would then be time to try to pressure north and south to work out a settlement. Already Africa has taken the lead. IGADD has reportedly informed Khartoum that it must be prepared to compromise to end the war through either secularism or division. The second session of the IGADD talks, convened in May 1994, marked a small breakthrough, producing an agreed agenda and a Declaration of Principles (DoP) upon which further peace talks are to be based and that would henceforth "constitute the basis for resolving the conflict in the Sudan." Nevertheless, the obstacles to a permanent peace remain formidable. While stating that the option of unity must be "given priority by all parties," the DoP clearly predicates this on certain contentious conditions, including the separation of religion and state, the equitable sharing of wealth, and complete social and political equality that recognizes Sudan's multiple identities guaranteed by a constitution that embodies internationally recognized human rights standards and is protected by an independent judiciary. In the absence of agreement on conditions conducive to unity, the IGADD principles affirm the south's right to self-determination (including independence) following a referendum and interim arrangements that would facilitate the overall settlement of the conflict.[14]

So far, IGADD's primary success has been to convince both sides that humanitarian issues should be addressed separately from political issues. A working committee for humanitarian relief aid managed to broker an agreement between Khartoum and the southern rebels to open air, river, and land routes across battle lines and "safe corridors" across the borders with Kenya and Uganda for the delivery of relief supplies. But less than a month after the IGADD talks were adjourned, Khartoum waged another military offensive, capturing the town of Kajo Kaji—a key supply point for the southern rebels. Still, most observers, including the IGADD mediators, agree that a military solution cannot bring a lasting peace. In May 1994, in an effort to bolster the IGADD peace initiative, President Clinton appointed Ambassador Melissa F. Wells as his special representative on Sudan with the objective of assisting "regional efforts to achieve a cease-fire and permanent peace agreement to end the civil war and to ensure the delivery of humanitarian assistance" to the affected population in the south.[15]

But clearly, and naturally, the burden falls on the Sudanese themselves. Although external involvement has had an important effect on the civil war, most Sudanese would admit that their internal crisis of identity constitutes its foundation. The reality is that external actors have been moved to act by regional and geostrategic considerations much more than for cultural reasons. No longer constrained by Cold War calculations, the international community has been called upon to moderate external involvement in the conflict and play a constructive mediating role. But in the end, the challenge of building a national identity that will give all citizens a sense of belonging and the opportunity to participate on an equal footing must be answered by the Sudanese.

Notes

1. Excerpt from a speech delivered at the opening of the Koka Dam Conference attended by north and south political forces in Ethiopia in March 1986. Mansour Khalid, "External Factors in the Sudanese Conflict," in Francis Mading Deng and Prosser Gifford, eds., The Search for Peace and Unity in Sudan (Washington, D.C.: Wilson Center Press, 1987), p. 110.

2. See Alexis Heraclides, "Secessionist Minorities and External Involvement," International Organization, vol. 44 (Summer 1990), pp. 341–377.

3. Ernest Gellner, Nations and Nationalism (Ithaca, N.Y: Cornell University Press, 1983), pp. 48–49.

4. Taisier Mohamed Ahmed Ali, "Roots of War in Sudan" (Paper presented at a conference entitled "Sudan: The Forgotten Tragedy," United States Institute of Peace, Washington, D.C., October 20, 1993), pp. 7–9.

5. Quoted in A. G. G. Gingyera-Pincwa, "The Border Implications of the Sudan Civil War: Possibilities for Intervention," in Dunstan M. Wai, ed., The Southern Sudan: The Problem of National Integration (London: Frank Cass, 1973), p. 132.

6. Mohamed Ahmed Mahgoub, Democracy on Trial: Reflections on Arab and African Politics (London: Andre Deutsch, 1974), p. 213.

7. Mansour Khalid, The Government They Deserve (London: Kegan Paul International, 1990), p. 151.

8. By 1985 the United States was supporting Sudan with $250 million and $40 million in economic and military aid, respectively. See Scott H. Jacobs, "The Sudan's Islamization," Current History 85 (May 1985), p. 231.

9. "Egypt and Sudan in Fresh Row," *Mideast Mirror,* May 25, 1994, p. 17.

10. Not only did Saudi Arabia cut off official assistance to Khartoum following the latter's demonstrated antipathy toward the Saudi royal family during the Persian Gulf crisis, it also began a campaign to persuade wealthy Saudis who gave millions of dollars to Islamic causes throughout the 1980s not to finance Sudanese Islamists. Youssef M. Ibrahim, "Saudis Seek to Cut Funds for Militants," *New York Times,* March 1, 1992, p. 8.

11. *The Economist,* April 18, 1992, p. 43.

12. Africa Watch, *Sudan: Eradicating the Nuba* (Washington, D.C.: Human Rights Watch, 1992).

13. "Sudan, Islam and Africa," *West Africa* (January 10–16, 1994), p. 7.

14. Ministry of Foreign Affairs, the Republic of Kenya, "Draft Declaration of Principles," Nairobi, Kenya, May 20, 1994.

15. The White House, Office of the Press Secretary, "Statement by the Press Secretary," Washington, D.C., May 20, 1994.

8

Ethnic Conflict and
Security in South Africa

MARINA OTTAWAY

One of the unexpected developments after the end of the Cold War has been an explosion of nationalism around the world, resulting in a sharp increase in the level of ethnic conflict. The political openings that have occurred in countries formerly dominated by socialist and authoritarian regimes have provided the space for new political groups to emerge. Alongside the new, democratic forces there have appeared other potentially dangerous forces that are threatening to democratization and stability; among these is ethnic nationalism.

Paradoxically, South Africa has moved away from the ethnic-based apartheid regime in the midst of this resurgence of nationalism. The logic of the transition from apartheid requires a rejection of ethnic divisions, but the political interests of some groups and the effect of events elsewhere has encouraged ethnic nationalism. In fact, ethnic conflict came very close to disrupting South Africa's transitional elections of April 27, 1994. Although catastrophe was avoided at the last minute and the elections were remarkably peaceful, the tensions are still there. It is possible that the new government will find a way of managing nationalist demands so as to avoid conflict, but it could also fail to do so. Such an outcome would have serious repercussions on the stability of South Africa and the entire region.

Ethnic Politics and Ethnic Nationalism in Africa

Discussing ethnicity, particularly in the African context, is always a delicate problem, but the vagueness of the concept of ethnicity and the misuse of the idea of tribalism do not justify avoiding discussion of ethnic conflict or denying its reality.[1]

There are real difficulties in defining an ethnic group or a nation (the two words are essentially synonymous). In theory, an ethnic group is characterized by a commonality of language, culture, and tradition that is based on a shared history. In practice, we know that ethnic groups are fluid, that their boundaries change, and that new ones emerge, often as a result of deliberate political maneuvers.[2] We also know that ethnic identities can remain dormant or become salient depending on circumstances. It is equally difficult to determine clearly to which group a specific individual belongs because history has given most of us a very mixed background. The boundaries of ethnic groups and the identity of individuals cannot be determined by simple, objective criteria; they must be understood in the context of particular political situations.

Ethnic divisions have affected African politics ever since the colonial boundaries were established: Colonial powers played ethnic groups against each other, and pro-independence parties and liberation movements were often divided along ethnic lines. But the postindependence governments condemned ethnic divisions and, in theory at least, sought to promote a broad nationalism embracing their entire country. The need to maintain unity and a common identity was a major argument used to justify the single-party system and the rejection of pluralist democracy. In reality, no African government was blind to the importance of ethnicity, and complex political maneuvers pitting "state versus ethnic claims," as one study put it, were carried out by all sides in the game.[3]

The continuing importance of ethnic claims in countries that theoretically rejected ethnic divisions strengthened the widely held conviction that African countries suffered from a special disability called tribalism. In reality, Africans were probably no more conscious of their separate ethnic identities than other people. The difference was that whereas ethnic or national identities were openly recognized as legitimate in many parts of the world, beginning with Europe, they were rejected in Africa. European nationalism was openly ethnic in nature, and African nationalism was supposedly multiethnic. In Europe, the boundaries of the state were supposed to be those of the nation, establishing the idea of the nation-state; but in Africa, the boundaries of the state were those established by the colonial powers, and the ethnic groups within each state were supposed to renounce their separate identities rather than use those identities to define new states. In European countries, ethnic minorities that refused to be assimilated were supposed to be entitled to protection and a special status, but when Africans failed to forgo their ethnic identities, they were denounced as suffering from tribalism. Instances of open, violent ethnic conflict, like those in Rwanda and Burundi, were few, but somehow they came to symbolize a tribal Africa in the eyes of many commentators.[4]

Although ethnic politics was pervasive and ethnic conflict occasionally flared up, ethnic nationalism—nationalism in the original, European sense—was rare in the first three decades of independence. There were few separatist or irredentist claims based on ethnicity: Biafra stands out as the major example of secessionist nationalism; Somalia's attempts to annex the Ogaden as the major example of irredentist nationalism. But Eritrean separatists, who achieved their goal of independence after three decades of fighting, never claimed that Eritrea was a nation. Rather, they argued it was a territory with a multiethnic population entitled to independence because it had been a separate colony. In Sudan, ethnic and religious differences were at the root of the conflict between north and south, but the southern movements were broadly multiethnic and afflicted by internal tensions. And in Ethiopia, the openly ethnic liberation movements of the 1970s remained uncertain whether their goal was to form new nation-states or to compete for power within a multiethnic Ethiopia.

Africa thus remained a continent of determinedly multiethnic countries. Aspirations to statehood or territorial claims based on national identity were rejected by the Organization of African Unity and the overwhelming majority of African countries. Respect for colonial borders was the fundamental principle of inter-African relations. The right to self-determination, in the African context, meant decolonization, not the right of different national or ethnic groups to have a country of their own. The only nationalism regarded as legitimate was one embracing the entire population of a country and seeking to coax the diverse population into becoming a nation. The state was expected to build a nation, but nations were not given the right to create a state.

Although the manifestations of the nationalist revival have been more dramatic in the former Soviet Union and in Eastern Europe, similar trends are beginning to appear in Africa. In all countries that held multiparty elections, not only did the population vote along ethnic and regional lines (which could be considered a continuation of ethnic politics of the earlier period), but political movements emerged with openly ethnic nationalist platforms.

Most African countries in the mid-1990s are still refusing to acknowledge the importance of ethnic nationalism, rejecting it as wrong and thus not deserving of attention. At the other extreme, Ethiopia is trying to devise a political system built entirely on ethnicity, but conflict continues unabated. South Africa, which in the transition process has been forced to make some concessions to nationalist demands and in doing so has curbed violence and avoided chaos, has the potential for setting an important example if it succeeds in managing nationalism on a sustained basis.

Ethnic Nationalism in South Africa

In the history of South Africa, ethnic nationalism was an ideology upheld by whites long before it became an issue among blacks. Afrikaner nationalism led to the formation of the independent Boer republics of the Transvaal and the Orange Free State in the middle of the nineteenth century and to their conflict with Britain.[5] But black ethnic nationalism is a much more recent phenomenon. The original resistance to European conquest cannot be defined as nationalism without severely distorting the concept. In the twentieth century, the strongest nationalism in South Africa, as in the rest of the continent, was not ethnic, but it embraced the entire black population living within the borders established by the European conquest. The African National Congress (ANC) and the Pan-Africanist Congress (PAC) appealed to all blacks; indeed, by the 1980s, the ANC was open to anybody, of any racial or ethnic group, who opposed apartheid.

The absence of a strong current of ethnic nationalism among blacks was particularly remarkable given the efforts made by the apartheid regime to promote such ideology. In fact, it is probable that the government's attempts to promote separate ethnic identities among blacks had the opposite effect; blacks resisted anything the government tried to impose because it always carried high costs for them. Only among Zulus, for reasons that will be discussed later, did there exist a stronger, separate identity.

In the early 1990s, with the end of apartheid approaching, ethnic nationalism became part of the struggle for power among competing movements and leaders trying to stake out a position in the new system. Once again, Zulu nationalism was especially important. At the same time, Afrikaner nationalism also revived, as Afrikaners, after almost half a century of security and "uplifting" under the National Party government, felt threatened by the impending change. As a result, Zulu and Afrikaner nationalism played a role in the political dynamics of the transition from apartheid. Zulu nationalism in particular is bound to remain a crucial political force in the future, with consequences that may well go beyond the boundaries of South Africa.

Afrikaner Nationalism

Until the early part of this century, the history of the Afrikaners was one of constant defeat at the hands of the British, culminating in the Anglo-Boer War of 1899–1902 and the loss of the independent Boer republics. Essentially, the Afrikaners were too few and too poor to resist domination by Britain, particularly after the discovery of diamonds and gold made South Africa an economic prize worth fighting for. Once the independent Boer republics were destroyed in the Anglo-Boer War, however, the British had no interest in maintaining South Africa as a colony when it could be turned into a white-governed member of the Commonwealth that offered Britain the same advantages of control without the headaches of administration. In 1910, therefore, the Union of South Africa became independent within the Commonwealth.

For the next forty years, the country was the scene of a struggle for control of the government between Afrikaners and South Africans of British descent. Originally, the latter had the advantage; they were richer and better educated, and, of course, Britain had won the war. But the Afrikaners—poor, uneducated, their communities devastated by the war—had numbers and determination on their side. In 1948, the National Party succeeded in winning the elections, marking the triumph of Afrikaner nationalism.

In typical liberation movement fashion, the National Party proceeded to set up a system that would benefit its people. The party had a clear goal of uplifting the Afrikaners out of dire poverty to a standard of living comparable to that of the English-speaking population. The even greater poverty of blacks received no attention. The means chosen to attain the goal were the same favored by all other African governments: heavy-handed state intervention in the management of the economy, the development of a large public sector, and the overstaffing of parastatals and government offices in order to create jobs. Politically, too, the National Party followed a typical African approach, setting up a de facto single party system, obliterating the distinction between government and party, and imposing the control of the party on all institutions, including the military and the bureaucracy. What the National Party did not manage directly through the institutions of government it controlled indirectly through the tight network of members of the Afrikaner Broederbond, who occupied leadership positions in virtually all important institutions.[6]

The policies that failed in other African countries succeeded in South Africa, thanks to the taxes paid by the gold and diamond companies and to the fact that only a small segment of the total population was the target of the government's largesse. Under the National Party, the gap between Afrikaners and English speakers largely disappeared. From a nation of poor farmers and urban workers struggling against the competition from Africans willing to work at lower wages, Afrikaners turned into a nation of civil servants and public sector employees.

Afrikaner nationalism, which before 1948 was directed in large part against the English-speakers, took on an antiblack character after 1948. Once the National Party was in power, the real threat came from the large black population, which risked engulfing the Afrikaners and all whites by their sheer numbers. The growth of independence movements in other African countries during the 1950s and the consequent decision by France and Britain to relinquish their colonies were particularly threatening, suggesting that South African whites would soon face the same threat of black nationalism.

Although they never hesitated to use force, the National Party leaders were aware that repression alone would not protect white power. As a result, they refined apartheid and started promoting black ethnic national-ism. Grand apartheid was a complex scheme to dress naked white domi-nation in the cloak of self-determination for each ethnic group in the hopes of disguising the real nature of the system and making it acceptable to its victims. Under the apartheid system, a rigid population registration system classified all individuals by race and ethnicity. Not only were whites and nonwhites kept separate, but the nonwhite population was classified in many groups: Coloureds, Asians, and nine different African ethnic groups were entitled to their separate development, the government claimed.[7] The architects of apartheid hoped that by building a system based on ethnicity rather than entirely on race, they could transform a situation in which blacks were in the majority into one in which no groups had a numerical advantage: South Africa, they argued, was a country of minorities entitled to self-determination. This policy would eventually turn the country into a constellation of independent states.

Crucial to the success of the maneuver was the development of ethnic nationalism among the various black groups. Separate homelands were or-ganized for each, with separate systems of education, cultural movements, and, eventually, the government hoped, "independent" governments firmly controlled from Pretoria. Not surprisingly, blacks refused to accept the bar-ren pieces of territory they were given as their countries or to agree that political rights in these so-called independent states were an adequate sub-stitute for political rights in a multiethnic South Africa. Although the gov-ernment managed to build up ethnic elites willing to accept independence in four of the homelands, the majority of the population continued to resist the apartheid solution. Furthermore, the project suffered a severe setback when Chief Mangosuthu Buthelezi, the chief minister of KwaZulu, refused to accept independence for the homeland. Since the Zulus, under the South African classification system, were one of the two largest population groups in the country, the failure to create an independent KwaZulu was a serious problem.[8]

It took the National Party a very long time to accept that the apartheid system was not working. Despite the obvious resistance by the black pop-ulation, the government forged ahead with the plan, trying to perfect it and to close the loopholes. The adoption in 1983 of a new constitution that al-lowed Coloureds and Indians to vote for their separate chambers in the parliament and theoretically to rule themselves through their own govern-ments was the last attempt to complete the apartheid edifice. Three years later, at its 1986 congress, the National Party admitted that blacks would have to be given political rights in South Africa. What the National Party envisaged was not a simple system based on majority rule but one based on separate representation and a degree of self-government for each pop-ulation group.[9]

The change in the National Party's stance was prompted by the failure of the homeland system and by the increasing level of political organization among urban blacks. In the early 1970s, blacks started once again organizing inside South Africa, putting an end to the long hiatus that followed the dismantling of the ANC and the PAC in 1960. By 1983, literally hundreds of township and student organizations had formed, and they came together under the umbrella of the United Democratic Front (UDF), actually the internal branch of the exiled ANC.[10] Black labor unions had also started organizing during the 1970s, and in 1985 they formed the new Congress of South African Trade Unions.[11] The National Party continued to use force to suppress black organizations, and it imposed a state of emergency in 1986. But the government knew it had to think of new solutions.

The changes of the 1980s also revived Afrikaner nationalism, this time as a movement by Afrikaner extremists against an Afrikaner-dominated government. In 1982, a splinter group broke off the National Party, forming the Conservative Party; but soon more militant, extraparliamentary organizations started forming. The best-known of these was the Afrikaner Weerstandsbeweging.[12]

This new Afrikaner nationalism was very different from the old. The goal of the National Party had been simple and clear: to win the elections and to govern the country for the benefit of the Afrikaners. But the new nationalists had confused goals and were divided, with new movements springing up and old ones disappearing continually. Initially, the nationalists appeared simply to be against any change, insisting that the apartheid blueprint be implemented. After 1990, as black political parties were permitted and negotiations started in earnest, many Afrikaner nationalist organizations redefined their goals as the exercise of their right to self-determination through the creation of an Afrikaner homeland.

The demand was extremely problematic because Afrikaners were not concentrated in one area and were therefore not the majority anywhere. As a result, different groups had very different visions of the homeland: The most ambitious claimed the entire territory of the old Boer republics; the visionaries a small enclave in the western Transvaal.

The insistence on a separate Afrikaner homeland was sufficient to create a strange marriage of convenience between Afrikaner extremists and homeland leaders who resisted reincorporation of their territories into South Africa. The Concerned South Africans Group (COSAG) came into existence in late 1992 in an attempt to prevent the ANC and the National Party from agreeing on a constitution that did not grant a high degree of autonomy to the regions. Only autonomy, they argued, would afford sufficient protection to the rights of the different groups that made up South Africa's population.

COSAG, which later became the Freedom Alliance, was doomed from the start. Its members had nothing in common except the desire to prevent an agreement whose terms they did not like. Homeland leaders were not concerned about the rights of Afrikaners, who in turn remained white supremacists. In the long run, the members of the alliance could not have agreed on the boundaries of their respective homelands. COSAG, however, was a convenient tool to force ethnic claims onto the political agenda.

Zulu Nationalism

Although the main current of black nationalism in South Africa was multi-ethnic, an ethnic nationalism had developed in the early part of the twentieth century among the Zulus, and it became particularly strong in the 1980s. It must be pointed out that Zulu nationalism was never an ideology embraced by all people classified as ethnic Zulus; on the contrary, many of them were strongly opposed to it, supporting the ANC instead. In fact, some violent encounters took place in KwaZulu and Natal (the white region in which the fragments of KwaZulu were embedded) between nationalist Zulus and Zulu supporters of the ANC.

It is not surprising that a nationalist tendency should have developed among the Zulus: A Zulu state had existed ever since Shaka had launched a program of conquest and founded an empire in the early part of the nineteenth century. In the process, a small and obscure Nguni clan, the Zulus, absorbed neighboring clans. Eventually, all Nguni-speaking inhabitants of the Natal region came to be seen as Zulus, despite the fact that the Zulu empire had controlled only the section of Natal lying north of the Tugela River. Because they had a centralized state and a military tradition that had been developed in Shaka's days, the Zulus were not easily subdued by the Afrikaners or the British. Many battles were fought before the British, after suffering a humiliating defeat, finally put an end to the Zulu empire in 1879.[13]

The Zulu king was exiled to Britain and a deliberate effort was initially made to break up the Zulu territory and erase the memory of the empire. But in the early part of the twentieth century, the South African government started perceiving the advantages of promoting a Zulu identity in order to divide the black population. The Zulu monarchy was allowed to revive as a symbol of Zulu separateness, and a cultural organization called Inkatha was allowed to organize.

It was important to the white regime that the Zulus embrace the homeland concept wholeheartedly. The monarchy could be resurrected and KwaZulu could be presented to the population as the continuation of the Zulu empire, the government hoped. But the government had not reckoned on Mangosuthu Buthelezi, who became both the ally and the enemy of the white regime, playing a game that he, and not the government, controlled. Buthelezi came from a family that, he claimed, had traditionally provided advisors to the Zulu kings. He became the chief minister of the homeland in 1953, overshadowing the king, a younger man with a weak personality. As a leader in a homeland created by the apartheid regime, Buthelezi was seen by many as a collaborator. Although he rejected the notion that KwaZulu was a creation of apartheid, he also refused to accept independence for KwaZulu under the conditions and within the boundaries established by the white government.[14]

Buthelezi's power depended on his control over the KwaZulu administration. Like all homelands, KwaZulu was run like an African single-party state. It had its strong leader in Buthelezi and, after 1975, its party in Inkatha YeNkululeko YeSizwe.[15] An Inkatha membership card was the key to receiving any service from the government, from a place in school for a child to the payment of an old-age pension. As labor unions and township organizations emerged during the 1970s, Inkatha's monopoly was challenged and Buthelezi feared his control would weaken, especially in the fast-growing townships that surrounded Durban and the industrial areas of Natal. As a result, he opposed the new organizations, which eventually brought him into opposition with the ANC. After the formation of the UDF in 1983, supporters of Inkatha and of the ANC became bitter enemies, starting a long cycle of violence between nationalist and nonnationalist Zulus that has continued even after the transitional elections of April 1994.

It is evident even from this brief account that Zulu nationalism is not a simple phenomenon. Although it undoubtedly has roots in the history of the Zulu empire and in the similarity of language and culture among people defined as Zulus, Zulu nationalism was deliberately encouraged by the government and by Buthelezi for their own political aims. Some see this manipulation as reason to dismiss the movement as artificial and thus not a legitimate expression of Zulu aspirations. But nationalism never arises spontaneously; it is always promoted by leaders and movements with a political agenda. Above all, once it is aroused, it does not disappear because scholars point out that it has weak historical or anthropological foundations. No matter what its origins are, Zulu nationalism is a real force in South African politics.

Ethnic Nationalism and the Transition from Apartheid

The National Party decision in 1990 to lift the ban on the ANC and other black political organizations and to open negotiations with its erstwhile enemies called into question the position of every group and the power of every leader and organization and threw the door of political competition wide open. No matter what the outcome of the talks would be, the future political map of South Africa was bound to be totally different from the one that had prevailed for almost half a century of National Party rule. It would have been more difficult, however, to predict that ethnic nationalism would be an important factor in the process.

The transition coincided with the dissolution of socialist regimes in the Soviet Union and Eastern Europe. In the world of the 1990s, socialism appeared dead as an actual political system and as a vision for the future, and nationalism, subdued in the days of the Cold War, was reemerging as a major political force everywhere.

Ten years earlier, the outcome of a South African transition would have been a foregone conclusion: the transformation of the ANC from the dominant liberation movement into the ruling political party in a centralized, authoritarian political system and the pursuit of economic development under heavy state control.[16] In the 1990s, these ideas were out of fashion, and any country that advocated them was bound to be ostracized by donors, lenders, and investors alike. Ten years earlier ethnic nationalism would have been promptly dismissed as tribalism or, in South Africa's case, as an attempt to prolong apartheid, but in a world that was witnessing the disintegration of the Soviet Union and Yugoslavia, nationalism had to be taken more seriously. Conversely, events elsewhere encouraged South African organizations to pursue the nationalist option.

The main players in the negotiations over the political system to replace apartheid were the National Party and the ANC. The National Party initially encouraged Inkatha's bid as a third player, hoping to form an alliance with Buthelezi against the ANC. But as a Zulu movement, Inkatha did not have sufficient support to be a national player, and an attempt in July 1990 to relaunch it as a national, multiethnic political party failed.[17]

The National Party also had to abandon its original strategy of establishing a political system based on political representation for major ethnic groups rather than on majority rule. Similarly, the ANC was forced to give up the idea that elections for a constituent assembly should be held immediately, without prior negotiations on the outline of the new political system. Slowly, a consensus emerged between the ANC and the National Party that the best hope for a peaceful transition resided in the formation of a government of national reconciliation in which all parties receiving a minimum percentage of the vote would participate. Power sharing at the center would be accompanied by decentralization, with the creation of nine provinces with their own elected assemblies.

The ANC and the National Party had each given up part of their initial demands to reach this agreement, but they had also received a lot in return. The National Party's position in the future government was ensured; in return, the ANC had a much greater chance to receive the cooperation of the security forces, the civil service, and the business community. The situation was very different for homeland leaders and Afrikaner nationalists. The homelands would be reincorporated into South Africa and would lose their identities in the surrounding provinces. The power of provincial assemblies and governments was not clearly spelled out in the interim constitution, but it appeared rather limited. The new system was not even clearly federal, although it could evolve in that direction.

Buthelezi had no intention of allowing himself to be negotiated into political oblivion. Turning unambiguously to nationalism, he denounced the agreement as a violation of the Zulu right to self-determination, even an insult to the Zulu nation. He advocated the regions' need to have a much higher degree of autonomy in order to safeguard their rights. The leaders of Bophuthatswana and the Ciskei, as well as Afrikaner nationalists, took up the idea, and COSAG emerged.

With Inkatha the only credible organization in the alliance, COSAG could not stop the transition. The leadership of Bophuthatswana had failed to gain popular support or to forge a political machine sufficiently strong to maintain control, and President Lucas Mangope was ousted in March 1994. The leader of the Ciskei, who had jumped on the nationalist bandwagon when it appeared to be going strong, had already begun to abandon his defiant stance. The Afrikaner nationalists were not winning much support from the white population, which was fearful but resigned to the change.

Even alone, Inkatha represented a threat. It could not stop the transition, but it could cause a lot of violence. By refusing to participate in the elections, it would raise questions about the fairness of the process and undermine the legitimacy of the provincial assembly and government in Natal. Ten days before the scheduled elections, when Buthelezi and the Zulu king reached an agreement with the ANC and the National Party, and Inkatha presented its candidates, there was enormous relief. Violence decreased sharply and the elections were uneventful. Inkatha won a small majority of the vote for the Natal assembly and enough votes on the national level to receive three ministerial posts.

Under the circumstances, the transition was extremely successful. It was also a partial victory for ethnic nationalism, ensuring Natal's autonomy and sealing its character as the Zulu homeland. The agreement between Inkatha, the National Party, and the ANC involved not only the recognition of the king as a constitutional monarch in KwaZulu but also the transfer to the king of millions of acres of land—about one-third of the new KwaZulu/Natal region—to be held in trust for his people.[18] On the eve of relinquishing power, the National Party succeeded in embedding into the makeup of the new South Africa a measure of Zulu autonomy and sovereignty. The subsequent creation of a council to supervise the use of that land decreased the personal power of the king, but it did not detract from the fact that the land transfer created an island of Zulu sovereignty in Natal.

Managing Ethnic Nationalism

In the aftermath of the elections that ended the apartheid regime, South Africa was basking in triumph, but catastrophe had been only narrowly averted, and the underlying problems remained. The Afrikaner extremists who had been planting bombs before the elections and the Zulu nationalists who had marched through the streets of Johannesburg brandishing weapons were still around. Afrikaner nationalists had not abandoned their demands for a homeland, and the victory of Inkatha in Natal accentuated the character of the province as a Zulu homeland.

The worst-case scenario, under the circumstances, was a return to violence—with more bombs, more killings between nationalist and non-nationalist Zulus, and an alliance between nationalists and elements of the security forces. The best-case scenario was the continuation of negotiations to reach a compromise solution on the many unsolved questions. To reach an agreement, the ANC and the National Party had postponed many decisions concerning the powers of the provinces, their relation to the central government, the role traditional authorities would play in the provincial legislatures and at the local level—all issues that related directly to the concerns of nationalists of all ethnic groups. The answers to these questions would determine whether ethnic nationalism would again become a disruptive force or whether it would be embedded in the political system. A high level of decentralization and regional autonomy and the recognition of traditional authorities would satisfy Inkatha—and would also upset ANC supporters in Natal. But they might also encourage the nationalism of other ethnic groups by making control over provincial governments appealing. Finally, concessions on decentralization sufficient to satisfy black nationalists would make it more difficult to ignore all claims by Afrikaner organizations. Finding a balance would not be easy.

The ANC was committed to nonracialism and by implication to non-ethnicism, and the National Party had renounced the possibility of building a system based on group representation. But in the negotiating process, both organizations had shown a high degree of realism about the necessity to make concessions to ethnic demands, meeting with the Zulu king and militant Afrikaners and writing a role, admittedly not clearly defined, for traditional authorities into the constitution. If the spirit of compromise continued to prevail following the elections, conflict could be minimized and solutions could emerge to the problem of how to govern a multiethnic, conflict-ridden society like South Africa democratically. It appeared extremely unlikely, however, that ethnic nationalism could be simply ignored without causing a return to violence. Pretending that ethnic nationalism did not exist, as many African regimes insisted on doing, would only lead to increased conflict.

Ethnic Nationalism and Regional Security

Ethnic nationalism in South Africa has implications that go beyond the borders of the country. A successful scenario—that of a democratic government sensitive to ethnic demands and willing to negotiate ways to accommodate them—could establish an example that Africa badly needs at the present time. A failure by South Africa to manage ethnic tensions would set a discouraging example for all of Africa and have direct, negative repercussions in southern Africa.

As Denis Venter notes in Chapter 9 of this volume, economically and politically, South Africa has a disproportionate weight in the region. Other countries are intertwined economically with South Africa. They were hurt in the 1980s both by Pretoria's policy of destabilizing neighboring countries inclined to help the ANC and by their own attempts to keep their distance from the white regime. With the normalization of relations with its neighbors, South Africa has already started reasserting its regional economic role. A strong South African presence in the economies of the neighboring countries is not without problems—South Africa could end up dominating and exploiting these weaker economies—but a South African economy devastated by political conflict would have a much more disastrous impact on its neighbors.

Politically, too, a conflict-ridden South Africa would have a destabilizing effect on the entire area. The last few years have already offered examples of the tragic impact of instability across borders. In the 1980s South Africa destabilized Mozambique by providing weapons to the Mozambican National Resistance. As the conflict in Mozambique wound down, AK-47s from the Mozambican civil war found their way back into South Africa, contributing to the escalating violence.

But more than weapons can move across borders. The effect of ethnic nationalism has been powerful everywhere, from nineteenth-century Western Europe to Eastern Europe and Central Asia today, so it is difficult to imagine that strong, unmanaged ethnic nationalism in South Africa would not serve as a demonstration elsewhere, for example, in Zimbabwe and Mozambique. The example of a South Africa successfully handling its own ethnic tensions by compromise and accommodation might help other parties find their own solutions. A South Africa reverting to ethnic conflict would certainly hurt its neighbors.

Notes

1. On tribalism, see Archie Mafeje, "The Ideology of 'Tribalism,'" *Journal of Modern African Studies* 9,2 (1971); and Aidan W. Southhall, "The Illusion of Tribe," *Journal of Asian and African Studies* 5,1/2 (1970).

2. On the fluidity of ethnic identities, see Nelson Kasfir, "Explaining Ethnic Political Participation," in Atul Kholi, ed., *The State and Development in the Third World* (Princeton, N.J.: Princeton University Press, 1986), p. 88 ff; and Crawford Young, *The Politics of Cultural Pluralism* (Madison: University of Wisconsin Press, 1976).

3. Donald Rothchild and Victor A. Olorunsola, eds., *State Versus Ethnic Claims* (Boulder, Colo.: Westview Press, 1983).

4. See, for example, Robert D. Kaplan, "The Coming Anarchy," *The Atlantic Monthly*, February 1994, pp. 44–76.

5. On Afrikaner nationalism, see T. Dunbar Moodie, *The Rise of Afrikanerdom: Power, Apartheid and the Afrikaner Civil Religion* (Berkeley: University of California Press, 1975).

6. J. H. P. Serfontein, *Brotherhood of Power: An Exposé of the Afrikaner Broederbond* (Bloomington: Indiana University Press, 1978).

7. The government recognized nine different major ethnic groups but set up ten separate homelands. The Xhosas were given two homelands, the Transkei and the Ciskei, separated by a swath of territory whites wanted to keep.

8. On Buthelezi's role, see Gerhard Maré and Georgina Hamilton, *An Appetite for Power: Buthelezi's Inkatha and the Politics of "Loyal Resistance"* (Johannesburg: Ravan Press, 1987).

9. See National Party, Position Paper Number 1: "Power-Sharing (and Related Concepts)," compiled by Stoffel van der Merwe, MP, July 1986.

10. See Mark Swilling, "The United Democratic Front and Township Revolt," in William Cobbett and Robin Cohen, eds., *Popular Struggles in South Africa* (London: Review of African Political Economy, 1988), pp. 90–113.

11. On the rise of black labor unions, see Steven Friedman, *Building Tomorrow Today: African Workers in Trade Unions, 1970–1984* (Johannesburg: Ravan Press, 1987).

12. On the new Afrikaner nationalist groups, see Helen Zille, "The Right Wing in South African Politics," in Peter L. Berger and Bobby Godsell, eds., *A Future South Africa: Visions, Strategies and Realities* (Boulder, Colo.: Westview Press, 1988), pp. 55–94. The constantly changing kaleidoscope of Afrikaner nationalist groups is extremely difficult to follow but is fairly well documented in the weekly newsletter *Southern Africa Report*, passim, particularly in 1993 and 1994.

13. See Donald R. Morris, *The Washing of the Spears* (New York: Simon & Schuster, 1965).

14. See Colleen McCaul, "The Wild Card: Inkatha and Contemporary Black Politics," in Philip Frankel, Naom Pines, and Mark Swilling, eds., *State, Resistance and Change in South Africa* (Johannesburg: Southern Books Publishers, 1989), pp. 146–173.

15. Inkatha was technically a cultural movement because the government did not allow the formation of parties in nonindependent homelands. This did not prevent Inkatha from functioning as a single party.

16. These ideas are explored at greater length in Marina Ottaway, "Liberation Movements and Transition to Democracy: The Case of the ANC," *The Journal of Modern African Studies* 29,1 (1991), pp. 61–82.

17. On the negotiations, see Marina Ottaway, *South Africa: The Struggle for a New Order* (Washington, D.C.: Brookings, 1993).

18. Paul Taylor, "Zulu Land Deal Creates Controversy for South Africa's New Leaders," *The Washington Post,* May 23, 1994.

9

Regional Security in Southern Africa in the Post–Cold War Era

DENIS VENTER

Profound change in global society, precipitated by the end of the Cold War, provides a compelling reason to rethink the concept of security, which has proven to be ambiguous at best. Security is often defined in reaction to threats of the state or of its interests.[1] The conventional military definition ossifies it in geopolitical terms "as the spatial exclusion of threats."[2] In such circumstances, state or national security merely become code words for safeguarding the security of a political regime and its social elite. Traditionally, security has almost exclusively involved military issues and threats to the state; but in the developing world, the notion of collective security (in the form of traditional alliances) rarely offers peace and security because very often nonmilitary internal and regional factors are of much more importance, among other ecological, ethnic, irredentist, and social concerns.[3]

For many people, security is threatened more often by the very government under whose sovereignty they live, either through its oppressive policies or as a result of its incapacity to sustain a good life for all.[4] It is therefore necessary to conceive of security without the centrality of the state: Peace and security need to be considered in relation to people.[5] Governments are not the only agents of security, and this is particularly true if a broad or holistic view of security is adopted. (Comprehensive security also requires vigorous civil societies, without which there cannot be mature [national or multinational] societies.) Broadening the security agenda to include political, economic, societal, environmental, and military aspects is to accept that human security is ultimately more important than state security.[6]

Individual security, however, raises a wider set of issues—such as human rights, economic development, and gender issues, in addition to food security, job security, resource security, and other associated aspects—and global security raises issues affecting, for example, the environment.[7]

134

It is therefore clear—as Gowher Rizvi, the south Asian strategist, states— that "security no longer . . . [can] be considered exclusively within the military sphere; it is concerned not only with safeguarding territorial integrity, but also with political, economic and social welfare, and above all, intercommunal harmony."[8]

This chapter looks closely at the sources of regional insecurity in southern Africa, what some of the possible mechanics for a regional security regime are, South Africa's role in the subcontinent, and how a regional security regime may be institutionalized now that the debilitating factors of insecurity (apartheid [domestic] and destabilization [regional]) have disappeared from the agenda. Security will be approached from a holistic, human angle and from, essentially, a South African perspective of the southern African region.

Sources of Regional Insecurity

Over the past five years, the political environment in southern Africa has undergone substantial change. Most of the major historical conflicts have been resolved or are in the process of being settled: Namibia has attained independence; Cuban and South African troops have been withdrawn from Angola; Mozambique's Frelimo and Renamo have signed and implemented a peace agreement; and South Africa has transformed itself into a multiracial democracy. Much of this progress is a direct consequence of the demise of the Cold War, which led to the cessation of superpower contestation on the subcontinent, a brief flurry of joint U.S.-Soviet efforts to resolve long-standing disputes in southwestern Africa, and a more prominent role for the UN in regional and national conflict resolution.[9] There has been a concomitant attenuation of ideology as a source of tension within and among African countries[10] and a significant movement toward political pluralism throughout the continent.

In terms of potential conflict areas in southern Africa, the following will pose serious threats to regional peace and security in the years to come:

- With South Africa's apartheid policies removed from the agenda, many of the region's simmering conflicts—which have been bottled up—may resurface. The main conflicts will likely involve border disputes or territorial claims.
- Inequitable distribution of resources both within and between countries may be another source of conflict. Because of economic decay and the added problems of drought and the ravages caused by structural adjustment programs, there is bound to be social strife and the consequent threat of major conflagrations.

- The potential for racial and ethnic conflict will likely be a continuing concern.
- Political pluralism may be a source of conflict in some countries,
  such as Swaziland, where the principle of multipartyism is not yet
  accepted. Although Zambia and Malawi managed to achieve peaceful transitions from one-party systems to multiparty politics, it is
  not yet certain that other countries will be as fortunate. Even in
  Zambia and Malawi, there are signs of stress as people struggle to
  learn the ethos of democratic pluralism and tolerance. Rapidly declining economies place even more pressure on the process of
  democratization.[11]

But southern Africa is also beset by a range of critical problems for
which no immediate solutions are in sight:

- The region suffers from chronic underdevelopment and the attendant conditions of poverty, unemployment, illiteracy, malnutrition,
  and inadequate social services. Efforts to redress the situation are
  inhibited by staggering balance-of-payments deficits, a debilitating
  debt crisis, and an unfavorable international economic climate.
- The structural adjustment programs of the World Bank and the International Monetary Fund, which tie foreign loans and aid to pre-
  scribed economic and political reforms, impinge on the independence of states, disadvantage the poorest sections of society, and
  have given rise to food riots and other forms of protest in several
  countries.
- Regional and national stability are undermined by internal political and ethnic conflict, authoritarian rule and disregard for human
  rights in some states, fledgling democracies in others, and large
  numbers of refugees and displaced people across the subcontinent.
- The region is wracked by an AIDS pandemic, rampant disease, and
  environmental degradation, arising from human mismanagement,
  limited resources, and natural phenomena. As recently as 1992, the
  most severe drought in eighty years threatened several million people with starvation.[12]

These problems are exacerbated by Africa's growing marginalization
in international politics and the world economy. The continent has never
presented an attractive opportunity for foreign investment, and the ending
of the Cold War has greatly diminished what little strategic value it once
had. The situation is compounded by the emergence of giant trading blocs
in North America, Europe, and the Pacific Rim with which Africa cannot
compete.

This leads us to ask some pertinent questions: Can southern Africa be considered a "security community," a group of states where peace is predictable? Is there any possibility that the region will develop in such a way that war and the threat of war will be rejected as legitimate or possible instruments of political power? However distant it may seem, is there at least the prospect of "common security" developing in southern Africa— the sort of common consciousness that involves the belief that security has to be achieved with others, not against them?

The acid test of a security community is whether or not the units target each other in a military sense. To what extent does southern Africa meet these criteria? In the past, because of the offensive strategy employed by South African forces, the criteria were clearly not met. What will be South Africa's strategy under a nonracial and democratic government? If it drops offensive doctrines, could the region become an anomaly to Deutsch's theory; that is, as we move further into the postapartheid era, will the separate units refrain from targeting each other but the region as a whole still not score highly in terms of value compatibility, economic ties, level of transnational links, institution building, responsiveness, and mutual predictability in behavior? Although the countries of the region may not threaten each other in the future, they face an enormous range of regional problems. Is southern Africa not a security community but rather a community of insecurity?

The essence of community building seems to be communication. The difficulties involving the cost and speed of communication channels across southern Africa are well known and result from a mixture of geographical, historical, economic, and political factors. They will not be easily overcome, but if we believe that ultimately the best route to security is through community building, then one might consider that cheaper transportation, efficient telecommunications systems, increased cultural exchanges, and so on should have priority on the broadened security agenda of governments in the region.[13] This argument will sound strange to those for whom security equals defense equals military might, but it is another way of thinking about minimizing the dangers of insecurity.

The Mechanics of a Regional Security Regime

The widely held expectations that South Africa will become the economic engine of southern Africa may be disappointed, partly because the postapartheid state has to generate wealth by external economic activities in areas as far removed as Western and Eastern Europe, the Middle East, and the Pacific Rim (and, naturally, in African states outside the subcontinent). Nevertheless, existing regional economic organizations and relationships

seem to provide relatively favorable conditions for the empirical development of mutually advantageous cooperation. And the current progressive
status of South Africa's economic relationships with the rest of Africa
bodes well for cooperation in other fields. The economic dynamic puts a
premium on common security arrangements, especially where power generation, water supply, and transport routes are concerned.[14]

For a security regime to be institutionalized in the region, several conditions will have to be met.[15] These conditions include strengthening and
sustaining both national and intraregional civil society; conceiving peace
and security as social and relational phenomena, transcending the jurisdiction of individual states (this, in turn, calls for rethinking the concept of
sovereignty); developing institutional and analytical capacities within state
and other bureaucracies; expanding and improving transport infrastructure
and other physical communications networks; and molding a regional
identity, at both the institutional and symbolic levels.

A number of measures could be taken to help accomplish these
goals:[16]

- Establishing a school of diplomacy for the region emphasizing
  training for peacemaking, conflict resolution, mediation, conciliation, arbitration, and sustainable development.
- Recasting military and police training in the region through region-
  specific military and police academies.
- Formulating a new legal basis for environmental protection and
  sustainable development and launching initiatives in these areas
  with nongovernmental organizations.
- Building a peacemaking, monitoring, and peacekeeping capability,
  as well as a conflict prevention, management, and resolution capacity under the auspices of the Southern African Development
  Community (SADC),[17] by utilizing the technical skills and political
  legitimacy of the UN and the Commonwealth.
- Promoting a regional convention on the monitoring, reduction, and
  ultimate abolition of arms transfers and working toward the denu-
  clearization of southern Africa and the southwestern Indian Ocean.

Given South Africa's full subscription to the conditions of the Nuclear
Non-Proliferation Treaty and the safeguards of the International Atomic Energy Agency, the first critical steps toward a comprehensive regional arms
control agreement have been taken. Nevertheless, the formality of a regional
nonproliferation treaty might be a useful platform for negotiating agreements to regulate the trade in and supply of arms generally. The first objective of a regional arms control agreement should be to restrict the arms trade
and to reduce military expenditure and the risk of new militarization.[18]

But all of these measures will be almost meaningless—and, indeed, social peace impossible—without appropriate programs for poverty alleviation, migration control, basic food security, access to primary health care, regional tourism, gender equity, human resource development, and participatory democracy based on public accountability; the development of agro-processing industries and alternative energy sources; the stimulation of economic activity and trade-financing facilities; and the coordination of resource management.[19]

South Africa and Southern Africa

A South Africa that exhibits even minimal calm and continuity is likely to remain the dominant force and the major economic, financial, technical, and military power in the region, contributing decisively to the subcontinent's security but perpetuating the existing fears of neighboring states about its regional preeminence.[20] Although the states of the region seem to have pledged themselves to cooperation and building harmonious relations, a quick glance at statistics shows exactly how lopsided the region really is.

Militarily and especially economically, South Africa is the giant not just of southern Africa but of sub-Saharan Africa, accounting for 45 percent of Africa's gross national product (GNP). South Africa's GNP is 50 percent greater than that of its nearest rival, Algeria, and two and a half times that of Nigeria or Egypt. Furthermore, South Africa's economic dominance of southern Africa is widely known. It contributes roughly 75 percent of the total GNP of the region; its GNP per capita is six times that of the average for the SADC and seven and a half times larger than that of the average for the Common Market of Eastern and Southern Africa and SADC countries combined.

South Africa's economic dominance raises the question of the country's ambitions and, more specifically, the likelihood that it might relish its role as the regional giant and might use this position to maintain or enhance its own political, diplomatic, and economic power.[21] "Giantism" has developed into one of some ten crises in South Africa's external relations,[22] and southern Africa has, indeed, reached a "unipolar moment."[23] In many ways, this is what the region has always feared. The strong resistance to the infamous Constellation of Southern African States idea was mainly about "supping with the apartheid devil," but it also concerned fear of South African domination. Clearly, SADC planning, which has always endeavored to draw South Africa into its cooperative net rather than the other way around, is precisely aimed at attenuating South Africa's domination of the region.[24]

But even with the best of intentions and will to create a mutually beneficial and nondependent regional economic cooperation system, South Africa will still dominate the region. The frustration experienced by the small states of the subcontinent brings to mind the lament of Mexican president (1876–1911) Porfirio Díaz: "Poor Mexico, so far from God, so near to the United States." South Africa's domination of its neighbors became even greater during its long and very damaging destabilization of the region.[25]

Should the unequal distribution of power endure, southern Africa's "unipolar moment" will become a permanent feature of the regional panorama. For a number of reasons, South Africa views the region with as much uncertainty and incredulity as the region views it. Reluctant to share the country's comparative advantage, successive South African regimes may dominate the region with a "carrot and stick" approach.[26]

In both the economic and security fields, the region will have to find ways to accommodate, manage, even curb South Africa's superior strength. The principal challenge lies in the fact that this strength also needs to be creatively channeled into the interests of the region as a whole.[27] Whatever the character of South Africa's government, its neighbors will feel some unease about its aims unless steps are taken to mitigate or ultimately transcend the pressures of the security dilemma. A "security regime" would achieve the former, a "security community" the latter.[28]

The most likely scenario for future relations in the southern African region may be "neoregionalism"—which means that the "center-hinterland relationships" would continue but without South Africa as the dominating center of gravity—as opposed to the alternatives of regional "restabilization" and "regional breakup and peripheralization."[29] This scenario presupposes a negotiated regional regime, which would necessitate replacing some South African products and services by sources from within the region (Zimbabwe, for example, could become an important supplier of manufactured goods) and reducing transport dependence on South Africa through the upgrading of infrastructural facilities in Mozambique and Angola. Therefore, to be meaningful, neoregionalism would require that states transcend their national goals and interests by acting and thinking regionally.

Institutionalizing Peace and Security

Peace presents southern Africa with a paradox. On the one hand, people need to be liberated from the state. On the other hand, it is purely academic to conceive of rudimentary peace, security, and development in the absence of strong, legitimate states. Consequently, building institutional capacity seems a necessary but insufficient condition for peace and security in

southern Africa; interstate cooperation and coordination must be strengthened also.[30]

At this point in time, a formal framework may perhaps be somewhat
premature. Weimer, Du Pisani, Gutteridge, and Nathan have argued the
need for confidence-building measures in the region; the legacy left by
"destabilization" seems to necessitate such a strategy.[31] But the end of the
Cold War and the resultant disengagement from regional conflicts by the
superpowers have left the way open for local initiatives to fill the power
vacuum with agreed arrangements. With the future of South Africa still
very precariously balanced and the region in a state of flux, it would be
unwise to leave regional security to chance. The danger is that the opportunity to properly consider regional security and cooperation may well
have passed in another year or two.

Proposals for a Conference on Security, Stability, Development and
Cooperation in Africa (CSSDCA) have been mooted under the aegis of the
Africa Leadership Forum and the initiative of African leaders such as former Nigerian head of state General Olusegun Obasanjo, former executive
secretary of the UN Economic Commission for Africa, Adebayo Adedeji,
and current secretary-general of the Organization of African Unity (OAU),
Salim Ahmed Salim. Indeed, the Kampala Forum was an effort to renew
the search for endogenous solutions to the continent's crises of insecurity,
instability, and underdevelopment. In essence, the CSSDCA was a carefully constructed showcase for a concept that in recent years has steadily
advanced to the center of African political thought and strategy: that without democracy, human rights, and popular participation, and without an
end to cross-border and civil wars, there can be neither security and stability nor economic growth, and therefore no release for the continent from
the tightening grip of violence, hunger, and debt. Moreover, without that
release, Africa as a bloc will become politically and economically even
more marginalized in a new global order, where success is determined by
economic strength rather than military power and ideological affiliation.[32]

At a conference held in Maputo, Mozambique, in 1990, the Conference on Security and Cooperation in Europe (CSCE) example and other
concepts relevant to confidence building and security in the region were
further explored. And significantly, within the SADC, similar ideas found
fertile ground: Witness the yearly Conference on Peace and Security in
Eastern and Southern Africa held in Arusha, Tanzania. As early as 1991,
even former South African president F. W. de Klerk expressed the view
that thought should be given "to the idea of multilateral regional talks [in
southern Africa] to foster confidence, economic growth, and security along
lines similar to the . . . CSCE."[33]

But academics have also contributed to the debate. Weimer sees the
value of a CSSDCA process in southern Africa principally in a social and

developmental context.[34] Drawing attention to poverty, hunger, unemployment, and sociocultural deprivation in the region, he regards a security regime, within the framework of something broadly similar to the CSSDCA, as the best way forward. Vale reminds us of the new perils and challenges awaiting the region after the end of apartheid, which include "near uncontrollable migration" and an imperative to restructure existing regional institutions such as the Southern African Customs Union (SACU) and the SADC for "the common good." Vale adds that the region as a whole will have to develop and maximize its relative strengths in a world in which Africa—including sub-Saharan Africa—will be increasingly marginalized.[35]

Vale also states the underlying logic of, and rationale for, a Conference for Security and Cooperation in Southern Africa (CSCSA) as follows:

> By embarking on a series of multilateral talks along the lines of the . . . CSCE, southern African states will enable an exploration of individual fears while simultaneously promoting regional accord. The underlying motive is rudimentary: while economic development in the region is essential, security questions for individual states are paramount. By catering for these at separate but parallel talks, a series of common understandings on the region's future can be reached.[36]

Nevertheless, in the security field, it is necessary to think about the extent to which we can generalize and apply concepts from one part of the world to another. For example, how relevant are the traditional concepts of statecraft, such as "national security" or "balance of power," and how applicable are they to the different context of southern Africa? Similarly, how transferable are institutions such as the CSCE? Although some ideas and practices may be transferable, they must be transplanted with care and with an eye to regional particularities.[37]

Moreover, is what is known as the security dilemma relevant to the southern African context? Apparently, it is not. The level of external security is relatively high because of geographical remoteness from the center of world affairs, the indifference of outside powers, and the general powerlessness of states within the region (as long as there is a clear reduction in the South African threat to the region as a result of its postapartheid foreign policy). In terms of international politics, therefore, the states of the southern African region are relatively secure legal entities, with no significant security dilemma pressures. However, internally, the situation has been much less satisfactory. Sovereignty is threatened more from within than from without: Clearly, there have been instances of significant domestic instability brought about by protracted civil wars in Angola and Mozambique, local political violence in South Africa, factional clashes in the Lesotho armed forces, and so on.

If the region is relatively free of external security dilemma pressures, then the implications for security policy are enormous. It means that priority has to be given to the domestic sources of instability. Security policy must be both more multileveled and more multifaceted: in other words, dealing not primarily with states or with issues of military strategy but with the whole range of threats to a nation's well-being. According to this reasoning, traditional security regimes, designed to mitigate security dilemmas, will not be as relevant to the southern African future as some might think.

One of the attractions of the CSCE model may be its nontraditional elements. Although this model was essentially statist in inspiration, its human rights provisions escaped from this bind; and its various "baskets" approach the security problem in a multifaceted way.[38] Southern Africa might be good ground on which to experiment with new modes of crisis control and conflict prevention and to move away from the general emphasis on formal organizations, with their rigid structures and agendas, which has usually precluded the establishment of an open forum to discuss problems, dangers, and incipient trends.[39] Thus it may be helpful to think of a complex of different regimes, with each one attempting to deal with different but overlapping sectors of the security problem. One advantage of seeking a combination of regimes is that complex structures are always likely to take more strain. Another is that it may well be easier to negotiate a series of single-issue regimes than a single comprehensive one. Indeed, progress in one might ease progress in another because of spillover effects.[40]

However, a CSCE process involving South Africa on equal terms with other countries in southern Africa and based on the idea of different baskets—dealing with security and disarmament; trade, production, labor, and general issues linked to institutional forms for economic integration; refugees and migration; and human rights, culture, and education—is appealing for a number of reasons. First, it would be an excellent instrument for confidence building and increased transparency with respect to armed forces and threat projections. Second, it could provide a useful framework for regional conflict management and conflict resolution. Third, it could provide a forum for exchange of ideas and comparison regarding domestic issues related to state-society relationships. And fourth, it could contribute to institutionalization, which, in turn, could further equity-based regional cooperation and integration on a wide range of issues, including those in the economic field.[41]

Thus, using the CSCE model, Vale suggests eight complementary regional baskets: security, economic development, law and human rights, education and technology, migration, health, gender issues, and agriculture.[42]

But he is mute on the tougher question of how a CSCSA could be institutionalized in practical terms. What, if anything, can southern Africa learn from the European experience with the CSCE? And, more important, can such a framework be sustained in the context of "soft," vulnerable states? Although South Africa may be harder, in relative terms, than the other states of the region, it, too, is a soft state in view of its doubtful capacity to meet existing and future domestic socioeconomic needs, its obvious inability to mobilize enough internal resources commensurate with its development needs, and the prospect that it may not be particularly well consolidated for years to come.

A CSSDCA or CSCSA process in southern Africa will be difficult to institutionalize without due consideration of these imponderables; however, this does not mean that it should not be attempted. Clearly, it may prove to be even tougher than the European experience, which had a relatively long genesis. There is also the additional consideration that a post-apartheid South Africa may attempt to manipulate regional institutions for its own particular purposes. These institutions may well become a competitive arena for competing social groups, which would effectively immobilize them and detract from their nonmaterial functions. Peace and security, after all, are also about nonmaterial, intangible things such as identity, social space, and human dignity.

Conclusion

Africa has acquired a reputation for the intractability of its problems, and outside countries are showing a particular reluctance to be drawn into its peacekeeping operations. Something must be done to limit conflict in Africa, which is more ravaged by civil war and other forms of armed conflict than any other part of the world. Current thinking is shifting toward political rather than military intervention: conflict prevention rather than conflict management or conflict resolution.

This thinking is in line with the approach of the OAU, which recently set up a Mechanism for Conflict Prevention, Management and Resolution. The Central Organ of the Mechanism, of which South Africa is one of eleven members, will operate at three levels: annual meetings of its members at the heads-of-state level, biannual meetings at the foreign ministerial level, and monthly meetings at the ambassadorial level—with special meetings called if necessary to deal with crises. Clearly, the Central Organ will have to coordinate its activities with regional peacekeeping initiatives: For example, the SADC—which has a formal mandate from member states to promote regional cooperation in the areas of politics and defense and security—has recently begun to assume regional security responsibilities with its proposal for establishing forums for conflict resolution and security and defense.[43]

Building on the concept of the Front Line States, the SADC is considering establishment of an Association of Southern African States (ASAS). ASAS will essentially be the political arm of the SADC, and its main responsibility will be to deal with conflict prevention, management, and resolution in the southern African region. Moreover, it is envisaged that ASAS should function independently of the SADC Secretariat; thus it will work in a flexible and informal manner and will be able to respond rapidly to incidents of regional insecurity.[44]

South Africa now seems poised to play its expected role in regional security, but some observers suggest that it must be cautious about being made the police force of the region and putting its military capacity at the disposal of the warring factions on the continent. They argue that South Africa cannot, by becoming militarily involved, singlehandedly rescue the people of Rwanda, or stop the civil war in Angola, or restore order in Mozambique, or create stability in Lesotho, and it should not try. It is in South Africa's interests to stabilize the subcontinent, if only to stop the vast and destabilizing flood of refugees and economic migrants across its borders, but that does not require military adventures or costly (and usually futile) peacekeeping operations.

Southern Africa is arguably the only part of the African continent that can look forward to a truly regional dynamic. But this dynamic will be forthcoming only if there is genuine and constructive cooperation among the countries of the region. SACU is, significantly, regarded as the most viable and most effective instrument of trade facilitation and customs management that exists in the southern African region, certainly, if not in Africa as a whole. South Africa should therefore use its energies to draw its neighbors into a functioning system of security and prosperity, which need not be a formalized organization but must extend real benefits. Moreover, regional cooperation and development integration rather than economic integration should initially guide the future of southern Africa; policy should concentrate on developing and extending regional technical-functional networks in the areas of transport, telecommunications, water management, and power generation.

The capability to cope with the aftermath of civil war and violent devastation, economic decline, colonialism, and apartheid in the southern African region has to be developed. Steps to consolidate security in a holistic sense, to restore law and order, and to prevent a recurrence of conflict are, however, likely to demand greater application and persistence than achieving the economic recovery that they will help make possible.

Be that as it may, the processes of political change in southern Africa have made possible a regional security regime, the soon-to-be established ASAS, which can take its place next to the SADC.

Notes

1. André Du Pisani, "Security and Peace in Post-Apartheid South Africa," *International Affairs Bulletin* 16,3 (1992), p. 5.

2. Simon Dalby, "Security, Modernity, Ecology: The Dilemmas of Post–Cold War Security Discourse," *Alternatives* 17 (1992), p. 98.

3. Lloyd J. Ching'ambo, "Towards a Defence Alliance in Southern Africa?" *Southern Africa Political and Economic Monthly* 5,8 (1992).

4. Ken Booth, "A Security Regime in Southern Africa: Theoretical Considerations" (Paper presented at a Conference on Security, Development and Cooperation in Southern Africa, Midgard, Namibia, May 23–27, 1993), pp. 4, 6.

5. See A. Linklater, *Men and Citizens in the Theory of International Relations* (New York: Macmillan, 1990). Also Ken Booth, "Security and Emancipation," *Review of International Studies* 17,4 (1991).

6. Barry Buzan, *People, States and Fear: An Agenda for International Security Studies in the Post–Cold War Era* (Boulder, Colo.: Lynne Rienner, 1991), pp. 26–28.

7. Larry Benjamin, "The Third World and Its Security Dilemma," *International Affairs Bulletin* 14,3 (1990), p. 20. Also Booth, "A Security Regime in Southern Africa," p. 8.

8. Peter Vale, "Southern Africa's Security: Something Old, Something New," *South African Defence Review* 9 (1993), p. 33.

9. Laurie Nathan, "'With Open Arms': Confidence and Security-Building Measures in Southern Africa" (Paper presented at the Seminar on Confidence and Security-Building in Southern Africa, Windhoek, Namibia, 1993), pp. 3–4.

10. Adebayo Adedeji, "Statement to the Kampala Forum on Security, Stability, Development and Cooperation in Africa (CSSDCA), May 19, 1991," in Olusegun Obasanjo and Felix G. N. Mosha, eds., *Africa: Rise to Challenge—Towards a Conference on Security, Stability, Development and Cooperation in Africa (CSSDCA)* (Abeokuta, Nigeria, and New York: Africa Leadership Forum, 1992), p. 297.

11. Ching'ambo, "Towards a Defence Alliance in Southern Africa?" pp. 35–36.

12. Nathan, "'With Open Arms,'" pp. 4–5.

13. Booth, "*A Security Regime in Southern Africa*," pp. 16–17.

14. William Gutteridge, "Prospects for Regional Security in Southern Africa," *South Africa International* 22,3 (January 1992), pp. 128–129.

15. Du Pisani, "Security and Peace," p. 11.

16. Du Pisani, "Security and Peace," pp. 11–13.

17. See Laurie Nathan and Joao Honwana, "The Establishment of SADC Forums for Conflict Resolution, and Defence and Security" (Paper presented to the Eighth Conference on Peace and Security in Eastern and Southern Africa, Arusha, Tanzania, August 22–24, 1994).

18. Gutteridge, "Prospects for Regional Security," p. 131.

19. André Du Pisani, "Post-Settlement South Africa and the Future of Southern Africa," *Issue* 21,1/2 (1993), pp. 67–68.

20. Greg Mills and Christopher Clapham, "Southern Africa After Apartheid: A Framework for Analysis," Working Paper Series (Bellville: University of the Western Cape, Centre for Southern African Studies, April 1991), p. 6. Also Hasu H. Patel, "Peace and Security in a Changing Southern Africa: A Frontline View," Working Paper Series (Bellville: University of the Western Cape, Centre for Southern African Studies, April 1992), p. 18.

21. Peter Vale, "Hoping Against Hope: The Prospects for South Africa's Post-Apartheid Regional Policy," Working Paper Series (Bellville: University of the Western Cape, Centre for Southern African Studies, July 1992), p. 11. Also Patel, "Peace and Security in a Changing Southern Africa," p. 18.

22. Deon Geldenhuys, "Ten Crises in South Africa's External Relations," *International Affairs Bulletin* 13,3 (1989), pp. 91–92.

23. Charles Krauthammer, "The Unipolar Moment," in Graham Allison and Gregory F. Treverton, eds., *Rethinking America's Security: Beyond the Cold War to a New World Order* (New York: W.W. Norton, 1992), p. 297.

24. Vale, "Hoping Against Hope," p. 11.

25. See Denis Venter, "South Africa and the African Comity of Nations: From Isolation to Integration," Research paper no. 56 (Pretoria: Africa Institute of South Africa, March 1992), pp. 14–34.

26. Vale, "Hoping Against Hope," pp. 12, 16.

27. Gutteridge, "Prospects for Regional Security," p. 128.

28. Booth, "A Security Regime in Southern Africa," pp. 25–26.

29. William G. Martin, "The Future of Southern Africa: What Prospects After Majority Rule?" *Review of African Political Economy* 50 (March 1991), pp. 120–121.

30. Du Pisani, "Security and Peace," p. 13.

31. Bernhard Weimer, "South Africa and the Frontline States: From Confrontation to Confidence-Building," *Southern Africa Political and Economic Monthly* 3,11 (August 1990). Bernhard Weimer, "Konferenz ueber Sicherheit und Zusammenarbeit im suedlichen Afrika?" *Afrika Spectrum* 26,3 (1991). André Du Pisani, "Ventures into the Interior: Continuity and Change in South Africa's Regional Policy, 1948 to 1991" (Paper presented at a conference on "South Africa into the 1990s and Beyond," Broederstroom, South Africa, April 15–19, 1991). Gutteridge, "Prospects for Regional Security." Nathan, "'With Open Arms.'"

32. Denis Venter, "The Kampala Forum and the CSSDCA Process: Vehicle for an African Regeneration?" Occasional Paper (Pretoria: Africa Institute of South Africa, 1995).

33. F. W. de Klerk, "The International Road Ahead for South Africa," Occasional Paper (Johannesburg: South African Institute of International Affairs, 1991), p. 5.

34. Weimer, "South Africa and the Frontline States."

35. Peter Vale, "The Case for a Conference for Security and Cooperation in Southern Africa (CSCSA)," in Anthoni Van Nieuwkerk Anthoni and Gary van Staden, eds., *Southern Africa at the Crossroads: Prospects for the Political Economy of the Region* (Johannesburg: South African Institute of International Affairs, 1991).

36. Vale, "The Case for a Conference for Security and Cooperation," p. 151.

37. Booth, "A Security Regime in Southern Africa," p. 23.

38. Booth, "A Security Regime in Southern Africa," p. 25.

39. Gutteridge, "Prospects for Regional Security," p. 131.

40. Booth, "A Security Regime in Southern Africa," p. 13.

41. Thomas Ohlson and Stephen J. Stedman, "Trick or Treat? The End of Bipolarity and Conflict Resolution in Southern Africa," Working Paper Series

(Bellville: University of the Western Cape, Centre for Southern African Studies, December 1991), p. 25.

42. Vale, "The Case for a Conference for Security and Cooperation," pp. 152–153.

43. See SADC Secretariat, *Windhoek Communique,* from the Workshop on Democracy, Peace and Security, Windhoek, Namibia, July 11–16, 1994. Also Nathan and Honwana, "The Establishment of SADC Forums."

44. See Aziz Pahad, "Regional Security in Southern Africa," *ISSUP Bulletin* 5 (1995), pp. 3–6.

10

ECOMOG, Liberia, and Regional Security in West Africa

ROBERT A. MORTIMER

As many a UN operation has demonstrated, peacekeeping is an inherently difficult and risky enterprise. Thus it should come as no surprise that the Economic Community of West African States (ECOWAS) Cease-Fire Monitoring Group (ECOMOG) encountered numerous setbacks and frustrations in its endeavor to restore peace to strife-torn Liberia. The novelty of ECOMOG lay in its regional origin and character, not in the nature of the mission that it undertook. It was an authentically West African initiative that, if it had been successful, might have been expected to breathe new life into regional cooperation under the auspices of the ECOWAS. Like peacekeepers elsewhere, however, ECOMOG ran into the dual perils of an intractable local situation and a lack of genuine consensus at the international level. Although ECOMOG may yet emerge as a forerunner of future ventures in African regional conflict management, its record of mixed results illustrates that intervention in civil war is a perilous undertaking and peace an elusive goal.

Most observers of the ECOMOG experience have emphasized Nigeria's key role in the operation. Just as ECOWAS arose from a sustained Nigerian diplomatic initiative in the 1970s, ECOMOG depended heavily upon Nigerian policy and resources. Yet within months of the August 1990 deployment of ECOMOG, it became clear that Nigeria required the collaboration of other regional powers in order to achieve the mandate of cease-fire and elections. This multilateral operation reached out to incorporate a larger number of actors, first within the West African region and then beyond.

Certainly the Liberian civil war may be viewed as a challenge to regional security. Not only did the strife disable a member state of the ECOWAS grouping, but the hostilities sent refugees spilling into the surrounding states of Côte d'Ivoire, Sierra Leone, and Guinea. Moreover,

149

foreigners in Liberia, including numerous Ghanaians and Nigerians, were caught up in the violence. The breakdown of civic order thereby entailed stakes for several of ECOWAS's members, yet this was far from the sole external dimension of the war. Like many civil conflicts, the Liberian war was an international affair from the outset. Charles Taylor's insurrection enjoyed the support of Côte d'Ivoire and Burkina Faso, the latter operating as a relay for an even more distant interventionist, Libya. This meant, of course, that ECOMOG did not have the wholehearted backing of the very organization from which it emanated. With support from within the ranks of ECOWAS itself, Taylor's National Patriotic Front of Liberia (NPFL) was emboldened and empowered to resist the multilateral force.

This chapter will show that the tribulations of ECOMOG stemmed in large measure from the lack of a genuine regional consensus regarding the anarchy in Liberia. Nor were the major powers, most notably the United States and France, in agreement about how to end the war. An uneasy truce and a de facto partition settled over Liberia in the months shortly following the deployment of ECOMOG. Because no one had the combination of will and resources necessary to end the stalemate, the Liberian people became the victims of a protracted conflict. Certainly the members of ECOMOG risked and in some cases lost their lives in the effort to restore peace, but they did not control the political processes that alone could allow them to succeed.

This chapter identifies three distinctive diplomatic periods in the multilateral intervention in Liberia: the Standing Mediation Committee phase (August 1990–June 1991); the Yamoussoukro Process phase (June 1991–June 1992); and the Committee of Nine/UN/OAU phase (July 1992–August 1995). This periodization differs from other analyses that focus more on the evolution of the military role of ECOMOG.[1]

The Standing Mediation Committee (SMC) Phase

Ostensibly a creation of ECOWAS, the origins of ECOMOG were in fact somewhat more obscure than might be commonly assumed. Indeed, ECOMOG took the world by surprise, landing on Liberia's shores on August 24, 1990, with a minimum of fanfare at a moment when the international media were focused on the recent Iraqi invasion of Kuwait. Although ECOWAS had held a summit meeting in May 1990, there had been no highly visible diplomatic event since then. More than other such peacekeeping operations, ECOMOG took shape in the shadows and interstices of regional politics, a factor that explains some of the difficulties that it encountered.

Nigeria's president Ibrahim Babangida used the Standing Mediation Committee (SMC) of ECOWAS to launch an intervention in Liberia's civil war, a rather flimsy base upon which to erect an ambitious project. Babangida would eventually tell the weekly *West Africa* that Lagos "believe[d] that it would have been morally reprehensible and politically indefensible to stand by and watch while citizens of [Liberia] decimate[d] themselves."[2] There is no reason to question Nigeria's moral qualms regarding the conditions in Liberia, which had indeed become intolerable by the summer of 1990; however, whether Nigeria had accurately assessed the political requirements of a successful intervention is another question. And however high their moral ground, Nigeria's leaders had to realize that any operation mounted from Lagos risked exacerbating West Africa's fears of Nigerian regional hegemony, which have consistently plagued attempts at the region's political and economic integration.

Such fears were all the more probable in the setting of the Liberian civil war, because President Babangida had cultivated friendly ties with Liberia's dictator Samuel Doe. President Doe, for example, had seen to it that the University of Liberia bestowed an honorary degree upon the Nigerian leader, who in turn made a generous donation to what became the Babangida School of International Affairs. Nigeria played a major facilitating role in rescheduling $30 million of Liberian debt with the African Development Bank and was reported to have supplied arms to the Doe regime. Because the mere suggestion of a Nigerian operation to rescue the embattled dictator could be expected to arouse antagonism, Nigeria chose to intervene in the civil strife through ECOWAS.

The problem was that the SMC did not really enjoy the political legitimacy necessary to pull off such an operation; it had existed for less than three months when it decided to launch ECOMOG. The SMC had been set up during the May 1990 ECOWAS summit meeting at the suggestion of Babangida. Its mandate was broad and general, namely to intervene—presumably as a mediator—whenever a conflict threatened the stability of the West African region. Because the resolution establishing the SMC referred to disputes between "two or more Member States," not to civil wars,[3] it is clear that the members of ECOWAS could not have anticipated the use to which the committee was shortly put. The summit appointed three Anglophone states (Gambia, Ghana, and Nigeria) and two Francophone members (Togo and Mali) to this new mediatory organ.

Committees of mediation have been a standard practice of Organization of African Unity (OAU) affairs, and the SMC was not seen to be of great consequence—until it became the springboard for launching ECOMOG. ECOMOG was initiated in a two-part sequence: First the SMC convened an emergency meeting in Freetown, Sierra Leone, in July 1990. At this meeting, the foreign ministers of the SMC states devised a peace plan that, among other things, called for a cease-fire in Liberia and Doe's resignation. The SMC instructed the executive secretary of ECOWAS, Abbas

Bundu, to carry out a mission to Liberia. There he met with both Taylor and Doe, the latter of whom indicated his willingness to go along with the plan. Up to this point, the standard techniques of mediation seemed to be working.

Soon, however, Taylor, whose troops had been steadily advancing on the capital, balked, declaring his intention to rout Doe rather than rely on the ECOWAS plan. Thus, in August 1990, the SMC convened once again and resolved to send in a multilateral force to effect its peace plan. At this point, Nigeria decided to push ahead without securing the political backing of the full ECOWAS membership. Support for ECOMOG came only from Anglophone countries, as SMC members Togo and Mali declined to contribute troops to the operation and President Blaise Compaore of Burkina Faso roundly condemned it.[4] Both Senegal and Côte d'Ivoire expressed reservations about the operation. Although Gambian president Dawda Jawara, who announced the decision, sought to rally support and Guinea contributed a small contingent, the intervention was essentially a Nigerian fait accompli. Babangida had made a bold bid under the apparent auspices of ECOWAS, but he had not secured the region-wide support that would be necessary to rein in Taylor's rebels.

Dispatched as a peacekeeping force to monitor a cease-fire decreed by the SMC, ECOMOG found itself engaged in hostilities during its first three months in Liberia. This initial round of overt hostilities between the interventionary force and the NPFL came to an end in November when Taylor, under both military and political pressure, agreed to come to the bargaining table. ECOWAS organized an "extraordinary summit" (the first it had ever called) in Bamako, Mali (a Francophone member state) on November 27–28, 1990. The Bamako summit raised hopes that a negotiated settlement was within reach; it called for, among other things, a national conference to be convened within sixty days and interim talks to be held in Banjul, Gambia, in December. The national conference was held in March 1991, without Charles Taylor, however; after two weeks of often acrimonious discussions, it ended in shambles. Moreover, during the conference, the NPFL launched an offensive into Sierra Leone, presumably to punish the country for its participation in ECOMOG as well as to pursue some pro-Doe soldiers who had fled across the border upon the death of their leader.

Thus, although the cease-fire of November 1990 marked a pause in the military confrontation between ECOMOG and the NPFL, it was not a significant diplomatic turning point. On the contrary, the diplomatic process remained primarily in the hands of the SMC, which, like ECOMOG, was seen as essentially an extension of Nigerian foreign policy.

The primary characteristic of this first phase was the preeminent role of the strongest member state of the SMC group, namely Nigeria. During this stage, ECOMOG became a party to the dispute rather than a buffer between disputants. Under the field command of Nigerian major general Joshua Dogonyaro, who effectively replaced a Ghanaian, Lieutenant General Arnold Quainoo, who initially led the operation, ECOMOG carried out an offensive that drove the NPFL forces back to the outskirts of Monrovia.[5] Its practical role became to protect Liberia's Interim Government of National Unity (IGNU) under Amos Sawyer, which was itself the product of an ECOWAS-sponsored conference. The NPFL refused to treat ECOMOG as a neutral body, characterizing it as a mercenary force or a puppet of Nigerian hegemony. It became necessary, therefore, to seek a new face for ECOMOG, a process that ended the SMC phase of the intervention in June 1991.

The Yamoussoukro Phase

From the moment that the SMC authorized the dispatch of ECOMOG, President Compaore of Burkina Faso was its most outspoken critic. The involvement of Burkina Faso in the Liberian civil war stemmed from the struggle for power between Compaore and Thomas Sankara in 1987, in which Taylor forged an alliance with Compaore: "Some people think that the Liberians training in Libya were employed in killing Sankara."[6] This speculation was due to the fact that Sankara was murdered shortly after the arrival of Taylor in Ouagadougou from Ghana and the fact that Libya, which felt that Doe had betrayed Colonel Qaddafi's hopes when the former came to power in 1980, had indeed trained a band of anti-Doe rebels who came under Taylor's command. Whether the Sankara hypothesis is well-founded or not, there is evidence that the Compaore regime served as a staging ground and transit point for weapons forwarded from Libya to the NPFL.

Some part of Compaore's decision to support the NPFL is no doubt attributable to Burkinabe relations with Côte d'Ivoire. Compaore was related by marriage to the late President Félix Houphouët-Boigny, an in-law of President William Tolbert, who was deposed and slain by Doe. Various authors have cited the personal antagonism between Houphouët and Doe as a partial explanation for Côte d'Ivoire's otherwise unlikely support of Charles Taylor.[7] Taylor launched his insurgency from Ivoirian territory in December 1989, but even more important, he continued to receive munitions and enjoy lines of communication across that border after ECOMOG arrived in Monrovia. Although the fall of Doe settled that old score, Houphouët was not happy to see a Nigerian-led force on the ground in Liberia. He had been suspicious of Nigerian hegemonic designs in West Africa since the late 1960s, when Côte d'Ivoire was one of only four African states to recognize the Biafran secession. The ECOMOG expedition reawakened Houphouët's old fears, and although he did not rail against it as overtly as Compaore did, he did nothing to restrain the NPFL either. The fact that various French firms were conducting profitable business relations in logging, diamonds, and rubber with the authorities in Gbarnga (Taylor's headquarters) may also explain Houphouët's tolerance toward the insurgents.

With the passage of time and the persistence of military stalemate, however, Abidjan's position became less tenable. It ran against the tide of a growing international sentiment, notably backed by the U.S. government, that a negotiated settlement needed to be found. External negotiators brought pressure to bear upon all parties to the conflict, including the government of Côte d'Ivoire. Even Nigeria urged Houphouët to place his regional prestige on the line by contributing to a settlement. These various appeals eventually produced the Yamoussoukro Process, a series of meetings hosted by Houphouët. The basic concept underlying these meetings was extremely simple: to "de-Nigerianize" ECOMOG by bringing in Senegalese troops and engaging the Francophone states in the diplomatic process. Among other things, this entailed the SMC temporarily taking a back seat.

The Yamoussoukro Process began on June 29–30, 1991, on the eve of the annual ECOWAS summit meeting. It brought together presidents Babangida, Jawara, and Gnassingbé Eyadéma of Togo, from the original SMC grouping, with Compaore, Houphouët and the primary antagonists, Taylor and Sawyer. At this meeting, Taylor appeared to agree to the idea of elections in Liberia within six to nine months. A few days later, the ECOWAS summit convened in Abuja, Nigeria, and applauded the Yamoussoukro initiative by creating a new organ under Houphouët's chairmanship known as the Committee of Five. Its membership—composed of Côte d'Ivoire, Senegal, Togo, Guinea-Bissau, and Gambia—was clearly designed to restore a major diplomatic role to the Francophone states, and the committee effectively supplanted the SMC as the primary diplomatic actor. The evolution from SMC to the Committee of Five was the first step in the process of expanding the international consensus regarding a Liberian settlement.

Although enlisting the cooperation of the Ivoirians was central to the Yamoussoukro strategy, it was not sufficient to break the deadlock. ECOMOG needed the backing of another country to counter Taylor's ostensible rationale for refusing to cooperate with it—namely, its allegedly Nigerian character. After some diplomatic arm twisting, Senegal volunteered to play this role; the arm twister was also a relatively new player in the Liberian crisis: the United States. The hostilities and atrocities in Liberia were something of an embarrassment to the U.S. government, which had long been assumed to hold a "special relationship" with that country. As the war dragged on, U.S. indifference to Liberia's crisis in the name of nonintervention had become increasingly problematic as a policy. The increase in the U.S. role, although modest, was a further step in the process of widening the circle of players.[8]

The prospect of Senegalese involvement began to materialize in July 1991 when U.S. Assistant Secretary of State for African Affairs Herman Cohen told the U.S. House Subcommittee on Africa that President Abdou Diouf "has said that he would send troops to the ECOMOG operation and that he would be personally involved."[9] The Senegalese president's personal involvement was not unexpected inasmuch as he had recently replaced Dawda Jawara as the presiding chairperson of ECOWAS and his country had just been named to the Committee of Five. That Senegal would send troops was less expected, however, for neither Senegalese public opinion nor the French government was enthusiastic about getting involved. However, in September 1991, the United States invited Diouf on a formal state visit to Washington, where he was strongly urged by President George Bush and Secretary of State James Baker to contribute a contingent of Senegalese forces to ECOMOG. As an incentive, the Bush administration pledged to pay a major portion of the operation's costs and provide logistical support. The Pentagon promptly came up with $15 million worth of military equipment for the Senegalese peacekeepers;[10] moreover, the United States forgave Senegal's $42 million public debt. These various inducements made the commitment palatable enough for Diouf to ignore French objections and to assume the domestic political risks that fatalities in Liberia might cost him.

The basic strategy of the Committee of Five process seemed sound: The United States would materially support the strengthening and political remodeling of ECOMOG, and President Houphouët would bring pressure upon the NPFL leader to collaborate with the regional peacekeeping force whose Nigerian character was now diluted. The disengagement would take place under the watchful eye of a committee that Houphouët himself chaired. Indeed, the Committee of Five sponsored three negotiating sessions in Yamoussoukro, Côte d'Ivoire, from July through October 1991.[11] This apparently well orchestrated strategy nevertheless failed for two primary reasons: It unrealistically relied on Houphouët to close the Ivoirian border, and it naively assumed the good faith of Taylor.

The assumption that the aging Houphouët was fully in control of Côte d'Ivoire's Liberian policy was mistaken. The "Vieux" or "Sage," as he liked to be called, had certainly authorized the original policy that permitted Taylor's band to launch the insurrection across the Ivoirian border on Christmas Eve 1989. Once Taylor took control of a large portion of Liberia, however, Ivoirian middlemen became involved in lucrative deals with French companies that were trading with the rebel authorities. These shadowy practices came to light in 1992, when Jean Christophe Mitterrand, François Mitterrand's son and his African affairs adviser, was forced to resign because of his involvement in this trade. Had Houphouët's attention been keenly focused on the traffic across the Ivoirian border, he would have been able to stop it, but the evidence suggests that his faculties and energies were already quite limited.[12]

The second failure of judgment lay in taking Taylor at his word when he declared that the problem with ECOMOG was Nigeria. In his testimony before the House subcommittee about Senegal's impending entry into ECOMOG, Assistant Secretary Cohen had stated: "Now this should give Charles Taylor the confidence that he needs."[13] Later, Cohen would acknowledge that he had misjudged Taylor's intentions.[14] The Senegal solution depended heavily upon the cooperation of the NPFL, which was simply not forthcoming.

In retrospect, it appears clear that Taylor preferred to fight as long as he had the means to sustain his forces, and certainly the Senegalese contingent of 1,500 troops, however well armed and commanded, did not change the military balance. Taylor's determination to continue to fight may well have been strengthened by the appearance of the United Liberation Movement for Democracy in Liberia (ULIMO), primarily a Krahn coalition (the ethnic group of slain president Doe), that began challenging the NPFL in the western regions of the country.

Because neither Taylor nor Houphouët fulfilled the role ascribed to him by the Yamoussoukro process, the addition of Senegal to the ECOMOG force did not achieve the desired objective. One final effort, both ironic and desperate, was made to save the Yamoussoukro approach. The irony was that the last "Yamu" meeting was held in Geneva, where the ailing Houphouët was spending increasing amounts of time for medical care. Adding to the irony was that this meeting of the Committee of Five was attended by only two of its members (Côte d'Ivoire and Senegal); also in attendance were Burkina Faso and Nigeria, whose positions were diametrically opposed, and their respective clients, Taylor and Sawyer. The Geneva meeting acknowledged the new factor on the ground—namely, ULIMO— and devised a new task for ECOMOG: to provide a buffer zone between ULIMO and the NPFL in the region along the border of Sierra Leone. The desperation was evident in the creation of yet a new timetable (the third) within which ECOMOG was to confine and disarm all combatants as originally provided for in the October 1991 (Yamoussoukro IV) accord.[15] But the Geneva timetable was not implemented by its June 2, 1992, deadline, and the Yamoussoukro diplomatic phase of the ECOMOG operation, for all practical purposes, came to an end.

From ECOWAS to the OAU and the Security Council

Under the headline, "Liberia Sinks Further into Civil War," *Jeune Afrique* reported in mid-July 1992 that Taylor's "men continue to fight, at the Sierra Leonean border, against those of ULIMO obliging ECOMOG to withdraw."[16] The military pressure on ECOMOG did not go unnoticed in Dakar, where two major inter-African conferences took place that same month. The second of these meetings was ECOWAS's annual summit, at which Abdou Diouf concluded his term as head of the organization and passed the torch to Nicephore Soglo of Benin. At the summit, Diouf not only called for a new ECOWAS strategy—an embargo against the NPFL— but outlined a third stage of the ECOMOG operation. This new stage entailed expanding the auspices under which the regional peacekeepers conducted their mission and enlisting the OAU and ultimately the UN in the pursuit of a Liberian settlement.

Diouf was well positioned to carry out this enlargement of the ECOMOG framework because he had recently agreed to preside as head of the OAU. At the Dakar summit, Diouf and OAU secretary-general Salim Ahmed Salim teamed up in an effort to extend the OAU's authority in civil conflicts like the one in Liberia. Salim prepared for the summit a detailed proposal calling for the creation of the Mechanism for Conflict Prevention, Management and Resolution. As the incoming OAU chairperson, Diouf lobbied vigorously for Salim's proposal; according to *Jeune Afrique*'s account of the summit, "All the principles were accepted by the Dakar summit. But the declaration which was to enact the proposal officially did not achieve consensus."[17] Much therefore depended upon Diouf's intentions to exploit the support for more active OAU involvement in civil wars.

Precisely because Senegal had sent its own soldiers into Liberia on behalf of the Yamoussoukro Process, Diouf was well aware of that strategy's shortcomings. He intended to strengthen the impact of ECOWAS and its interventionary force by marshaling the full authority of the OAU behind the regional organization. Although the strategy looked sound on paper, it was overtaken by events on the ground, in this instance a strong counteroffensive carried out by ULIMO. In fact, ULIMO's growing strength complicated ECOMOG's task severely: Sierra Leone (a component part of the ECOMOG force) was by now strongly backing ULIMO because it feared that Taylor would take over in Liberia. The 1992 coup that carried Valentine Strasser to power only strengthened Sierra Leone's commitment to ULIMO; Strasser himself had served with ECOMOG and had developed a strong antipathy to Taylor.[18] Before Diouf could effectively implement his OAU strategy, full-scale war involving the ECOMOG force erupted, and the diplomatic situation escalated beyond the OAU to UN involvement.

On October 20, twelve ECOWAS leaders met urgently in Cotonou, Benin, to call upon ULIMO and the NPFL to reestablish a cease-fire. Although the Yamoussoukro IV accord remained the point of reference for a settlement, the Cotonou "mini-summit" set up a new monitoring committee, a decision that indicated discreetly that the Committee of Five was no longer in charge of the search for a settlement. The new committee had nine members, reflecting the long-term trend toward expanding the number of actors in the diplomatic process: four from the Committee of Five (Côte d'Ivoire, Senegal, Togo—i.e., the Francophones—and Gambia); two from the SMC (Nigeria and Ghana, hence the return of the principal Anglophones); Burkina Faso and Guinea (pro- and anti-Taylor, respectively); and, finally, Benin in its new capacity as chair of ECOWAS.[19] The monitoring committee, however, had no greater leverage over the situation on the ground than had its predecessors. *Africa Report* cited a cable from the American ambassador in Benin suggesting that "President Soglo . . . has thrown up his hands over Liberia, deciding that Nigeria has taken over ECOMOG and that ECOWAS is too divided to have a common policy for a peaceful resolution to the problem. Let them fight, he mutters often, until they are exhausted."[20] Soglo's discouragement was indicative of a bleak reality: Despite a myriad of diplomatic meetings, the fighting of October–November 1992, like that two years earlier, was basically between the NPFL and Nigeria.

Little surprise, then, that the follow-up to the Cotonou cease-fire appeal, which went unheeded, took place in Abuja, Nigeria. On November 7, the nine members of the monitoring committee called again for a cease-fire. They also declared that a land, sea, and air embargo, initially approved in principle at the July summit of ECOWAS and invoked at the October Cotonou meeting, was now "deemed to have entered into force."[21] In imposing sanctions, however, ECOWAS recognized that it had to secure a stronger international mandate and appealed to both the OAU and the United Nations for their active support. The NPFL accepted the cease-fire, but then promptly broke it. Nigerian aircraft of the ECOMOG force pounded away at "Taylor-land," carrying out Operation 120 Hours, five days of constant bombardment designed to inflict a crippling blow.

The recourse to the UN Security Council on November 19, 1992, significantly extended the diplomatic framework of regional peacekeeping, but it was intended first and foremost to enhance ECOWAS's own effort. In his remarks to the Security Council on behalf of ECOWAS, Benin's foreign minister Theodore Holo emphasized that the war had become a threat to the entire subregion of West Africa and that the "international community is now obliged to establish peace in Liberia. . . . I believe that the United Nations must be linked with the disarmament and demobilization in order to inspire confidence among the different parties to the fighting."[22]

The Council unanimously backed the sanctions earlier approved by ECOWAS; via Resolution 788, it declared a general and complete arms embargo against Liberia, specifying that the embargo did not apply to ECOMOG. The resolution called upon secretary-general Boutros Boutros-Ghali to appoint a special representative to Liberia, a post to which Trevor Gordon-Somers was promptly named. On November 23, Taylor announced that the NPFL would cooperate with the UN, whose involvement, he declared, was "an opportunity to end the three-year-old senseless war."[23]

However senseless the war, it did not end with the UN-decreed embargo, nor did the UN send any additional force into the field to strengthen ECOMOG militarily. Rather, the stalemate of old was restored while a new negotiating phase began. The appeal to the UN nevertheless added a new dimension to the bargaining process; as Gordon-Somers explained, his mandate was to work with ECOWAS—and hence ECOMOG—not to replace it. At its Abuja meeting, ECOWAS had also requested the OAU to appoint a liaison to work with the new monitoring committee. The former president of Zimbabwe, Canaan Banana, was shortly named to this position. Thus, two new negotiators were brought into the peacekeeping process. They would be instrumental in finally getting the warring parties to the negotiating table in July 1993.

The path to the summer peace talks was strewn with another round of hostilities. The fact that Senegal—mainly for domestic reasons—withdrew its 1,500-person contingent in January 1993 and that Nigeria compensated for its departure by sending in 5,000 of its own troops maintained the tension at the military level. The NPFL continued to receive supplies via Côte d'Ivoire, and ECOMOG aircraft bombed the Ivoirian town of Danane near the Liberian border at the end of February, highlighting the fact that the underlying Nigerian-Ivoirian disagreement about Liberia was still unresolved.

Taylor appeared determined to keep fighting as he told the journalist Jean-Karim Fall, "We cannot negotiate with ECOMOG, we shall never negotiate with ECOMOG."[24] His forces were suffering reverses, however; for example, ECOMOG offensives recaptured the airport at Robertsfield and then took Buchanan, an important port that the NPFL had long held. Later in April 1993, UN mediator Gordon-Somers led a joint UN/OAU delegation to Taylor's headquarters in Gbarnga. Upon his return, he announced that all parties would be invited to a new round of peace talks. The insertion of a UN negotiator into the operation was critical: Soglo had become exasperated with the conflict and determined to negotiate a settlement within the UN/OAU framework.[25]

During the three months between Gordon-Somers's mission to Gbarnga and the actual peace talks in Geneva, Taylor's military position continued to deteriorate. ULIMO had driven NPFL forces out of most of western Liberia. ECOMOG, with its additional contingent of Nigerian soldiers and renewed willingness to use air power, maintained its offensive. A massacre of 300 civilians at Harbel attributed (perhaps erroneously) to NPFL elements further discredited Taylor's camp. The determination of Nigeria's Major-General Adetunji Olurin, who had assumed command of ECOMOG in 1992, to tighten the noose was evident to all.[26] Military pressure, reinforced by the Security Council embargo, ultimately forced Taylor to consider the UN mediation offer. In effect, the peacekeepers took an active military role against one of the parties in order to reactivate the diplomatic process.

Gordon-Somers decided that the shores of Lake Geneva, far from the killing fields of Liberia, might provide the calm and the perspective necessary to achieve an enforceable agreement. The UN special representative cochaired the talks with Executive Secretary Bundu of ECOWAS and Canaan Banana, who was representing the OAU. For the first time talks were held under the auspices of regional, continental, and global organizations. Each component was necessary to the agreement hammered out in a week of bargaining between the NPFL, ULIMO, and IGNU. The UN agreed to provide an observer force, the UN Observer Mission in Liberia, to monitor the monitors. The OAU agreed to supplement ECOMOG with forces from African states previously unengaged in the conflict—in effect, to de-Nigerianize the force, as Senegal had earlier tried. Troops from Tanzania and Uganda eventually arrived in Liberia at the end of 1993 and early in 1994 but subsequently withdrew without having achieved ECOMOG's ultimate objective of disarming the factions and restoring peaceful political processes. ECOWAS, as the sponsor of ECOMOG, remained the principal agent in the plan, an arrangement consistent with Boutros-Ghali's conception, spelled out in his 1992 *Agenda for Peace,* which envisaged the UN playing a support role to regional initiatives.

Negotiated in Geneva, the accord was actually signed in Cotonou on July 25, 1993. The accord essentially defined ECOMOG's role as it had previously been conceived: to monitor a cease-fire and to supervise a process of disarmament. Soglo assumed an oversight role regarding the political arrangements defined in the Cotonou Agreement, and ECOMOG appeared finally to be able to complete its mission.

Yet in the years following the Cotonou Agreement, the warring parties failed to implement its key provision, namely disarmament; on the contrary, new military factions sprang up in regional pockets. Although a council called the Liberian National Transitional Government was seated in March 1994 with a mandate to prepare elections by September, the will to disarm was absent. As the prospect of September 1994 elections receded, the incoming chairperson of ECOWAS, President Jerry Rawlings of Ghana, took charge of brokering a settlement among the warlords, organizing a series of meetings from September 1994 to May 1995. The Cotonou

Agreement remained the point of reference, and the level of violence declined somewhat, but the political stalemate continued to defy resolution into mid-1995. Two years after the Geneva/Cotonou agreement, ECOMOG controlled the key area around Monrovia, essentially enforcing a status quo in a land wasted by its own internal divisions. In September 1995, yet another council formed, this time with the direct participation of the NPFL and ULIMO leaders, rekindling hope that the war might finally end.

Conclusion

ECOMOG has sparked interest as an exercise in regional peacekeeping.[27] Whether relying on regional organizations like ECOWAS has more advantages than disadvantages remains an open question. In Liberia's case, the principal advantage was simply the motivation of the regional states to end the carnage produced by the first eight months of civil war. Yet supporters of Taylor have argued that the war was drawing to an end at the moment that ECOMOG intervened; from this perspective, the intervention could be seen as ultimately prolonging the agony.

The great disadvantage of regional peacekeepers may well turn on the issue of impartiality. Classic peacekeeping theory assumes the neutrality of the interventionary force; it relies as well on the assumption that the local disputants are willing to cooperate with the peacekeepers or at least tolerate them as a buffer. In Liberia, this precondition was never really met, because the shadow of hegemony loomed over ECOMOG from the outset. As Karl Magyar has put it simply, "Without Nigeria's involvement, there would have been no ECOMOG."[28]

Even granting Nigeria the benefit of the doubt regarding its initial humanitarian impulse, the intensity of the conflict propelled Nigeria into a stronger commitment with the passage of time. Nigeria's power became increasingly stronger in the ECOMOG operation, and the country succeeded in turning the peacekeeping operation into an enforcement operation without losing general international backing. Although the commitment may have proven longer and more costly than Babangida had initially expected, he managed to pull his iron out of the fire with considerable diplomatic success.

The record indicates that ECOMOG could not have achieved its objectives without enlisting extraregional support, and Nigerian diplomacy was quite successful in gaining broader international legitimization for an operation of its own inspiration. Certainly, Charles Taylor made the task easier by his own mercurial behavior and by the atrocities that discredited his movement. By engaging Houphouët in the second phase and then the OAU and the UN in the third phase—allowing Abdou Diouf and then

Nicephore Soglo to bear much of the diplomatic burden in the name of ECOWAS—Nigeria largely diffused the hegemony issue.

ECOMOG is an important episode in post–Cold War inter-African relations. The multilateral intervention restored a semblance of order to a chaotic situation, and without it, the war could have taken an even higher toll in lives and destruction. Yet as a case study in regional peacekeeping, ECOMOG is problematic: Although it presided over a truce of sorts for a couple of years, it acted more as an enforcement agent against the NPFL rebellion in 1990 and the Taylor offensive of October 1992. The multilateral, Nigerian-dominated force is more a classic study of competing national interests in the West African subregion.

The Liberian civil war triggered old impulses of regional rivalry at the same time that it gave rise to new instruments of multilateral warfare and diplomacy. The new African political order is likely to continue to manifest the interplay of diverse conceptions of national interest, especially between the potential regional hegemon and the lesser powers. But a precedent for collective action, however tortuous its course in Liberia, has been set, and it may enable the region's states to navigate more surely in the post–Cold War waters.

Notes

1. Africa Watch, for example, in its document, "Liberia, Waging War to Keep the Peace: The ECOMOG Intervention and Human Rights" (June 1993) identifies the following periods: August–November 1990: intervention and achievement of cease-fire; November 1990–October 1992: fragile truce; October 1992–August 1995: renewal of hostilities between ECOMOG and NPFL.

2. *West Africa,* February 4–10, 1991, p. 140, as cited in Earl Conteh-Morgan, "ECOWAS: Peace-making or meddling in Liberia?" *Africa Insight* 23,1 (1993), p. 37.

3. Decision A/DEC 9/5/90 Relating to the Establishment of the Standing Mediation Committee, *Official Journal of the ECOWAS* 21 (November 1991), p. 5.

4. The decision of August 7, 1990, creating ECOMOG stated that it was "to be composed of military contingents drawn from the Member States of the ECOWAS Standing Mediation Committee as well as from Guinea and Sierra Leone." *Official Journal of the ECOWAS,* 21 (November 1991), p. 7.

5. Nigerian sources have been critical of General Quainoo's conservative, old-school UN style of peacekeeping, which was seen as inappropriate to a situation in which a cease-fire had not yet been established. See, for example, Gani Yoroms, "ECOMOG and West African Regional Security: A Nigerian Perspective," *Issue: A Journal of Opinion* 21 (1993), p. 89. See also Nkem Agetua, *Operation Liberty: The Story of Major General Joshua Nimyel Dogonyaro* (Lagos: Hona Communications Ltd., 1992).

6. S. Bryon Tarr, "The ECOMOG Initiative in Liberia: A Liberian Perspective," *Issue: A Journal of Opinion* 21 (1993), p. 80.

7. See, for example, Tarr, "The ECOMOG Initiative," p. 78.

8. The portion of the chapter on U.S. and Senegalese involvement draws upon my chapter "Senegal's Role in ECOMOG: The Francophone Dimension," in Earl Conteh-Morgan and Karl Magyar, eds., *Peace-keeping in Africa: ECOMOG in Liberia*, forthcoming.

9. U.S. Congress, House Committee on Foreign Affairs, Subcommittee on Africa, *Crisis in Liberia: The Regional Impact*, hearing, July 16, 1991, 102d Cong., 1st sess. (Washington, D.C.: GPO, 1992), p. 33.

10. Section 506b of the Foreign Assistance Act authorizes such transfers to assist governments in peacekeeping. The United States has contributed an additional $8.6 million to ECOWAS for the peacekeeping operation. U.S. humanitarian assistance to Liberian victims of the war totaled $259 million for the period 1990 to mid-1993. Africa Watch, "Liberia, Waging War," p. 29.

11. At the first of these meetings in July, Sawyer and Taylor, accompanied by Jimmy Carter, met with the presidents of the Committee of Five member states (Eyadéma of Togo was represented by his minister of justice) and agreed to cooperate in creating conditions conducive to free and just elections. At the September meeting, Senegal announced its decision to contribute troops, and the Liberian parties agreed to set up an electoral commission. In October (Yamoussoukro IV), with eleven member states and the secretary-general of the OAU in attendance, Sawyer and Taylor agreed to a sixty-day timetable for the encampment and disarmament of the belligerents. For greater detail, see Tafsir Malick N'Diaye, "Conflict Prevention and Conflict Resolution in the African Context: Peacekeeping in Liberia," *Issue: A Journal of Opinion* 21 (1993), pp. 71–72.

12. Tarr, "The ECOMOG Initiative."

13. U.S. Congress, *Crisis in Liberia,* p. 33.

14. "L'Afrique, la France, et nous," *Jeune Afrique* 1667 (December 17–23, 1992). The French journalist Marie-Pierre Subtil, made the following observation on the Yamoussoukro IV accord: "Yet it is still necessary that the hotheaded Charles Taylor respect the engagement that he has just made at Yamoussoukro. That would constitute a first." *Le Monde,* November 1, 1991.

15. On the Geneva meeting and the details of the timetable, see N'Diaye, "Peacekeeping in Liberia," pp. 72–73.

16. *Jeune Afrique* 1645 (July 16–22, 1992), p. 29.

17. Sennen Andriamirado, "OUA: ce que va faire Abdou Diouf," *Jeune Afrique* 1644 (July 9–15, 1992), p. 20.

18. On this point and the ULIMO offensive more generally, see Geraldine Faes, "Taylor perd du terrain," *Jeune Afrique* 1652 (September 3–9, 1992).

19. Togo and Gambia had figured in both the SMC and the Committee of Five, and the new committee had a 6–3 ratio of Francophones to Anglophones despite the return of the principal military antagonist of the NPFL, Nigeria.

20. Peter da Costa, "Talking Tough to Taylor," *Africa Report,* January–February 1993, p. 21.

21. *Africa Research Bulletin,* November 1992, p. 10792.

22. *Africa Research Bulletin,* November 1992, p. 10793.

23. *Africa Research Bulletin,* November 1992, p. 10793.

24. *Le Monde,* April 9, 1993. See also Taylor's press conference of March 26, 1993, in *Foreign Broadcasting Information Service, Africa,* March 29, 1993.

25. Questioned in Abidjan on May 12, 1993, Soglo expressed his irritation with ECOWAS's preoccupation with Liberia: "It's necessary that not all our energy

is expended on that one question of Liberia. . . . Instead of talking about regional integration, we are talking about the problem of Liberia. . . . It's a mess." Cited in Mark Huband, "Targeting Taylor," *Africa Report*, July–August 1993, p. 30.

26. See, for example, the comment by a humanitarian relief worker ("Olurin is unclouded by doubt. Taylor is clearly evil, and he is a liar, and Olurin clearly sees it as part of his mandate to kill him if he can") and that by Ghana's minister of information ("There's a Nigerian passion to annihilate Charles Taylor"), both cited in Huband, "Targeting Taylor," pp. 30, 31.

27. On this general theme, see Paul E. Diehl, "Institutional Alternatives to Traditional U.N. Peacekeeping: An Assessment of Regional and Multinational Options," *Armed Forces and Society* 19,2 (1993), pp. 211–218.

28. Karl Magyar, "ECOMOG's Operations: Lessons for Peace-keeping," in Conteh-Morgan and Magyar, eds., *Peace-keeping in Africa*, forthcoming.

11

The Involvement of ECOWAS in Liberia's Peacekeeping

MARGARET ADERINSOLA VOGT

The Economic Community of West African States (ECOWAS) Monitoring Group (ECOMOG) that was deployed to Liberia provides lessons for the study and design of security management mechanisms for both the entire African region and other parts of the world. The ECOWAS intervention in Liberia marked the first time that a subregional organization mounted a multilateral force with the sole objective of policing and restoring order in a member state in which central authority had collapsed. It had the stated objective of providing support to facilitate humanitarian activities.[1]

The Historical Background

The Liberian civil war erupted in 1989 when Charles Taylor, a former official in the government of Samuel Doe, recruited and trained a handful of men in Libya. He then assembled his forces in Côte d'Ivoire and launched an offensive against security posts in the county of Nimba in Liberia. Many Liberians who were disaffected with the extreme authoritarian and brutal style of Doe's rule joined the rebel movement, the National Patriotic Front of Liberia (NPFL), with the hope that it would end the killing of innocent people and the abuse of peoples' rights. The event that most deeply affected Liberians was the killing of some 3,000 people in Nimba county by Samuel Doe in retaliation for their support of the attempted coup by his former chief of staff and ally, Thomas Quiwonkpa.[2] Taylor had participated in this coup attempt and escaped from the country after it failed.[3]

The Taylor-led revolt quickly gathered momentum as many Liberians perceived the NPFL as a liberation force. Unfortunately, as the insurgent forces successfully fought their way to Monrovia, a split occurred within the NPFL; a group headed by Prince Yedou Johnson broke away and

165

formed the Independent National Patriotic Front of Liberia (INPFL). The civil war degenerated into a pogrom as the NPFL, the INPFL, and the Armed Forces of Liberia attacked people they perceived as supporters of their opponents and killed hundreds of civilians. The situation became particularly disturbing when the Nigerian, Ghanaian, Guinean, and German embassies were specifically targeted. A large number of civilian refugees who had sought shelter in these embassies were taken as hostages; many of them were killed and embassy property was destroyed.

In many African countries, pressure mounted for measures to be taken to evacuate Liberia's civilian population.[4] Nigerian president Ibrahim Babangida argued that "Liberians are our brothers, and Nigerians over there together with them see themselves as part of the society. I don't think it is right for government to create distinction among fellow Africans over the evacuation exercise."[5] The ECOWAS Standing Mediation Committee (SMC) proposed the deployment of a monitoring force, ECOMOG, to facilitate the rescue of trapped civilians from Monrovia.[6] This plan was strongly opposed by Charles Taylor, who promised to attack the force as soon as it landed in Monrovia. Some of the member states of ECOWAS, especially Burkina Faso, accused members of the SMC of overextending their mandate by establishing an intervention force, arguing that a subregional organization established for the purposes of economic integration did not have any business deploying a military force.[7] However, the decision to deploy ECOMOG was later approved by consensus at the first ever extraordinary session of the Authority of Heads of State and Government held in Bamako, Mali, in November 1990.[8]

When ECOMOG was finally deployed on August 24, 1990, with a force of about 3,500 troops under the command of Lieutenant General Arnold Quainoo of Ghana, its mandate was more limited than had been initially assumed; the force was set up to establish a bridgehead and to facilitate the evacuation of thousands of civilians stranded behind battle lines. However, ECOMOG was not adequately equipped for operation, and the force was unable to achieve its objectives at first attempt.[9] To prevent ECOMOG from landing, Charles Taylor's NPFL had occupied the port area and opened fire on the multilateral force. It took extensive military intervention and assistance from the INPFL to dislodge the NPFL and to create a moderately safe area for the ECOMOG force to land. In fact, it was Johnson who welcomed the first ECOMOG force to Monrovia.[10]

Thus, from its inception, the ECOMOG mandate was compromised because of its de facto alliance with one of the warring factions. Because a friendly working disposition had been established between the ECOMOG forces and the INPFL, Johnson was permitted easy access to the ECOMOG force headquarters. On September 9, 1990, he launched an attack on Samuel Doe when he was visiting the headquarters for the first time. Doe was abducted and later killed by Johnson.

Doe's death introduced a new phase in the ECOMOG operations. The Ghanaian force commander was replaced by Nigeria's Major General Joshua Dogonyaro, and the mandate given to the force was expanded. ECOMOG was now allowed to utilize offensive-defensive military strategy to effect the pacification of the Monrovia area and to deter continued attacks on itself.[11] It was also to establish and enforce an embargo on the transport of arms and ammunition to the warring factions. ECOMOG was expanded to more than 14,000 troops and deployed in Liberia for over three and a half years. Although it has succeeded in establishing credible peace and stability in Monrovia and a large section of the countryside, the political and military situation in Liberia has not been stabilized enough for internationally supervised elections to be conducted.

The deployment of ECOMOG marks the first occasion that a regional organization (in this case, a subregional body) has mobilized the military forces of its member states and deployed them in combat for an extensive military operation. The ECOMOG experience has proven that, contrary to the arguments raised against the formation of an African High Command, it is not impossible for African states to mobilize and launch military operations to deal with collective security problems. Once a good number of important members of the organization are sufficiently interested and committed to providing the necessary support, consensus can always be gathered from other member states.

However, ECOMOG also confirmed some of the worst fears of the skeptics. As a prime mover of ECOMOG, Nigeria was considered indispensable, committing over 10,000 soldiers to the operations and paying more than three-quarters of the bills. But Nigeria's strong support also created the impression that it had a vested interest in the outcome of the Liberian crisis. Without the facilitating role played by Nigeria, Ghana, and the other states, ECOMOG would not have been a reality, and the situation in Liberia would have degenerated into a major regional crisis.

The Problems of ECOMOG

The problems of the ECOWAS multilateral action in Liberia can be grouped into two principal sets.[12] The first set of questions addresses theoretical issues concerning the concept of multilateral intervention itself, and the second set concerns organizational, structural, and procedural issues. On philosophical grounds, some of the members of the subregional organization were critical of what they perceived as an overextension of

ECOWAS's jurisdiction, from economic issues to the adoption of military mandates. They argued that an organization that was established primarily, if not solely, for the facilitation of economic integration lacked a mandate to take on political and security-related responsibilities, even if done for humanitarian reasons. Some member states felt that due consultation had not been carried out before the force was deployed.[13] The first set of questions include the following:

1. Can a regional economic grouping of states assume security-related responsibilities? If so, what conditions must govern the decision to intervene, and who determines when these conditions are met? What happens when security- and military-related problems disrupt and overshadow the processes of economic integration?

2. Is it philosophically right for a multilateral organization to intervene militarily into internal security situations? Did ECOWAS have that mandate, and which legal instruments in the status of the organization provided it with such authority?[14]

3. The acceptance of jurisdiction in domestic problems of member states, even on economic questions, ascribe supranational characteristics to the subregional organization. However, ECOWAS presently lacks the political capabilities to assume supranational responsibilities. What are the implications of pursuing regional integration policies in a situation of endemic internal disintegration?

4. Where does a regional organization affix the limits of state sovereignty? Where do sovereign responsibilities end and supranational responsibilities begin?[15] Should a multilateral force engage in peace enforcement, even in support of a humanitarian action? What are the conditions under which this can be done, and how can the organization ensure a mix of forces to achieve the multiple objectives of peacekeeping, peace enforcement and peace building, all in one mission? What impact does enforcement have on the perception of neutrality of the multilateral force, and what types of damage control mechanisms can be adopted to reduce the negative effects and consequences of enforcement actions?

The second set of questions include:

1. Does the 1981 protocol on defense, on which the entire concept of intervention was built, provide enough scope and authority for the full implementation of the basic philosophies of the protocol?

2. Should the creation of a central decisionmaking organization be an essential step prior to the deployment of a regional multilateral force?

3. What are the implications for ECOWAS of the deployment of a multilateral force based on the 1981 protocol without the implementation of the structural organization provided for in the 1981 protocol?[16]

4. How did the ECOMOG force structure affect its operational competence, and how can any problems be ameliorated? How should the twin operational concepts of peacekeeping and peace enforcement be implemented in practical terms in order to reduce the negative impact of one over the other?

5. Would the networking of the subregional security system into the regional security organizational structure enhance the operational efficiency of regional multilateral action, and what impact would it have on the concept of neutrality?

6. What are the lessons of the ECOMOG experience regarding the financing of peacekeeping? How can the questions of finance be more adequately addressed?

The question of the competence of an economic grouping of states in dealing with regional security questions was first addressed by Ibrahim Babangida, who argued that effective economic integration strategies cannot be conducted in a security vacuum. Effective economic interaction can best be conducted, according to Babangida, when there is full and effective security of life and property and freedom of movement of peoples.[17] Some critics of ECOMOG argued that the regional organization had exceeded its mandate by assuming the security responsibility, claiming that the body did not have the organizational structure to handle such a responsibility.

The involvement of ECOWAS in the Liberian crisis greatly polarized the member states of West Africa. Burkina Faso and Côte d'Ivoire initially supported the rebel incursion into Liberia. (The former Ivoirian president later withdrew that support, at least officially, and subsequently hosted a series of peace initiatives to resolve the Liberian crisis.) The deployment of ECOMOG was strongly opposed by several of the Francophone West African states, exacerbating the language-group division in the subregion. The critics of ECOMOG argued that the SMC did not have the political authority to commit the subregional organization to peacekeeping.[18] Privately, some of the member states were suspicious of Nigeria's intentions in Liberia and felt threatened by its display of military power. The other member states of ECOWAS queried the criteria used to determine the choice of Liberia for a peacekeeping initiative and thought they had not been sufficiently consulted on the matter.

If the decision to deploy forces to Liberia was based on the need to facilitate the evacuation of the noncombatant peoples, would the same measures be adopted in similar conflict situations? Who is to assess when a situation is ripe for intervention if there is no permanent central decisionmaking organism empowered to act in the event of a breakdown of order within a member state? The adoption of such a broad mandate may overstretch the capacity of the organization; nevertheless, the capacity for a more extensive military intervention can be developed.

Critics of ECOMOG argued that the force deployed to Liberia already represented an intervention force because the acceptance of all the warring factions had not been secured. The argument put forward by ECOWAS was that the neutrality of the force was widely acknowledged prior to the NPFL attack against ECOMOG on October 15, 1992.[19]

One of the cardinal tenets of traditional peacekeeping is that a force can be deployed only after the consent of all the warring factions is secured; such a force is usually designed to maintain and supervise pre-agreed cease-fires and buffer zones in an interpositionary deployment between the warring factions. These conditions were not met in Liberia; however, the ECOWAS secretariat argued that since there was a collapse of central authority, signified by the inability of the government to provide the minimum conditions necessary for the maintenance of law and order, the subregional body was justified in taking action out of humanitarian considerations. The report of the executive secretary of ECOWAS to the SMC described the following scene in Monrovia: "The orgy of killings and wanton destruction continued unabated, involving thousands of innocent civilians—barbaric acts that contravened all recognized standards of civilized behavior. Thousands of foreign nationals, including community citizens, were also trapped in Liberia without any means of escape or protection."[20]

The need to create some legitimizing political frame in Liberia prompted ECOWAS to convene a conference of Liberian nationals after Doe's death in September 1990. A meeting of all the warring factions in Freetown, Sierra Leone, was held to negotiate a cease-fire and to work out an end to the conflict. This effort failed, however, because the NPFL did not send any representation. The ECOWAS secretariat then developed the ECOWAS Peace Plan, using the 1981 Protocol on Mutual Assistance on Defense as its legal foundation. The secretariat and members of the SMC argued that Burkina Faso and Côte d'Ivoire had, by providing base facilities for the NPFL rebellion, broadened the scope of the rebellion from a purely internal issue. Charles Taylor accused the Nigerian government of hiding behind the ECOWAS shield to continue its protection of Doe's regime.[21]

A product of the Peace Plan, the Interim Government of National Unity (IGNU) provided the political legitimization for the activities of ECOMOG. IGNU was able to speak on behalf of a broad spectrum of Liberian people and to negotiate with ECOWAS for the needs and interests of the country. Hence, accusations by the NPFL that ECOMOG was an alien force of aggressors could be dismissed by a large number of Liberians, who welcomed the assistance of the subregional body to return their country to order. ECOMOG was able to isolate the NPFL and eventually persuaded it to agree to a cease-fire.

Multilateral Intervention in Internal Security Situations

The deployment of ECOMOG in Liberia also signifies a major breach in established tenets of relations among African states that argue against the interference by states in the internal affairs of other states. The Organization of African Unity (OAU) charter clearly enjoins member states not to interfere in the internal affairs of other states; in fact, it is one of the most strictly adhered to tenets in the charter. Some critics, though, contend that it is often used as a convenient ploy to justify inaction against states that violate the basic principles of good governance.[22]

There have been occasions when the charter's stipulation has been contravened; for example, during the time of Idi Amin, when Tanzanian troops were deployed to Uganda and occupied Ugandan territory. However, the justification for Tanzania's action was provided by prior Ugandan aggression against that country, and Tanzania had lodged an official complaint at the OAU. In Liberia, the ECOWAS secretariat justified the deployment of ECOMOG as the only option left for the subregional states in a situation of complete breakdown of sovereign authority. The concept of inviolability of sovereignty and territorial integrity had already been compromised when Liberian authority could not prevent the violation of the rights and security of individuals and of foreign nationals, embassies, and properties in Liberia. It can also be argued that the 1981 Protocol on Mutual Assistance on Defense[23] allowed the subregional organization the right to intervene in internal conflict situations where clear evidence exists of external intervention. Additionally, the 1978 Protocol on Non-Aggression, in articles 2, 3, and 4, enjoins each member state to refrain from committing, encouraging, or condoning acts of subversion, hostility, or aggression against the territorial integrity or political independence of other member states. The protocol further states that each member state shall "undertake to prevent foreigners, resident on its territory or non-resident foreigners, using its territory as a base, from committing such acts." By allowing the NPFL to organize and launch its invasion of Liberia from their territories, both Côte d'Ivoire and Burkina Faso opened the door to the internationalization of the crisis.[24]

Is it right to insist on the concept of noninterference in the face of complete breakdown of central authority? Was the Doe regime in July 1990 in a position to exercise sovereign authority? Although Doe was ensconced in the presidential palace, the security situation had deteriorated to the point where he feared for his life and would not risk venturing out. It was at this stage that Doe reportedly wrote to the ECOWAS heads of state, asking their assistance in settling his country's crisis. Nevertheless, the organization lacks supranational authority to undertake some of the responsibilities it assumed in Liberia. Until 1990, compliance to the organization's rules was purely voluntary; there were no sanctions that it could apply against states that violated its codes of conduct.[25]

Is the ECOMOG experience replicable? Under what conditions can a similar force be deployed? The role of countries such as Nigeria and Ghana in the deployment of ECOMOG to Liberia was critical, for they had the ability to deploy their forces in such a multilateral operation at their own expense and to maintain the logistical requirements of the operations. Even though Nigeria's dominance of the force was strongly criticized, it is clear that without Nigeria, there would have been no sustainable Liberian operation.

Should a force that was deployed to facilitate the provision of humanitarian assistance have implemented an enforcement action? The NPFL criticized ECOMOG's several bombing raids and pointed to them as further proof of the aggressive intentions of the states contributing troops, especially Nigeria. ECOMOG argued that the first mandate to embark on enforcement actions in November 1990 was essential to the continuation of the objectives of peacekeeping in Liberia. Faced with incessant attacks from both the INPFL and the NPFL, ECOMOG wanted to create what has become known in contemporary UN peacekeeping parlance as "safe havens." ECOWAS was concerned about both creating a zone that would be sufficiently secure in order to provide a shelter for the thousands of refugees from the hinterland and securing the establishment of the interim administration. Under the command of General Dogonyaro, the warring factions were pushed out of the Monrovia area and soon signed the first cease-fire accord.

The next major offensive took place in October 1992, after "Operation Octopus," the attack launched on Monrovia by the NPFL, and the massacre of nine Senegalese soldiers, reportedly by Taylor's force. It took a full-scale land, sea, and air battle to contain the situation and to force the NPFL back to the bargaining table. Naturally, this offensive affected the way in which the warring factions, especially the NPFL, perceived the partiality of the ECOMOG force. The perception was further distorted by the fact that the subregional organization was not directly involved in the distribution of humanitarian assistance, which rendered the argument that the peacekeeping force was deployed to facilitate humanitarian action difficult to accept.

The issue of the distribution and handling of humanitarian assistance would have been greatly facilitated had IGNU under Amos Sawyer worked harder to establish relations with the other factions, especially the NPFL, and bridges of communications with the government at Gbarnga. Instead, Taylor was treated as a belligerent, and the IGNU chose to ostracize him.

Although IGNU initially insisted that all international humanitarian aid had to be routed through Monrovia, the humanitarian agencies insisted on complete independence of action in the distribution of assistance to the interior because they found IGNU's scope of operations too restricted. The ECOWAS secretariat supported the attempt to restrict the distribution of relief materials on the grounds of an inability to provide effective security. It argued for the need to balance the interest of ensuring the provision of relief and the imperatives of avoiding any activity that might compromise the security of peace enforcers. It argued further that when peace enforcement, rather than peacekeeping, is adopted as the strategy, security agencies have the responsibility and duty of directing all operations.[26] The field commander of ECOMOG was finally able to create "corridors of tranquility" for the delivery of humanitarian assistance.[27]

Some scholars have argued that ECOMOG has "complicated their task by adopting the politically sensitive protocol on defense,"[28] whereas others have argued that "the states of West Africa have accomplished what states of the entire continent have not: acceptance of a mutual security agreement."[29]

Should the same force that is deployed for a peacekeeping action be used for peace enforcement activities? This switch has not always been easy to make. The historical experience of ECOMOG has been that oftentimes commanders are changed whenever there is a change of mandates; for example, the Ghanaian commander, Lieutenant General Quainoo, was changed to Nigeria's General Dogonyaro in November 1990 when an order for a military offensive was issued to pacify the Monrovia area and its environs. Dogonyaro was replaced by General Rufus Kupolati, who argued that his mandate was to establish a peacekeeping force. He proceeded to open up lines of communication with the NPFL in order to encourage the rebel force to accept the mediatory roles of ECOMOG and Nigeria. In the 1992 siege on Monrovia, Major General Ishaya Bakut, who had pursued a more reconciliatory policy, was replaced by General Adetunji Olurin, who declared war on the NPFL and succeeded in breaking the siege on the capital. Currently, Major General John Inienger, who assumed office after Olurin in 1993, is pursuing a more traditional peacekeeping strategy.[30]

It can be argued that the most extensive spate of diplomatic activities have occurred during the periods when the more traditional peacekeeping mandates are in operation. Others would contend that there is more meaningful progress when enforcement action is embarked upon because it pushes the various parties to make concessions and to seek accommodation. Apart from the change of military commanders, the adoption of enforcement mandates has always been followed by the introduction of additional weaponry with greater firepower. These heavy weapons are usually withdrawn immediately after the declaration of a cease-fire.

The Proliferation of Warring Factions in Liberia

The Liberian crisis entered a new and more complicated epoch after the NPFL-led "Operation Octopus" in October 1992. The Liberian political scene witnessed a proliferation of new factions, all vying for political and military advantages. The first of these new factions was the United Liberation Movement for Democracy in Liberia (ULIMO), which was formed in mid-1991. Initially, the movement's proclaimed objective was to discourage the alliance between Foday Sankoh of Sierra Leone, leader of the Revolutionary United Front and ally of Taylor, and Charles Taylor's NPFL and to force the latter to accept and adhere to the agreements concluded. The main thrust of the faction's military campaign was directed at Taylor-held positions. After the repulse of the attack on Monrovia, not only did the NPFL lose substantial territory to ULIMO, but its southeastern flank came under threat from the Liberian Peace Council (LPC). Furthermore, a splinter group evolved within the NPFL itself, led by the former defense spokesperson, Thomas Woewiyu. The LPC, the Woewiyu faction of the NPFL, the breakaway faction of ULIMO led by Roosevelt Johnson and the remnants of the Armed Forces of Liberia also formed the coalition that successfully expelled Charles Taylor from his headquarters in Gbarnga in September 1994.[31]

The proliferation of new factions and the dislodging of the NPFL from its power base occurred after the signing of the Cotonou Agreement. The parties to the agreement included the chairman of the first transition government, Amos Sawyer, the Alhaji Kromah–led faction of the ULIMO, and the NPFL, led by Charles Taylor. The Cotonou Agreement covered issues pertaining to cease-fire and arrangements for the monitoring of its violation, disarmament of the factions' forces, and the general disarmament and demobilization of all the fighting forces and noncombatant but armed groups.

The factions agreed to disarm to ECOMOG, following the procedure provided for in the previous peace agreements arrived at in Yamoussoukro, Côte d'Ivoire, and Geneva, but this time around, the ECOMOG forces would be expanded, with contingents from East African countries. The UN Observer Mission in Liberia (UNOMIL) was to monitor and verify the disarmament process.[32] It was believed that the involvement of the expanded ECOMOG and UNOMIL would add greater credibility to the delicate process of disarmament. Before their deployment, the cease-fire was to be monitored by a Joint Cease-fire Monitoring Team, consisting of members representing the three signatories (the interim government of Liberia, NPFL, and ULIMO), ECOMOG, and a mission of UN observers.

The proceedings at the Cotonou conference were further influenced by the domestic political crisis that Nigeria was experiencing at the time. The political chaos that attended the nullification of the June 12, 1993, elections diverted the attention of the Nigerian military government from foreign policy issues. The general feeling in the subcontinent and even among Nigerians was that a country that could not organize a smooth democratic transition program lacked the credibility to implement such a process in another country.[33] Cotonou was further perceived as an opportunity by the Francophone countries to take control of the peace process from the Anglophones in general and from Nigeria in particular.

The agreement provided for the replacement of the IGNU by a five-member Transitional Council, three of whose members would be nominated by the three parties to the agreement; the remaining two members were to be nominated jointly from a list of nine candidates after due consultation. The agreement also contained provisions for the holding of elections in February and March 1994; following the election of a National Assembly and cabinet, the transition government would be disbanded. The implementation of the political aspects of the Cotonou agreement, however, became problematic. While the factions appointed members to the Liberian National Transitional Government (LNTG), the peace process was interrupted by increased fighting. The NPFL refused to proceed with the agreement's disarmament provisions, arguing that its position was highly threatened by new armed factions, many of whom Taylor claimed were being financed by the Nigerian elements in ECOMOG. Furthermore, Taylor objected to the nomination of his former defense spokesperson, Thomas Woewiyu, now one of the prime movers of the coalition mobilized against the NPFL, and he insisted on being the first vice president of the Transitional Council, with a provision for him to head the interim administration should the position become vacant.

These issues were the subject of discussion and negotiation, first at Akosombo, Ghana, in September 1994, then at Accra, Ghana, in November–December 1994, and finally at Abuja, Nigeria, in May 1995. At the Akosombo meeting of the SMC, the Armed Forces of Liberia, led by Hezekiah Bowen, the ULIMO (Mandingo) faction of Alhaji Kromah and the NPFL were the only parties to the agreement. None of the new factions—the ULIMO (Krahn) faction of Roosevelt Johnson, the breakaway NPFL faction led by Woewiyu, and the LPC, led by George Boley—was represented. By September 1994, these new factions had become major players in the Liberian military and political chessboard. Their exclusion was generally criticized, especially by the chair of the LNTG, David Kpormakpor, and by the members of the National Conference, then convened in Monrovia.[34]

The scenario became even more complicated when the NPFL's Gbarnga headquarters came under an intensive and successful assault from the ULIMO Mandingo as soon as Charles Taylor and his delegation landed in Accra for the conference. The NPFL has since then been unable to reestablish full authority at Gbarnga.[35] The ECOWAS summits held in Cotonou and Abuja were not successful in resolving all the contending issues nor in moving the peace process forward. The disagreement over the composition of the Council of State and especially the issue of the vice chairmanship of the council remained unresolved even after these meetings.[36]

The deadlock in the peace process, the continued violations of the cease-fire, and the proliferation of new factions have all exacerbated the division in the ranks of ECOWAS's member states. The Accra and Abuja summits exposed the growing dissension between Ghana and Nigeria over the approach that needed to be taken on the Liberian crisis. Jerry Rawlings, president of Ghana and the current chair of ECOWAS, appeared to have closed ranks with Charles Taylor's most devoted advocates in the subregion, Burkina Faso and Côte d'Ivoire. At the Abuja summit, he accused his peers, the heads of state of the subregional countries, of pursuing hidden agendas: "Our community is in danger of being torn asunder by the insincerity we continue to show in our dealings with the other over Liberia."[37]

Frustrated over the human and material resources that have been invested in Liberia without much progress in the peace process, the people of both Ghana and Nigeria have put increasing pressure on their heads of state to withdraw from Liberia. Although Ghana has threatened to withdraw from ECOMOG if the peace process is not pursued with seriousness, Nigeria has reiterated its commitment to the resolution of the crisis in spite of its enormous financial burden. Charles Taylor's refusal to attend any other summit after Akosombo further diminished the prospect of meaningful dialogue. However, one of the most meaningful steps toward the resolution of the Liberian crisis might have taken place in June 1995, when Taylor paid an important visit to Abuja during which he held closed-door consultations with the Nigerian head of state and held meetings with the political and military leadership.

The most significant aspect of the visit was Taylor's acknowledgment of the contribution that Nigeria, along with other member states of ECOWAS, had made in the past four years to the resolution of the Liberian conflict. Apologizing on Nigerian television for his past antagonism toward ECOMOG and Nigeria in particular, Taylor stated his belief that the Nigerian contribution was made in a genuine search for peace in Liberia: "The Nigerian presence was as a result of a genuine fraternal desire to see peace restored to the country and that he would now *work* towards the same aim with his Nigerian brothers."[38] Some have argued that perhaps Taylor's change of attitude was influenced more by the NPFL's loss of political and military influence rather than a new-found wisdom. Be that as it may, if this optimism can be sustained, it will have a positive impact on the peace process.

Structural and Operational Problems of ECOWAS

The 1981 protocol, the legal justification of ECOMOG, provides for multilateral mulitary support for a state that is the subject of aggression through the use of allied armed forces from member states. However, ECOWAS had taken no measure to earmark forces in advance of a crisis as provided under this protocol.[39] The two institutions that were to provide the leadership and policy directives to the multilateral force, the Defense Council and the Defense Commission, were not established at the time of the deployment of ECOMOG.

The result was that ECOMOG was dominated by Nigeria, which provided over 10,000 of its troops and approximately 70 percent of its funding. These initiatives, combined with the Nigerian government's aggressive defense of ECOMOG's actions, contributed to the perception that the force was controlled by Nigeria. The other force-contributing states insisted that the use and deployment of their forces would have to be authorized by their governments. Furthermore, there was no clear indication that the ECOWAS secretariat exercised central authority over ECOMOG, the force commander receiving most of his instructions from his home government.

Thus the ECOWAS secretariat had a most tenuous control of ECOMOG. This deficiency has been partly corrected with the expansion of ECOMOG's composition to include elements under UN sponsorship. In addition, ECOMOG's decisionmaking structure has been slightly streamlined. The lack of a tight central controlling mechanism, however, provided flexibility in ECOMOG's strategy; it could respond to the situation existing on the ground without the delay commonly associated with the decisionmaking of the UN on peacekeeping and international security issues. For example, in October 1991, following the NPFL attack on Monrovia, it was possible for ECOMOG to assume an enforcement posture without being inhibited by a lengthy political debate. Again, in November 1991, it assumed an enforcement posture to clear the Monrovia area of all warring factions and to create a safe haven for refugees.

The ECOWAS military experience parallels that of other ECOWAS protocols. Even when these protocols are signed and ratified, the organization does not have the power to enforce compliance. Consequently, the success of any agreement depends on the voluntary adherence of its member states. The organization does not have the power or the capacity to impose sanctions on its member states. The future success of ECOWAS in dealing with security issues depends on its ability to (1) fully implement the 1981 protocol on defense, establishing the institutional frame for its operationalization, and (2) provide legal and political reorientation to give the organization a supranational character. At the moment, too much emphasis is placed on sovereign equality and national interest; ECOWAS would be given a new lease on life if it were allowed to assume supra-national powers. This is the thrust of the recommendation of the Charter Review Committee, established to propose mechanisms for improving the effectiveness of the organization's implementation capacity.

The Organization of African Unity and the UN in the Liberian Crisis

In 1990, when ECOWAS embarked on the intervention in Liberia, one of its justifications was the apparent diversion of the world's attention from African issues at a time when the continent was, as it still is, in turmoil. The events in the Persian Gulf and the unrest in Eastern Europe and the former Soviet Union following the end of the Cold War captured the attention of the international community. The mediation efforts of the sub-regional organization have not been fully successful, however, in resolving the root cause of the Liberian problem. There is still no national government in Liberia, the creation of the transitional government is proving difficult, and the implementation of the disarmament process has remained problematic. The warring factions have justified the refusal to disarm by pointing to the evolution of new factions.

The interim government has succeeded in establishing firm control, with the assistance of ECOMOG, in Monrovia and some other major population areas such as Buchanan. This has encouraged masses of Liberian refugees to return and has provided a safe haven for people fleeing the war areas in the hinterland. By 1993, it was estimated that about 80 percent of the population of Liberia lived in Monrovia and its environs. The rest of the country has been reduced to war zones where contending military factions have carved out competing spheres of influence.

What lessons does the Liberian crisis offer for the management of security in Africa? The post–Cold War scene in Africa is characterized by a disturbing wave of internal conflicts, many of them posing the danger of state disintegration. The ad hoc and accidental intervention that was carried out in Liberia without a properly conceived and managed machinery cannot and should not be the answer. A carefully organized operational procedure for the arrangement of all conflicts needs to be evolved at the continental level so that there is a clearly defined hierarchy of action. The primary responsibility for deciding to intervene (especially when it comes to the deployment of forces) should be at the continental level because the formal introduction of troops into a conflict is probably better managed and has more credibility when there is a clear supranational authority.

At its Cairo summit in 1993, the Organization of African Unity (OAU) agreed to a conflict management mechanism to be managed by a central political decisionmaking organ. The summit rejected a regional peace-keeping force because of political considerations such as sovereignty and territorial integrity. In fact, the OAU has deployed ad hoc observer missions to some conflict situations (Rwanda, Angola) as part of a UN initiative, has sent a political election observer mission to Congo, and is currently planning to participate in the management of the Liberian crisis alongside ECOMOG. Because such initiatives are not based on clearly defined mandates and lines of command and control, they run the risk of failure. Should they fail, the effect would be to further undermine the confidence of the people in regional organizations.

While a restructuring of the secretariat to enhance efficiency may help, the lack of supranational authority by the organization and its inability to apply sanctions is a major handicap. The philosophical focus of the organization needs to be changed from that of a club of states to a functional, people-oriented organization. The OAU has established a central organ for conflict prevention, management, and resolution that will facilitate the deployment of peacekeeping forces in collaboration with the UN, which is a major step toward enhancing the capacity of the organization to act quickly.[40] This central organ met in Tunis in May 1995 and welcomed the ECOWAS decision to convene a summit conference on Liberia at Abuja.

The final report by the Committee of Eminent Persons, established to review the ECOWAS treaty, extensively analyzed existing mechanisms, highlighting the basic flaws and recommending areas of amendment and refinement. Apart from calling for an expansion of the institutional capacity of the secretariat through the appointment of deputy executive secretaries and a military advisor, the panel endorsed the declaration of political principles at the Abuja summit in 1991. It also called for the inclusion of this declaration in the preamble of the modified protocol on nonaggression. The appeal for the appointment of a military adviser is designed to enhance political and military cooperation among member states. Even more important is a recommendation that a regional observer be established who would monitor and mediate relations among states, especially at the border areas, and who would take concrete measures to diffuse tensions by organizing meetings "between relevant ministries on various aspects of interstate relations."[41] The group also advocates a much clearer statement in the protocol on mutual assistance on defense and on intervention in domestic political conflicts, arguing that the declaration of political principles should be operationalized in a constructive and objective manner.

The establishment of an ECOWAS security observation and peace-keeping system was also endorsed. The panel called for the provision of support to member states "facing crisis threatening internal peace, stability and security or for the observation of democratic elections."[42] Ideally, this would be carried out strictly within the context of the declared principles on political action. If not, ECOWAS may become a tool in the hands of those wanting to suppress the process of change.

The proposals relating to aspects of security management certainly require more extensive refinement and fine-tuning to fit into a continent-wide security management mechanism. The provision for the establishment of a military observer group should include the collection of information on conflict situations that can be linked to an OAU network. The peacekeeping forces proposed would most likely consist of previously earmarked contingents that can be pooled when needed. Logistical planning, preparing standard operational procedures, equipping and training need to be organized at the level of the secretariat and should be coordinated with the procedures at the OAU level so as to facilitate a cross-utilization of forces across the continent.

In sum, all regional and subregional organizations derive their authority to act on international security issues from the UN. In Liberia, the UN was not formally introduced until the regional organization confronted difficulties in compelling member states to observe ECOWAS-imposed embargoes. There is a need for the regional and subregional organizations to operate strictly within the UN guidelines and in close collaboration with the secretariat in order to tap from the wealth of expertise available at the continental level and to facilitate UN intervention when deemed desirable.

Some assessment of UNOMIL's contribution to the solution of the Liberian crisis is necessary. The expansion of the original effort of the West African states and the introduction of the Security Council jurisdiction have encouraged some of the great powers to contribute more financial support to Liberia and have reduced the perception of partiality of the peacemaking effort. However, UNOMIL has not made much difference to the actual progress of the peace process because it still operates under the shadow of ECOWAS and depends fully on ECOMOG for military support and protection. The confidence of the warring factions has not been sufficiently gained for large-scale disarmament.

The forces from the East African region that were introduced into the expanded ECOMOG were relatively small, about 1,558 people at its peak in 1994. With the withdrawal of this contingent from ECOMOG, one hopes that the UN will not decide to withdraw its political presence from Liberia, as it did in Somalia. It would be more useful if the UN expanded its security presence through greater collaboration and integration with both the OAU and ECOWAS so that the political objectives of the international community in Liberia could be enhanced. However, in the final analysis, the Liberian crisis will be solved only when the Liberians themselves are ready.

Notes

1. Decision A/DEC.1/8/90 on the establishment of an ECOWAS Cease-fire Monitoring Group for Liberia, First Session of the Community Standing Mediation Committee, Banjul, August 6–7, 1990.

2. "Liberia: Unarmed Civilians Killed," *Amnesty International Newsletter* 20, 10 (October 1990), p. 1.

3. For an extensive analysis of the historical background of the Liberian crisis, see Amadu Sesay, "Historical Background to the Liberian Crisis" in M. A. Vogt, ed., *The Liberian Crisis and ECOMOG* (Lagos: Gabumo Publishing Company, 1992).

4. Concerning calls for the evacuation of Nigerians from Liberia, see *The Guardian*, June 5, 1990.

5. *The African Concord,* August 27, 1990.

6. The decision to create ECOMOG was made at the first session of the Community Standing Mediation Committee held in Banjul, August 6–7, 1990. Decision A/DEC.1/8/90, p. 4.

7. *The African Concord*, September 28, 1990.

8. Decision A/DEC.2/11/90: Relating to the Adoption of an ECOWAS Peace Plan for Liberia and the entire West African Sub-Region, art. 1, par. (b).

9. The initial force that was deployed to Liberia consisted of a good number of ships from the merchant marines, with a few strike ships for convoy protection. See M. A. Vogt, "The Problems and Challenges of Peace-making: From Peace-keeping to Peace Enforcement," in Vogt, ed., *The Liberian Crisis and ECOMOG.* p. 154. See also the account of C. Y. Iweze, the first ECOMOG chief of staff, that many of the troops arrived in Liberia without their personal weapons and that some countries sent paramilitary forces "whose roles in their countries were essentially those of customs and immigration duties" in "Nigeria in Liberia: The Military Operations of ECOMOG," *Nigeria in International Peace-keeping 1960–1992* (Lagos: Malthouse Press Limited, 1993), p. 220.

10. See Iweze's account of the lack of clarity and political direction from the ECOWAS headquarters and how the force related to the various warring factions in his article "Nigeria in Liberia," p. 224.

11. A. Olaiya, "ECOMOG Mission and Mandate," *The Peacemaker* 1,1 (September 1991–March 1992), p. 11.

12. For an exhaustive account of the ECOMOG operations, especially at the first stages of the operations, and a thorough analysis of the operational lessons, see Iweze, "Nigeria in Liberia."

13. *Africa Confidential* 31,19 (September 1990). Also, see the excerpts of the press briefing by Blaise Compaore, president of Burkina Faso, in reaction to the decision to deploy ECOMOG in *The Guardian,* August 15, 1990.

14. The critics of ECOMOG rely on the clauses in the OAU charter, article 3, section 2, committing its members not to interfere in the internal affairs of other states. The legal argument was most forcefully pursued by Blaise Compaore in his press conference referred to in note 13, which was also reported in the *Newswatch,* August 27, 1990, p. 16. Dr. Akinola Aguda of Nigeria also argued that the rescue of their nationals does not provide sufficient justification for intervention by the ECOWAS states in Liberia. See *The African Concord,* July 21, 1991.

15. The commission that was later established to examine the charter of ECOWAS in the contemporary international security environment and to recom-

mend amendments to the charter extensively reviewed the question of supranationality. This was reported in the *Final Report by the Committee of Eminent Persons for the Review of the ECOWAS Treaty* in article (v) of issues discussed, p. 19 of the report to the ECOWAS executive secretary, June 2, 1992.

16. The 1981 Protocol on Mutual Assistance on defense was signed in May 1981 and has since been ratified. The protocol's signature was informed by the wave of foreign military aggression against some African countries. The Portuguese invasion of Guinea-Bissau and the mercenary invasion of Benin created fears that military action would be taken at will against the territorial integrity of African countries that are perceived as revolutionary. The Beninois government blamed the attack on its capital, Cotonou, on France and accused that country of masterminding the attack with the collaboration of some African countries. For the full text of the protocol, see *The Economic Community of West African States: Protocol Annexed to the Treaty,* pp. 135–136.

17. Lecture by General Ibrahim Babagida, "The Imperative Features of Nigerian Foreign Policy and the Crisis in Liberia: 1990," reproduced in George Obiozor et al. *Nigeria and ECOWAS Since 1985: Towards a Dynamic Regional Integration* (Enugu: Fourth Dimension Publishing Company Ltd.), pp. 103–111.

18. The secretary-general of ECOWAS strongly emphasized the link between physical security and economic security through integration, arguing that the former was not achievable in the absence of the latter. See *West Africa*, July 1–7, 1991, p. 1085.

19. Abbass Bandu, "ECOMOG Operation in Liberia: A Political and Diplomatic Perspective," paper presented at the Nigerian National War College, October 5, 1993, p. 29.

20. See *West Africa*, July 1–7, 1991, p. 1085.

21. *African Research Bulletin* 27,8 (August 1–31, 1990), p. 9802.

22. The stipulation on noninterference in the internal affairs of states is contained in article III of the OAU Charter.

23. The Protocol on Mutual Assistance on Defense was signed in Freetown, Sierra Leone, on the May 29, 1981. The protocol was signed by all member states except Cape Verde. It has since entered into force, even though the major organs are yet to be established.

24. The legal arguments on the establishment of the force are extensively discussed by Jinmi Adisa, "The Politics of Regional Military Cooperation: The Case of ECOMOG," in Vogt, ed., *The Liberian Crisis and ECOMOG.*

25. The legal arguments against the action of ECOWAS in Liberia was extensively argued by Dr. Akinola Aguda in *The African Concord*, August 27, 1990.

26. Colin Scott et al., "Humanitarian Action and Security in Liberia: 1989–1994," Occasional Paper #20 (Providence, R.I.: Thomas J. Watson, Jr., Institute for International Studies, Brown University, 1995), p. 12.

27. Dr. Abass Bundu, "The ECOMOG Operations in Liberia: A Political and Diplomatic Perspective" (Lecture delivered at the Nigerian National War College, Course 2, October 1993), p. 26.

28. The issue of intervention on humanitarian grounds is discussed by Earl Conteh-Morgan in "Conflict and Militarization in Africa: Past Trends and New Scenarios," *Conflict Quarterly*, Winter 1993, p. 39.

29. Quoting from an article by Claude E. Welch, Jr., "The Military Factor in West Africa: Leadership or Regional Development," in Julius E. Okolo and Stephen Wright, eds., *West African Regional Cooperation and Development* (Boulder, Colo.: Westview Press, 1990), p. 174.

30. The changes of the ECOMOG mandate, often signified by the redeployment of the force commander, is extensively discussed in M. A. Vogt, "Problems and Challenges of Peace-Making."

31. "Liberia: After Akosombo," *African Confidential* 35,22, November 4, 1994.

32. Cotonou Agreement, sec. E, art. 6.

33. See Cecilia Anthony-Williams, "Open the book on ECOMOG," *The Guardian,* February 16, 1994, p. 31. Also see the Emmanuel Efeni, "Lessons from Liberia" in *The Guardian,* November 17, 1993, p. 9.

34. See "Liberia: After Akosombo," p. 3.

35. *African Confidential* 35,22 (November 4, 1994).

36. "Deadlock on Liberia" in *West Africa* 4051 (May 29–June 4, 1995).

37. *West Africa* 4051 (May 29–June 4, 1995), p. 836.

38. "Breaking the Ice," *West Africa,* June 12–18, 1995, p. 920.

39. The Gowon Commission that reviewed the ECOWAS treaty suggested the adoption of a supplementary protocol to complement the protocol on Mutual Assistance on Defence, which in Article 12 provides for the appointment of a deputy executive secretary (military). *Committee of Eminent Persons,* June 1992.

40. *Report of the secretary-general on the Various Initiatives on Conflict Management: Enhancing OAU's Capacity in Preventive Diplomacy, Conflict Resolution and Peace-keeping* (Council of Ministers, 62d Ordinary Session, June 21–23, 1995, CM/1883[LXII]).

41. *Final Report by the Committee of Eminent Persons,* p. 40.

42. *Final Report by the Committee of Eminent Persons,* p. 40.

PART 3

Extracontinental Actors
and Regional Security

12

Removing the Shackles?
U.S. Foreign Policy Toward Africa
After the End of the Cold War

PETER J. SCHRAEDER

Every few years it has been a ritual exercise for Africanists to ponder continuity and change in U.S. foreign policy toward Africa. The time frame of analysis is usually the post–World War II era, with 1958—the year marking official recognition of Africa through the creation of the U.S. State Department's Bureau of African Affairs—serving as a convenient starting point.

A fairly consistent conclusion of these analyses is that U.S. policies toward Africa were marked by continuity rather than change during the Cold War era. For example, in 1983 at a presidential address to the annual meeting of the African Studies Association, Crawford Young underscored the policy's "essential continuity." Although he carefully added that "noteworthy fluctuations" have occurred, he nonetheless concluded that "these variations have been above all of style, tone, and the subtler chemistry of policy articulation, and not its underlying substance."[1] In 1988, another scholar concurred, noting that U.S. foreign policy toward Africa during the Cold War era "has demonstrated remarkable coherence and regularity despite the differences between Republican and Democratic administrations and the tenure of nine different Assistant Secretaries of State for African Affairs."[2]

With the end of the Cold War, however, scholars and policy analysts looked forward to the possibility of long-awaited and much desired changes in the United States' African policies. Michael Clough, senior fellow for Africa at the Council on Foreign Relations, captured the optimism of Africanists by arguing that the U.S. was "free at last" of the conceptual and ideological "shackles" of the Cold War era and therefore should create a new relationship with the African continent.[3] Indeed, the end of the Cold

War rendered obsolete a formerly interventionist policy built upon the twin themes of anticommunism and containment, especially after Washington's primary perceived adversary—the former Soviet Union—had followed in the footsteps of other great empires throughout history, fragmenting into a host of smaller, independent, and noncommunist countries.

The primary purpose of this chapter is to assess the evolution of U.S. policies now that the shackles of the Cold War have been removed. I will first briefly describe U.S. images of Africa and the essence of U.S. foreign policy toward Africa during the Cold War era.

Africa as a Foreign Policy Backwater

The earliest recorded incident of North America's involvement with Africa took place in 1619, when a Dutch ship sold twenty Africans into slavery in the British North American colonies.[4] From this inauspicious beginning, the colonies eventually became part of a worldwide slave-trading network, the legacy of which nearly four centuries later would be more than 30 million citizens—roughly 12 percent of the U.S. population—claiming an African-American heritage.

Despite historical and cultural ties between the U.S. and the African continent, there exists no consensus within the policymaking establishment over Africa's importance. The African-American lobby TransAfrica and the Congressional Black Caucus are quick to emphasize the importance of the ethnic link. Other members of Congress underscore the humanitarian or moral imperatives that link the United States to Africa; of particular concern are Western efforts to alleviate chronic drought and famine. The U.S. Department of Commerce, noting the potential market of nearly 600 million people for U.S. goods and services, as well as significant levels of U.S. oil and mineral imports from West Africa and southern Africa, respectively, underscores the economic links of the relationship. The Department of State focuses on political linkages—most notably the weight of more than fifty votes within the UN and the importance of the Organization of African Unity. The U.S. Department of Defense naturally focuses on military linkages, including Africa's geographical proximity to strategic "chokepoints" such as the Strait of Bab el Mandeb in the Horn of Africa and the Cape of Good Hope in southern Africa.

Despite these linkages, Africanists generally agree that the United States' African policies have been marked by indifference, at worst, and neglect, at best.[5] Africa has been treated as a backwater in official policymaking circles in terms of the time and resources allocated to it. A spirited exchange between Senator Jesse Helms and Senator Daniel Patrick Moynihan illustrates the gap of knowledge about Africa among some elected officials. The debate concerned an amendment put forth by Helms, who, concerned with perceived communist advances in Africa (most notably the presence of Soviet military advisers in Mozambique and Cuban troops in Angola), sought a ban on aid to any African country hosting foreign troops on its soil.

> But, Mr. Moynihan said, what of Chad, which is "fending off the Red armed hordes" with the help of the French? And what of Djibouti, which is doing the same? Mr. Helms was puzzled. Djibouti? Where is this Djibouti? Mr. Moynihan sprang to his feet, strode to the wall of the hearing room, clambered atop a chair and referred to a big map. He pointed to the Horn of Africa. "Communists to the left," [Ethiopia] he said, gesturing broadly. Another gesture: "Communists to the right" [Somalia]. A stab of the finger on the map: "Djibouti—right in the middle." Mr. Helms appeared enlightened, even chastened. The amendment was defeated.[6]

Although Moynihan correctly identified the foreign troops stationed in Africa, his analysis of the situation was not without error. The "Red armed hordes" that the French were credited with stopping in Chad were, in reality, Libyan troops under the leadership of Muammar Qaddafi. Furthermore, his designation of Somalia as a communist country was outdated. By 1987, Somali leader Mohammed Siad Barre had broken his country's alliance with the former Soviet Union and had largely abandoned Marxism in favor of a U.S. alliance and an export-oriented capitalist path of development.[7]

The lack of substantive knowledge of Africa is especially acute at the level of the mass public, which maintains what can be called a *National Geographic* image of the continent.[8] Although some topics, such as racial politics and the transition to democracy in South Africa, receive regular press coverage and have somewhat improved the public's awareness, the mention of Africa typically conjures up stereotypical images of lush jungles and wild animals, poverty and famine, corruption and "tribal" warfare, and rampant sexuality leading to the explosion of AIDS.

This image is reinforced by the nature of U.S. media programming and the safari tradition of U.S. journalism. Media programming, when it does focus on Africa, usually concentrates on the sensationalist and often negative aspects of the continent.[9] Unless field reporters can produce a "hard" news story that can attract attention back home—such as interviews with U.S. Marines detailing the hardships of being deployed in Somalia during the 1992 Christmas season as part of Operation Restore Hope—editors interested in what will sell make it difficult to place a feature story in the press. Even the traditional crisis-oriented stories that usually make it onto Western television are often blocked from airing: For example, despite the availability of excellent film footage documenting the emerging Ethiopian famine of 1983–1985, editors initially refused to televise the material because they "thought that there was no news in another African famine."[10]

The safari tradition of U.S. journalism (i.e., sending generalists to Africa on short-term assignments) reinforces the checkered view the public has about the continent. Helen Kitchen, a former journalist and respected Africanist, notes that although much of the reporting by U.S. newspaper and wire correspondents is informed and conscientious, follow-up is inconsistent. She laments that what one still gets from the U.S. media is "discontinuous segments of the day-to-day history of Africa."[11] For example, the dearth of newspaper reports on Somalia less than six months after the withdrawal of U.S. troops (as opposed to extensive daily coverage while U.S. troops were present) might lead the average reader to assume that the conflict has been resolved and the Somali people are being fed.

Even the scholarly community has focused an inadequate amount of attention on the United States' African policies.[12] The study of Africa within the three disciplines perhaps best suited to ensuring a well-informed foreign policy—history, political science, and international studies—has been relegated to a low-level status.[13] Scholars within these disciplines historically have given academic priority to studies that focus on traditional U.S. security concerns, such as East-West relations and the nature of the Atlantic Alliance, or geographical regions of perceived greater importance, such as Southeast Asia, Central America, and, more recently, Eastern Europe and the Middle East.

Although advances have been made, the fact that Africa remains poorly understood by the policymaking establishment, the general public, the media, and the academic community translates into a poor base for formulating effective foreign policy. Disagreement within the U.S. policymaking establishment over how to respond to the invasion of Zaire by exiles based in neighboring Angola prompted former British prime minister James Callaghan to remark: "There seem to be a number of Christopher Columbuses setting out from the United States to discover Africa for the first time. It's been there a long time."[14]

Unfortunately, the United States has had to "rediscover" Africa at several junctures during the post–World War II era. U.S. policymakers have tended to ignore the African continent until some sort of politico-military crisis grabs their attention. One undesirable outcome of such an approach is that policy often becomes driven by events, as opposed to the more desirable outcome of events being shaped by policy. Perhaps the greatest danger in such a strategy is that poor understanding can foster poorly devised policies that ultimately are destined to fail. As the United States prepares to enter the twenty-first century, it will become increasingly important to shed its Christopher Columbus image and formulate effective policies that are proactive rather than reactive.

Discovering Africa Through the Prism of the Cold War

As the nationalist urges of independence movements swept the countries of Africa during the 1950s, marking the beginning of the end of European colonialism, two politicians of widely divergent perspectives emphasized the necessity of rethinking U.S. foreign policy toward the continent. "For too many years," Vice President Richard M. Nixon noted in 1957 after returning from a twenty-two day tour of the African continent, "Africa in the minds of many Americans has been regarded as a remote and mysterious continent which was the special province of big game hunters, explorers and motion picture makers."[15] Recognizing the importance of an emerging Africa in the international scene—especially within the context of the East-West struggle—Nixon recommended that President Dwight D. Eisenhower authorize the creation of a separate Bureau of African Affairs within the State Department, an idea that reached fruition in 1958.

Also speaking out in 1957, Senator John F. Kennedy derided what he perceived as Washington's inability to come to grips with the question of colonialism and the growing forces of nationalism in Africa.[16] Kennedy later warned that the "only real question is whether these new nations [of Africa] will look West or East—to Moscow or Washington—for sympathy, help, and guidance in their effort to recapitulate, in a few decades, the entire history of modern Europe and America." In order to blunt what he perceived as the steady decline of U.S. prestige in Africa at the expense of growing Soviet influence, Kennedy concluded that "we must embark on a bold and imaginative new program for the development of Africa."[17]

Despite their partisan rivalries, both Nixon and Kennedy shared Cold War beliefs that stressed the necessity of enlisting Africa in the United States' quest to halt the spread of communism and contain Soviet expansionism. Most important, these beliefs were shared in varying degrees by all U.S. presidents from the 1950s to the end of the 1980s and served as the basis for a variety of interventionist episodes in Africa during the Cold War era.[18] These episodes ranged from offers of economic and military aid to leaders of anticommunist client states, such as Emperor Haile Selassie of Ethiopia; the imposition of economic sanctions against radical leaders backed by the Soviet Union, such as Egypt's Gamal Abdul Nasser; Central Intelligence Agency (CIA)–sponsored covert action campaigns, including the successful assassination of Patrice Lumumba, the radical nationalist prime minister of Zaire; the funding of paramilitary guerrilla insurgencies, such as the U.S. assistance to the guerrilla forces of Jonas Savimbi to overthrow a self-proclaimed Marxist regime in Angola; and, finally, the direct application of U.S. military force, including Lyndon B. Johnson's decision to send U.S. combat troops to Zaire.

Two themes aptly illustrate how U.S. policymakers perceived Africa's role in the various strategies of containment that were initially outlined by the Truman administration. First, rather than viewing African countries as important in their own right, U.S. policymakers saw them as a means for preventing the further advances of Soviet communism; therefore, U.S. relationships with African regimes evolved according to their relative importance within an East-West framework. For example, the United States courted Haile Selassie from the 1940s to the 1970s because of Ethiopia's strategic location and its partnership in a global telecommunications surveillance network directed against the Soviet Union.[19] When the security relationship between the United States and Ethiopia shattered during the 1970s, the United States turned to Siad Barre primarily because access to bases in Somalia could enhance the U.S. military capability to counter any Soviet threats to Middle Eastern oil fields.[20] Similarly, Washington policymakers viewed Mobutu Sese Seko and a host of Afrikaner governments positively because Zaire and South Africa possessed strategic resources and could also serve as bulwarks against communism.[21] In each of these cases, an overriding preoccupation with anticommunism led Washington to overlook the authoritarian excesses of these regimes in favor of their willingness to support U.S. containment policies in Africa.

The second major outcome of Washington's containment policies in Africa was the emergence of the continent as a battlefield for proxy wars as both the United States and the Soviet Union became involved in regional conflicts. In almost every case, regional conflict was exacerbated by one superpower's reaction to the other's involvement in a particular crisis situation. Indeed, Soviet involvement, as well as its mere threat, was enough to capture White House attention and usually provoke an escalation of the conflict. In the case of Zaire, the political instability of the early independence years, coupled with only relatively limited amounts of Soviet involvement, was enough to warrant authorized covert assassination attempts and two military operations involving limited amounts of U.S. troops and transport aircraft.[22] During the 1975–1976 Angolan civil war, Soviet-Cuban involvement led to a tacit alliance between the United States, South Africa, and Zaire in which Washington supported the direct involvement of Zairian and, more onerous for most African countries, South African troops.[23] In these and other cases, local conflicts having little to do with the ideological concerns of communism or capitalism threatened to become East-West flashpoints in the face of growing U.S.-Soviet involvement.

The Cold War foundations of the United States' African policies were dramatically called into question by the fall of the Berlin Wall in 1989, the overthrow of communist regimes in Eastern Europe, and the fragmentation of the Soviet Union. Although the Russian Republic pledged to seek further cooperation with the United States in a variety of realms—including the resolution of regional conflicts in Africa—the fragmentation of the former Soviet Union signaled a significant shift in the international balance of power. As U.S.-Russian cooperation continues to replace the former antagonistic relationship, Washington's Cold War–driven policies have changed and will continue to change in all the regions of the world, including Africa.

Trends in U.S. Policy in the Post–Cold War Era

Although they do not constitute an exhaustive list, eight trends capture the evolving nature of U.S. foreign policy toward Africa in the post–Cold War era. A first trend is the reinforcement of the historical tendency among U.S. policymakers to treat Africa as a back-burner issue. Although many Africans are quick to note the tremendous negative impact of the Cold War on Africa, ironically, this struggle did lead to greater U.S. attention to the continent. In fact, African leaders were often able to use U.S.-Soviet competition as a bargaining tool to obtain substantial increases in economic and military aid. However, as political changes in the former Eastern bloc began to dominate the agenda of the U.S. policymaking establishment, African diplomats and scholars correctly discerned the downgrading of African issues. As succinctly noted by Michael Clough, this has resulted in a de facto policy of "cynical disengagement" in which policymakers are guided by three principles: (1) "Do not spend much money [on Africa] unless Congress makes you"; (2) "Do not let African issues complicate policy toward other, more important parts of the world"; and (3) "Do not take stands that might create political controversies in the United States."[24]

A second trend has been budget cutbacks in U.S. government offices related to Africa and growing pressures to trim already reduced levels of economic and military aid. Budgetary cutbacks are an outgrowth of the perception among U.S. officials that the continent is less important in the post–Cold War era and are reinforced by popular pressures to trim the budget deficit and enhance spending for domestic social programs. For example, in order to staff growing numbers of consulates and embassies in Eastern Europe and the newly independent republics of the former Soviet Union, the State Department trimmed approximately seventy positions from its Bureau of African Affairs and closed consulates and embassies in Cameroon, the Comoro Islands, Kenya, and Nigeria.[25] The U.S. Agency for International Development (USAID) similarly cut a variety of programs and staff positions related to Africa and reportedly only the "11th-hour intervention" of the Congressional Black Caucus prevented the Foreign Affairs Committee of the U.S. House of Representatives from merging its subcommittees on African and Latin American affairs.[26] Even the CIA announced in June 1994 that it planned to close fifteen stations in Africa and withdraw dozens of case officers. "We have never been in Africa to report on Africa," explained one CIA official. "We went into Africa as part of the covert activity of the Cold War, to recruit [as spies] Soviet, Chinese, Eastern European and sometimes North Korean officials under circumstances that were easier to operate under than in their home countries."[27]

The amount of U.S. assistance given to Africa from fiscal year (FY) 1985 (just prior to the passage of the Gramm-Rudman-Hollings Deficit Reduction Act) to FY 1994 (the last budget prepared by the Bush administration) offers a revealing barometer of changing U.S. interests in Africa.[28] During this period, U.S. military assistance (minus the roughly $2 billion given annually to Egypt) declined from $279.2 million to $3.8 million. Other forms of security assistance, such as Economic Support Funds, similarly dropped from $452.8 million to $15 million. The majority of Africanists are quick to note, however, that reductions in these forms of assistance are not necessarily a bad thing, especially when one notes that development assistance increased from $1.14 billion in FY 1985 to $1.34 billion in FY 1994. Although this increase should be applauded, the tabulation of overall aid flows suggests Africa's growing marginalization within the policymaking establishment in the post–Cold War era. Whereas Africa received roughly 10.3 percent ($1.87 billion) of an overall budget of $18.13 billion in FY 1985, this figure had declined to 7.6 percent ($1.36 billion) of an overall budget of $17.99 billion in FY 1994.

The first foreign assistance budget request completely prepared by the Clinton administration (FY 1995) reflects how aid to Africa will be affected by a Democratic administration determined to slash the deficit and focus on the U.S. economy "like a laser beam."[29] Because the administration has restructured aid according to four new general categories—sustainable development ($990.4 million), humanitarian assistance ($68.3 million), building democracy ($23.8 million), and promoting peace ($0.5 million)—the figures are not directly comparable with earlier statistical summaries. Still, two major conclusions can be drawn: First, the Clinton administration is continuing to emphasize development as opposed to military/security-related forms of assistance. Second, the marginalization of Africa is continuing in terms of both the gross amount ($1.08 billion) and the percentage (6.03) of targeted aid from an overall foreign assistance budget of $17.94 billion. This trend intensified in spring 1995 as the new Republican-controlled Congress implemented a campaign pledge to further cut foreign assistance programs, particularly those within the development category managed by USAID.

A third trend of the post–Cold War era is the reinforcement of Washington's tendency to relegate responsibility for overseeing its African policies to those national security bureaucracies that make up the executive branch: the State Department, the Defense Department, and the CIA, as well as their specialized agencies devoted specifically to Africa. Of all regions in the world, Africa has traditionally attracted the least interest and attention from the United States. This trend has continued under the Clinton administration, most notably because of the president's desire to downplay foreign policy and instead focus primarily on U.S. domestic concerns.[30] As a result, U.S. policies toward Africa are increasingly subject in the post–Cold War era to the influence of bureaucrats within the national security bureaucracies.

The most important outcome of this bureaucratic influence within the policymaking process is that U.S. policies on Africa have become fragmented, interpreted differently according to the established organizational missions of each bureaucracy. The primary mission of the State Department's Bureau of African Affairs, for example, is the maintenance of smooth and stable relationships with all African governments. The emphasis is on quiet diplomacy and the negotiated resolution of any conflicts that may arise. In sharp contrast, the primary mission of the CIA's Africa Division has traditionally been to carry the ideological battle against the former Soviet Union and communism to the African continent. Openly contemptuous of self-proclaimed Marxist and other "leftist" regimes, liberation movements, and, more recently, "radical" activists (such as Libya's Muammar Qaddafi) and political movements (such as Islamic fundamentalism), the CIA prefers close liaisons with the security services of European allies and friendly African regimes. As for the Pentagon, the primary mission of the Office for African Affairs (International Security Affairs) is to ensure continued access to strategically located bases and other facilities for responding to local crises and, most important, military contingencies in Europe or the Middle East.

The U.S. response to the escalating civil war in Liberia demonstrates the importance of the national security bureaucracies in shaping its policies toward Africa in the post–Cold War era.[31] Unlike its direct handling of more hard-line military operations in Panama and Kuwait—both of which were initially opposed by the State Department's Bureaus of Latin American Affairs and Near Eastern and South Asian Affairs, respectively—the White House deferred to the Africa bureau's desire to remain relatively neutral in the civil war and seek the negotiated departure of Liberian dictator Samuel Doe.[32] Conscious of African concerns over unilateral superpower intervention on the African continent, the bureau managed to gain White House approval to seek the negotiated departure of President Doe and, failing that, support of a multilateral occupation force led by Nigeria and solely made up African troops. Although the White House ultimately did send in the U.S. Marines, their actions were solely limited to ensuring the safe departure of approximately 1,100 U.S. civilians and diplomatic personnel residing in the country. At no point did U.S. forces seek to militarily determine the outcome of fighting between government forces and guerrilla factions vying for control.

A fourth trend in the post–Cold War era is growing U.S. concern—particularly within the Department of Defense—over threats posed by "low-intensity conflict" (LIC) and "radical" African leaders. LIC is defined as encompassing the lower end of the "spectrum of violence" and therefore includes the following categories of operations: counterinsurgency (aid to an allied government to defeat a guerrilla insurgency); proinsurgency (aid designed to foster a guerrilla insurgency against a foreign government); peacetime contingency operations (such as short-term rescue missions); terrorism counteraction; antidrug operations; pacification or control of ethnic groups; humanitarian assistance; and military civic action.[33]

Two fundamental assumptions lie at the heart of this rising strategic consensus within the policymaking establishment: (1) "Vital U.S. interests are threatened by radical and revolutionary violence" in Africa and other regions of the Third World; and (2) the U.S. "must be prepared to use military force" to protect these interests.[34] "Tribal wars and instability [in Africa] do not bode well for us," explained one U.S. official in justification for contingency planning against LIC groups in Africa. "Africa's a huge piece of land that we, as a world power, must fly around, sail around, traverse," he continued. "It's not as strategically important as Japan, NATO, Europe—but it's there."[35]

Various portions of the U.S. policymaking establishment are also increasingly concerned with the potential threat posed by what they perceive as radical African leaders. As demonstrated by U.S. attempts to assassinate Patrice Lumumba during the early 1960s and the Reagan administration's attacks against Qaddafi during the 1980s, the perceived threats posed by radical African leaders have attracted the attention of the highest levels of the U.S. policymaking establishment. Opposition to these leaders during the Cold War era was most often based on the belief that they contributed to the political designs of the Soviet Union. During the 1990s, U.S. hostility toward these leaders has been based on their acceptance of such ideologies and movements as Islamic fundamentalism and their ability to destabilize U.S. allies and clients and in general stymie U.S. regional policies. This concern was most forcefully laid out in an article written by Tony Lake, national security adviser in the Clinton administration, in which he addresses the necessity of counteracting "backlash" states within the international system.[36]

In the case of Somalia and Operation Restore Hope, for example, both the Bush and Clinton administrations demonized General Mohamed Farah Aidid as one of the chief stumbling blocks to the country's pacification and the creation of an enduring political settlement.[37] This characterization, reinforced by press accounts of Aidid's "barbaric" and "ruthless" nature, ultimately led to a series of shortsighted military policies designed to isolate and defeat his portion of a clan militia army known as the United Somali Congress (USC). Not only did such an approach create a false impression of Aidid's military strength (he controls only portions of southern Mogadishu and parts of central Somalia), but it was based on the false assumption that stability and order would be restored once he was captured and his USC force defeated.

The reality of the ongoing conflict in Somalia is that Aidid is only one of several militia leaders who control various portions of the country and that there are many other "Aidids" who could potentially assume the mantle of leadership and pursue similar policies if he were either captured or killed. According to some Somali specialists, the key to success in Somalia would not be the military isolation of Aidid but a diplomatic initiative that would bring Aidid and all other militia leaders into the process.[38] Unfortunately, this approach was adopted by the Clinton administration only after dozens of U.S. soldiers were either killed or wounded and the body of one soldier was dragged through the streets of Mogadishu following an unsuccessful raid on Aidid's headquarters in October 1993.

A fifth trend in the post–Cold War era is a growing perception within the policymaking establishment that Islamic fundamentalism is a threat to U.S. interests on the African continent.[39] Many officials note that the decline of the former Soviet Union and communism has created a power vacuum on the African continent that potentially could be filled by what they perceive as "radical" forms of Islamic fundamentalism, particularly the Shia variant espoused by Iran. This view was confirmed by a leaked National Security Review of U.S. policy toward Africa for the 1990s, which indicated that Islamic governments and movements, particularly those sponsored by Iran, Libya, and the Sudan, posed a direct threat to U.S. interests in Africa.[40] This perception is not new; rather, it is the result of the United States' growing preoccupation with Islamic leaders and movements since the Iranian revolution of 1978 and the 444-day hostage crisis that followed.[41]

The the United States' perception of Islamic fundamentalism is clearly demonstrated by its foreign policy toward the Bashir regime of the Sudan.[42] A close ally of the United States during the 1980s, Sudanese president Ja'afar Nimeiri was overthrown in a 1986 military coup d'état, an event leading to the intensification of a guerrilla war led by the Sudan People's Liberation Army, and another successful military coup led by General

Omar Hassan Bashir in 1989. Sudan earned the denunciation of the Bush and the Clinton administrations for two reasons: First, State Department officials express concern over the fact that the Bashir regime is buttressed by the National Islamic Front, an extremely well organized and vocal fundamentalist group led by Hassan Turabi. Of even greater concern to U.S. policymakers is Bashir's strict enforcement of shari'a (Islamic law) and, most important, his apparent decision to allow Iranian-sponsored bases that CIA analysts claim are designed to train Islamic militants for "terrorist" actions throughout Africa. "By January 1992, U.S. officials were telling reporters that Sudan might become a base for exporting Islamic revolution across Africa," explains Raymond W. Copson, a researcher for the Foreign Affairs and National Defense Division of the Congressional Research Service, "although some nongovernment specialists doubted that troubled Sudan would prove very useful to the fundamentalist cause over the long term."[43]

In a sense, the anticommunist logic of containment of the Soviet Union during the Cold War era may be in the process of being replaced by an anti-Islamic variant focused specifically on the fundamentalist regimes in the Middle East and North Africa. "Like the Red Menace of the Cold War era," explains Leon T. Hadar, a vocal critic of those who perceive Islam as a threat to U.S. foreign policy, "the Green Peril—green being the color of Islam—is described as a cancer spreading around the globe, undermining the legitimacy of Western values and threatening the national security of the United States."[44] An important component of this trend is that African regimes have sought to manipulate the threat of Islamic fundamentalism in order to obtain greater levels of U.S. foreign assistance and attention.

A sixth trend of the post–Cold War era has been growing U.S. diplomatic involvement in the resolution of regional conflicts in Africa.[45] An early example of what such diplomacy could yield was demonstrated by the 1988 U.S.-brokered accords that offered South Africa's withdrawal from Namibia and independence for that country in exchange for the withdrawal of Cuban troops from Angola—a country that served as a proxy East-West battlefield in the 1970s and 1980s. On March 21, 1990, Namibia achieved independence under the leadership of African nationalist Sam Nujoma as a multiracial, multiparty democracy on the African continent. Two important ingredients that facilitated the resolution of this long-standing regional conflict were Assistant Secretary of State for African Affairs Chester Crocker's tireless efforts to make the United States a peace broker in the negotiating process and the former Soviet Union's willingness to pressure its Angolan and Cuban allies to accept a negotiated settlement.[46] Both of these factors—which built upon the willingness of regional African participants to seek a negotiated settlement—obviously were by-products of a decline in Cold War tensions in the late 1980s.

The case of Namibia is not unique; rather, it is indicative of how the United States and the other great powers can work together as "facilitators" of resolving regional conflict in Africa.[47] As outlined by Donald Rothchild, there were at least nine forms of U.S. diplomatic involvement in conflict resolution in Africa during the post–Cold War era:

- conflict prevention (the assemblage of information, measures of reconciliation, and pressure for human rights and democratization);
- behind-the-scenes support for the mediation of disputes by African third-party actors;
- the backing of a regional actor;
- assistance for an extracontinental actor;
- the promotion of an international organization's initiative;
- pressure on local actors to negotiate;
- humanitarian intervention and diplomatic facilitation;
- the organization of a regime transition; and
- direct third-party mediation between internal parties.[48]

However, an important constraint on U.S. efforts at resolving regional conflict is the historical neglect of Africa by the White House. In order to be successful, U.S. efforts ideally require the interest and support for activist measures at the highest levels of the policymaking establishment. Indeed, resolving issues such as the ongoing civil wars in Liberia, Somalia, and Sudan will be extremely difficult even if the Clinton administration makes peace in these countries its number-one priority. Unfortunately, the highest levels of the U.S. policymaking establishment remain primarily concerned with Western and Eastern Europe, the newly independent countries of the former Soviet Union, and flash points in other parts of the Third World.

A seventh trend of the post–Cold War era is the promotion of multiparty democracy as a precondition for the improvement of economic and political relations with Washington. The downfall of single-party regimes throughout Eastern Europe and the former Soviet Union—the intellectual heartland of single-party rule—raised important questions concerning the viability of this model in Africa. Most important, just as political democratization became a precondition for dramatically expanding levels of U.S. aid to the former Eastern bloc countries, this concept has filtered through the other regional bureaus of the State Department, including the Africa bureau. In fact, the Clinton administration codified U.S. support for the democratization process into an official doctrine—the so-called policy of enlargement—intended to replace the now outmoded strategy of containment.[49]

The Clinton administration's policy of enlargement and its predecessor under the Bush administration have contributed to positive developments on the African continent. In the case of Nigeria, for example, it has been argued that intense diplomatic pressures on the part of the Clinton administration and the European Union were critical in preventing the Nigerian military regime from canceling presidential elections that were ultimately held on June 12, 1993.[50] Although the military regime ultimately annulled the results of those elections, leading to a major transitional crisis, the stance of the United States was much appreciated by the Nigerian population and emboldened proponents of democracy to maintain their campaign of disobedience.

Among the other concrete positive outcomes of U.S. democratization policies include the funding of a variety of U.S.-based democratization institutes that have sent observer teams to facilitate multiparty elections; the provision of foreign assistance to fledgling democracies to consolidate newly created democratic institutions, most notably independent judiciaries and legislatures; and the promotion of short-term visits by groups of Africans to the United States and U.S. citizens to Africa to strengthen links between elements of civil society in both regions.

Despite these positive outcomes, two important contradictions confront policymakers. The first is related to the decline in U.S. foreign aid to the African continent. African countries, even if they do adopt political reforms, are unlikely to receive greater amounts of resources from a shrinking foreign aid budget. Although democratization can be rewarded in a variety of other ways (e.g., preferential trading privileges), levels of foreign assistance nonetheless remain the yardstick by which African leaders judge the commitment of the industrialized North to their democratic rhetoric.

A second and more serious contradiction is the growing perception of the Islamic fundamentalist threat. Specifically, a tension has always existed between Washington's often-stated preference for democracy in Africa and perceived national security interests. For example, during the Cold War era, when the ideal of democracy clashed with the national security objective of containing communism on the African continent, containment often prevailed at the expense of democracy. A succession of U.S. administrations were willing to downplay the internal shortcomings of a variety of U.S. allies on the African continent in favor of their strong support for U.S. policies of anticommunism and containment.

Although expectations were initially high among U.S. policy analysts and academics that Washington could focus on the normative goal of promoting democracy and human rights in the emerging post–Cold War international system, the U.S. response to events in Algeria in 1991 seems to indicate that containment of Islamic fundamentalism is as at least one security objective that overrides the preference for democratization. In sharp contrast to U.S. denunciations of authoritarianism in other regions of Africa, the Bush administration remained silent when the Algerian army

annulled the first multiparty elections in Algeria since independence and assumed control of the country in a military coup d'état. The reason for si-
lence was not that U.S. officials firmly believed the Algerian generals were
guarantors of democracy but rather that an Islamic fundamentalist party, the
Islamic Salvation Front—which, among other campaign promises, had
called for the strict enforcement of shari'a—was on the verge of taking
power through the ballot box.[51] In this regard, the Clinton administration
has adopted the view that whereas "radical revivalism must be combatted
by all means" in northeast Africa (especially in Egypt), areas outside of this
zone (for example, northwest Africa) are of less strategic importance due to
their distance from major petroleum sources, and therefore U.S. involvement against fundamentalist movements there can be minimized.[52] It is for
this reason, for example, that the Clinton administration, much to the con-
sternation of French diplomats, has emphasized the necessity to seek a negotiated settlement for the Algerian civil war—even if this entails the eventual recognition of an Islamist, albeit democratically elected, regime.

The eighth and final trend of the post–Cold War era is Washington's
gradual abandonment of ideologically based policies in favor of the pursuit
of economic self-interest. This general tendency has heightened economic
and political competition between the United States and other Western
powers, most notable of which is the rising French-U.S. conflict within the
financially important telecommunications and petroleum industries in
Francophone Africa.[53] There seems to be a contradiction, however, between official government actions and increasing support for the private
sector. For example, when the Republican majority in the U.S. Congress
slashed already reduced levels of foreign assistance in spring 1995 based
on its perception of Africa's strategic and economic unimportance, Herman Cohen, assistant secretary of state for African affairs under the Bush
administration, was presiding over a conference in Libreville, Gabon, designed to strengthen U.S.-African trade and investment. Despite their hes-
itation to provide the African continent with financial assistance, few
members of Congress would disagree with Cohen's primary themes: (1)
The U.S. can no longer afford to accept France's determination to maintain
its privileged *chasse gardée* ("private hunting ground") within the economic realm; and (2) foreign policy should serve as the facilitator of U.S.
private enterprise in all regions of the world, including Africa.[54]

Removal of the Shackles?

The removal of the Cold War shackles from U.S. foreign policy has important implications for the creation of a new African political order. In a
positive sense, the decline of the Cold War suggests decreasing amounts of

U.S. covert and military intervention on the African continent, as well as less military assistance for authoritarian clients who used the threat of Soviet expansionism to attract White House attention and support. The promotion of democracy may become the centerpiece of U.S. policy, and the possibilities are good for continued cooperation among the great powers in facilitating resolution of regional conflicts. Even if the United States and other major powers of the world adopt neutral stances, the stage may be set for African solutions to African problems, and therefore the creation of a new African political order based on African interests and aspirations. However, U.S. policymakers must resist the urge to replace one set of shackles (anticommunism) with yet another (anti-Islamic fundamentalism). Most important, they must resist the temptation to become complacent in the post–Cold War era and should actively seek to promote sustainable development and democratization on the African continent. Well-fed peoples who share in the fruits of their political systems will pose no threat to the United States; instead, they will provide markets and political allies that can only strengthen the U.S. position in the world.

Notes

This chapter draws upon Chapters 1 and 6 of Peter Schraeder's book *United States Foreign Policy Toward Africa: Incrementalism, Crisis and Change,* vol. 31 of *Cambridge Studies in International Relations* (Cambridge: Cambridge University Press, January 1994).

1. Crawford Young, "United States Foreign Policy Toward Africa: Silver Anniversary Reflections," *African Studies Review* 27,3 (September 1984), p. 14.

2. N. Brian Winchester, "United States Policy Toward Africa," *Current History* 87,529 (May 1988), p. 193.

3. Michael Clough, *Free at Last? U.S. Policy Toward Africa and the End of the Cold War* (New York: Council on Foreign Relations Press, 1992), p. 2.

4. Peter Duignan and L. H. Gann, *The United States and Africa: A History* (Cambridge: Cambridge University Press, 1984), p. 9.

5. See, for example, Immanuel Wallerstein, *Africa and the Modern World* (Trenton, N.J.: Africa World Press, 1986), p. 80.

6. "Putting Djibouti on the Map for Senator Jesse Helms," *New York Times,* April 24, 1987, p. A14.

7. See David D. Laitin and Said S. Samatar, *Somalia: Nation in Search of a State* (Boulder, Colo.: Westview Press, 1987), esp. chap. 5.

8. See Catherine A. Lutz and Jane L. Collins, *Reading National Geographic* (Chicago: University of Chicago Press, 1993).

9. For an overview, see Beverly G. Hawk, ed., *Africa's Media Image* (New York: Praeger, 1992). See also a special issue, "The News Media and Africa," edited by Hawk, of *Issue: A Journal of Opinion* 22,1 (1994).

10. Hawk, *Africa's Media Image;* "The News Media and Africa."

11. Helen Kitchen, *U.S. Interests in Africa* (New York: Praeger, 1983), p. 9. See also Kitchen, "Still on Safari," in L. Carl Brown, ed., *Centerstage: American Diplomacy Since World War Two* (New York: Holmes and Meier, 1990), pp. 171–192.

12. However, recent publishing trends suggest that Africa is potentially gaining an increased amount of attention within the academic community. See Peter J. Schraeder, "Reviewing the Study of U.S. Policy Towards Africa: From Intellectual 'Backwater' to Theory Construction," *Third World Quarterly* 14,4 (1993), pp. 775–785.

13. See Robert H. Bates, V. Y. Mudimbe, and Jean O'Barr, eds., *Africa and the Disciplines: The Contributions of Research in Africa to the Social Sciences and Humanities* (Chicago: University of Chicago Press, 1993).

14. Quoted in Helen Kitchen, "The Making of U.S. Policy Toward Africa," in Robert I. Rotberg, ed., *Africa in the 1990s and Beyond: U.S. Policy Opportunities and Choices* (Algonac, Mich.: Reference Publications, 1988), p. 14.

15. Richard M. Nixon, "The Emergence of Africa, Report to President Eisenhower by Vice President Nixon," *Department of State Bulletin* 36,930 (April 22, 1957), p. 640.

16. John F. Kennedy, "The Challenge of Imperialism: Algeria," in Theodore C. Sorensen, *"Let the Word Go Forth": The Speeches, Statements, and Writings of John F. Kennedy* (New York: Delacorte Press, 1988), pp. 331–337.

17. John F. Kennedy, "The New Nations of Africa," in Sorensen, *"Let the Word Go Forth,"* pp. 365, 368.

18. For an overview of U.S. containment policies, see F. Ugboaja Ohaegbulam, "Containment in Africa: From Truman to Reagan," *TransAfrica Forum* 6,1 (Fall 1988), pp. 7–34.

19. For discussion, see Harold G. Marcus, *Ethiopia, Great Britain and the United States, 1941–1974: The Politics of Empire* (Berkeley: University of California Press, 1983).

20. For discussion, see Jeffrey A. Lefebvre, *Arms for the Horn: U.S. Security Policy in Ethiopia and Somalia, 1953–1991* (Pittsburgh: University of Pittsburgh Press, 1991).

21. See, for example, Sean Kelly, *America's Tyrant: The CIA and Mobutu of Zaire* (Washington, D.C.: The American University Press, 1993); and William Minter, *King Solomon's Mines Revisited: Western Interests and the Burdened History of Southern Africa* (New York: Basic Books, 1986).

22. See Madeleine G. Kalb, *The Congo Cables: The Cold War in Africa—From Eisenhower to Kennedy* (New York: Macmillan, 1982).

23. Of course, U.S. policymakers went to great lengths to deny that a tacit alliance with South Africa existed. See, for example, Nathaniel Davis, "The Angolan Decision of 1975: A Personal Memoir," *Foreign Affairs* 57,1 (1978), pp. 109–124. See also John Stockwell, *In Search of Enemies: A CIA Story* (New York: W. W. Norton, 1978).

24. See Michael Clough, "The United States and Africa: The Policy of Cynical Disengagement," *Current History* 91,565 (May 1992), pp. 193–198.

25. See Steven A. Holmes, "Africa, From the Cold War to Cold Shoulders," *New York Times*, March 7, 1993, p. E4.

26. See Holmes, "Africa, From the Cold War to Cold Shoulders," p. E4.

27. Quoted in Walter Pincus, "CIA Plans to Close 15 Stations in African Cutback," *Washington Post*, June 23, 1994, p. A20.

28. Figures for FY 1986 are "obligations" as found in U.S. Agency for International Development (USAID), *U.S. Overseas Loans and Grants, Series of Yearly Data (Volume IV, Africa), Obligations and Loan Authorizations, FY 1946–1990* (Washington, D.C.: USAID, 1990). Figures for FY 1994 constitute "estimated obligations" and were provided by USAID, Bureau for Legislative Affairs.

29. Figures for FY 1995 were provided by USAID, Bureau for Legislative Affairs.

30. Even under President Jimmy Carter—recognized by Africanists as pursuing one of the most enlightened policies toward the continent during the post–World War II period—Africa ranked last in terms of foreign policy attention. Despite the fact that Africa accounted for 10.9 percent of the Carter administration's foreign policy actions in 1977, this figure still trailed all other regions of the world (the second to lowest region was the Soviet Union and Eastern Europe, with 14.6 percent) and in fact decreased in importance by nearly 50 percent over the next three years. For an explanation and discussion of these figures, see Jerel A. Rosati, *The Carter Administration's Quest for Global Community: Beliefs and Their Impact on Behavior* (Columbia: University of South Carolina Press, 1987), pp. 123, 130, 139, and 147.

31. For an overview of the U.S. position at the early stages of the conflict, see U.S. Congress House Committee on Foreign Affairs, Subcommittee on Africa, *U.S. Policy and the Crisis in Liberia*, Hearing, June 19, 1990, 101st Cong., 2d sess. (Washington, D.C.: GPO, 1990).

32. For an overview, see Holly Burkhalter and Rakiya Omaar, "Failures of State," *Africa Report,* November–December 1990, pp. 27–29.

33. See Michael T. Klare, "The Development of Low-Intensity Conflict Doctrine," in Peter J. Schraeder, ed., *Intervention into the 1990s: U.S. Foreign Policy in the Third World* (Boulder, Colo.: Lynne Rienner, 1992), pp. 37–54.

34. Klare, "Low-Intensity Conflict Doctrine," pp. 37–54.

35. See Robert L. Pfaltzgraff, Jr., and Richard H. Shultz, Jr., eds., *Ethnic Conflict and Regional Instability: Implications for U.S. Policy and Army Roles and Missions* (Carlisle Barracks, Pa.: Strategic Studies Institute, U.S. Army War College, 1994), p. 51.

36. Tony Lake and F. Gregory Gause III, "Confronting Backlash States: A Debate," *Foreign Affairs* 73,2 (1994), pp. 45–55.

37. For a critical overview of Operation Restore Hope, see Ken Menkhaus, "Getting Out vs. Getting Through in Somalia: U.S. and U.N. Policies in Somalia," *Middle East Policy* 3,1 (1994), pp. 146–162.

38. See, for example, Ken Menkhaus and Terrence Lyons, "What Are the Lessons to Be Learned From Somalia?" *CSIS Africa Notes,* no. 144 (January 1993).

39. See John L. Esposito, *The Islamic Threat: Myth or Reality?* (New York: Oxford University Press, 1992).

40. See National Security Review 30, "American Policy Toward Africa in the 1990s," signed by President George Bush in January 1993. See also Ian O. Lesser, *Security in North Africa: Internal and External Challenges* (Santa Monica, Calif.: RAND, 1993).

41. Among the other events that have heightened concerns among policymakers that Islamic leaders and movements may pose grave threats to U.S. security interests are the 1983 bombing of the U.S. Marines barracks in Lebanon, which resulted in the deaths of 241 Marines; Libya's interventions in neighboring territories during the 1980s; terrorist attacks by radical Muslim groups against foreigners living in Egypt and Algeria; the bombing of the World Trade Center in New York by Islamic militants; Arab support for the Muslim forces fighting in Bosnia; and Iraq's invasion of Kuwait in 1990, an event that resulted in the military involvement of over 400,000 U.S. military personnel in a war against Iraq at the beginning of 1991.

42. For a good overview of U.S. policy toward Sudan, see U.S. Congress, House Committee on Foreign Affairs, Subcommittee on Africa, and Select Com-

mittee on Hunger, International Task Force, *War and Famine in the Sudan,* Joint Hearing, March 15, 1990, 101st Cong., 2d sess. (Washington, D.C.: GPO, 1991).

43. Raymond W. Copson, "Sudan: Foreign Assistance Facts," *CRS Issue Brief,* February 18, 1992.

44. Leon T. Hadar, "What Green Peril?" *Foreign Affairs* 72,2 (1993).

45. See Francis M. Deng and I. William Zartman, eds., *Conflict Resolution in Africa* (Washington, D.C.: Brookings, 1991).

46. For an insider's account, see Chester A. Crocker, *High Noon in Southern Africa: Making Peace in a Rough Neighborhood* (New York: W. W. Norton, 1992).

47. See Donald Rothchild, "Regional Peacemaking in Africa: The Role of the Great Powers as Facilitators," in John W. Harbeson and Donald Rothchild, eds., *Africa in World Politics* (Boulder, Colo.: Westview Press, 1991), pp. 284–306.

48. See Donald Rothchild, "The United States and Conflict Management in Africa," in John W. Harbeson and Donald Rothchild, eds., *Africa in World Politics,* 2d ed. (Boulder, Colo.: Westview Press, 1995).

49. See Anthony Lake, "From Containment to Enlargement," address at the School of Advanced International Studies, Johns Hopkins University, Washington, D.C., September 21, 1993.

50. See Tunji Lardner, "Rewriting the Tale of the 'Dark Continent,'" *Media Studies Journal* 7,4 (1993), p. 101.

51. See, for example, Alfred Hermida, "Democracy Derailed," *Africa Report* 37,2 (March–April 1992), pp. 13–17.

52. See François Soudan, "Le Maghreb vu d'Amérique," in *Jeune Afrique* 1770 (December 8–14, 1994), pp. 14–15.

53. For an extensive analysis that also includes Japan, see Peter J. Schraeder, "From Berlin 1884 to 1989: Foreign Assistance and French, American, and Japanese Competition in Francophone Africa," *The Journal of Modern African Studies* 33,3 (1995).

54. See Henri Vernet, "La Potion Libérale de l'Oncle Sam," *Jeune Afrique* 1783 (March 9–15, 1994).

13
Moscow's Cold War and Post–Cold War Policies in Africa

JEFFREY A. LEFEBVRE

From the time the first Russian explorers set foot on the African continent in the fifteenth century until the latter half of the 1950s, Africa remained on the margins of Russian foreign policy. Even with the onset of the Cold War in the late 1940s, Africa remained a low strategic priority for Moscow.[1] Nonetheless, the Soviet Union maintained an interest in the region if only because it was one of the weak links in the world capitalist system. In Africa, Moscow could maneuver to enhance Soviet influence and establish its credentials as a great power; secure regional strategic, political, and economic interests; and divert Western attention and resources from Europe, where the Soviet Union felt most vulnerable militarily.[2] To achieve these interrelated objectives, Moscow relied upon two policy instruments: support for national liberation movements (NLMs) and the provision of military and economic assistance.[3]

The manner in which Moscow executed these policies in Africa fluctuated between pragmatic realism and ideological dogmatism. Western analysts have identified at least three and as many as ten shifts between so-called right-wing and left-wing tendencies from the days of Lenin through Gorbachev.[4] The right-wing approach favored support for sympathetic noncommunist movements or governments and strengthening ties with geopolitically important developing countries, even if capitalist in orientation. Conversely, the left-wing approach emphasized ideology as a litmus test, whereby support was given primarily to Marxist-Leninist vanguard parties or movements. These policy shifts resulted from ideological as well as pragmatic considerations, such as Moscow's view of East-West relations, the availability of regional opportunities, and constraints imposed by domestic political and economic circumstances. Nikita Khrushchev's rhetorical support for NLMs and pragmatic use of military and economic aid gave way in the 1970s to Leonid Brezhnev's heavy reliance upon

206

military support for anti-Western NLMs and self-proclaimed Marxist-Leninist governments in Africa. Under Gorbachev, Moscow returned to a Khrushchev-like pragmatism toward Africa that involved cooperation with the United States, the nurturing of positive-return economic relationships, and strategic disengagement. Boris Yeltsin's "democratic" Russia has thus far continued this pragmatic, nonideological approach.

From Khrushchev's Friendly Hand to Brezhnev's Activism

In February 1956, Nikita Khrushchev delivered a secret report to the 20th Party Congress calling for "peaceful coexistence" with the West and sanctioning the concept that there were "different paths to socialism" that could be achieved without recourse to violent revolution or war. The disintegration of the Western colonial order and the emergence of the Non-Aligned Movement had opened up new opportunities for Moscow in the Third World. But Stalinist orthodoxy, which insisted upon the exclusiveness of the Soviet path to socialism, had to be abandoned. To help the developing countries free themselves from continued economic and military dependence upon the West, Khrushchev offered to extend a friendly hand by providing Soviet aid "free from any political or military obligations."[5]

Khrushchev's friendly hand policy did not discriminate on the basis of ideology, although three "radical" West African countries—Ghana, Guinea, and Mali—did receive special attention from Moscow, accounting for 44.5 percent of Soviet aid to sub-Saharan Africa between 1959 and 1964.[6] But Moscow also provided economic and military credits and aid to moderate African states such as Ethiopia, Kenya, and Somalia. Soviet ties to Africa, however, were relatively limited and geopolitically marginal compared with Moscow's interest and involvement in Egypt and Iraq.

Peaceful coexistence with the West did not mean that Moscow had abandoned the doctrine of supporting national liberation struggles. But the Soviet Union was not in a position to provide extensive aid to NLMs owing to its limited power projection capabilities, its fear that a small war might escalate into a superpower nuclear exchange, and its desire to reserve what resources it had available for foreign aid to progressive anti-Western and important moderate noncommunist countries.[7] Although Khrushchev's rhetoric—such as his January 6, 1961, "sacred" wars of national liberation speech—and Moscow's involvement in the 1960–1961 Congo crisis painted a different picture in the eyes of the West, Soviet support for African liberation struggles in the late 1950s and early 1960s was nonetheless modest.[8] Soviet backing for the National Liberation Front (FLN) in Algeria during its eight-year (1954–1962) war for independence from France, the pro-Moscow leadership of the Popular Movement for the Liberation of Angola (MPLA) in its struggle against Portugal in Angola, and the Eritrean insurgents in Ethiopia during the 1960s was, respectively, indirect, marginal, and nonexistent.

Nonetheless, during the Khrushchev years, Moscow greatly expanded its diplomatic presence in Africa, thereby extending the Soviet Union as a global power.[9] However, following Khrushchev's political demise in 1964, Moscow shifted its diplomatic focus away from Africa to the Middle East and Southeast Asia. In the mid-1960s, some of Moscow's principal radical beneficiaries in Africa and Asia had fallen in coups. These setbacks not only produced a new realism in Moscow regarding the development of "revolutionary democracies" but also resulted in a reduction of Soviet aid to the African continent.[10] Although Moscow continued to deal with important states such as Nigeria, Zaire, and Ethiopia and increased its influence in Sudan and Somalia, by the end of the 1960s, the Soviet Union seemed to be more interested in pursuing détente with the United States than in exporting revolution.

However, in the mid-1970s Moscow reengaged in Africa in a more assertive and ideologically driven manner. Three external political and strategic developments produced this leftward shift. First, the expulsion of Soviet military advisers from Egypt in July 1972 and Washington's diplomatic victory in the October 1973 Arab-Israeli war, which resulted in Egypt and Sudan realigning with the United States, had exposed the weak and tenuous nature of Moscow's position in the Arab world. Second, the Soviet Union had achieved strategic parity with the United States, thereby nullifying the threat of American nuclear blackmail and reducing the likelihood of superpower nuclear war, especially over strategically marginal Africa. Moreover, under the direction of Admiral Sergey Gorshkov, the Soviet Union had developed a "blue water" fleet that could play a political role in countering "imperialist aggression" and defending the "national liberation movement" in the Third World.[11] Third, and of special importance to Kremlin ideologues, by the mid-1970s, a number of African governments had openly declared themselves socialist and some had even embraced Marxism-Leninism. But if these governments were left undefended, Soviet analysts reasoned, a "counter-revolutionary" wave might sweep through Africa and turn the continent into another Latin America, full of bourgeois nationalist military regimes hostile to communism.[12] Thus, in the mid-1970s, the "Brezhnev Doctrine" was applied to Africa. Socialism, in Eastern Europe as well as Africa, was deemed to be irreversible.

Moscow's renewed interest in supporting NLMs and defending the socialist revolution in Africa was demonstrated in Angola in the mid-1970s. Until 1974, Soviet support for southern African liberation struggles had been modest, given that the region was dominated by South Africa and

Portugal, and the NLMs were themselves weak.[13] However, the April 25, 1974, coup in Lisbon by military officers opposed to Portugal's overseas military campaigns in Angola, Mozambique, and Guinea-Bissau dramatically altered the situation in southern Africa. The superpowers briefly engaged in a proxy war over the future of Angola: Moscow used the Congo as a staging ground for supplying arms to the MPLA faction, and the CIA, with the support of Zaire, provided covert aid to the Front for the Liberation of Angola (FNLA) until the U.S. Congress passed the Clark Amendment in early 1976 terminating such support. Although it was the Cuban military intervention in early November 1975 that ultimately allowed the MPLA to declare itself the legitimate government of Angola, Moscow claimed victory and on October 9, 1976, signed a Treaty of Friendship and Cooperation with Angola.

A year later, Moscow seized a new opportunity in the Horn of Africa.[14] Following the September 1974 military coup in Addis Ababa that overthrew Emperor Haile Selassie, relations between the United States and Ethiopia deteriorated. In December 1976, Colonel Mengistu Haile Mariam signed a secret arms agreement with Moscow that he implemented after assuming power in a bloody shootout with his rivals in February 1977. Within three months, the U.S.-Ethiopia military relationship was formally terminated.

But by embracing revolutionary Ethiopia, the Soviet Union eventually lost Somalia. Although the government in Mogadishu had embraced Marxism-Leninism in October 1970, permitted the Soviets to develop military facilities at Berbera on the Gulf of Aden, and, in July 1974, signed a Treaty of Friendship and Cooperation with Moscow, the Soviet Union was an impediment to Somalia's pursuit of irredentism in the Horn, especially with respect to Ethiopia's Ogaden region. Brezhnev attempted but failed to reconcile the two rivals by enlisting the services of Cuba's Fidel Castro—who in the spring of 1977 proposed the creation of a Marxist-Leninist Red Sea confederation that would include Ethiopia, Somalia, and South Yemen. When war broke out in the Ogaden between Somalia and Ethiopia in the summer of 1977, Moscow chose to sacrifice Somalia's friendship and the military facilities at Berbera for its ties to Ethiopia. Apparently wary of Mogadishu's close links to pro-Western Arab regimes, and believing that the embattled revolutionary regime in Addis Ababa would make a more dependable and dependent ally in the long run, Moscow eventually threw the full weight of its support behind Ethiopia, which included a massive military airlift of approximately $1 billion worth of arms and more than 10,000 Cuban troops. On May 28, 1978, less than two months after its victory in the Ogaden War, Ethiopia signed a Treaty of Friendship and Cooperation with Moscow.

In Angola and again in Ethiopia, the Soviet leadership displayed a willingness to send massive amounts of military assistance and Cuban troops to Marxist-Leninist governments. The fact that the majority of African states were sympathetic to the MPLA in Angola and Ethiopia's position in the Ogaden War lowered the level of political risk for Moscow to engage in this type of activism, or what some U.S. officials saw as adventurism.[15] Whereas during the ten-year period preceding the Angolan intervention (1964–1973), Moscow had delivered approximately $200 million worth of arms to a dozen sub-Saharan African states, from 1974 to 1982, Ethiopia and Angola alone received in excess of $4 billion worth of Soviet arms transfers.[16]

Brezhnev's foreign policy approach toward Africa was based on the concept that two realms existed in the world: one of détente and peaceful coexistence with the West and one of class conflict in the Third World where Moscow sought to expand its influence and run the risk of confrontation with the West.[17] Africa fell into the latter realm. But because U.S. and Soviet strategic interests in sub-Saharan Africa were considered marginal, the risk of war seemed minimal. By pushing the limits of détente in the mid-1970s, the Soviet Union had again become a major actor in Africa and one that now posed a significant challenge to Western influence on the continent. In the course of events, Moscow had also knocked China out as a major ideological rival in Africa.[18] However, Soviet gains in Angola, Ethiopia, and Mozambique were offset by the loss of Somalia, Sudan, and Egypt and also contributed to a deterioration in U.S.-Soviet relations, which resulted in a more activist and militaristic U.S. policy in southern Africa and the Horn of Africa in the 1980s.

Gorbachev's "New Thinking" in Africa

Following the death of Leonid Brezhnev in November 1982, Kremlin watchers in the West detected a right-wing shift in Soviet foreign policy that accelerated after Mikhail Gorbachev assumed power in March 1985.[19] By the early 1980s, Moscow's attempt to secure its influence in the Third World by supporting Marxist-Leninist regimes was proving costly largely because of the aggressive globalism of the Reagan administration. The United States had encircled Ethiopia in the Horn by arming Sudan, Somalia, and Kenya, was providing aid to Jonas Savimbi's National Union for the Total Independence of Angola (UNITA) rebels in Angola and to anticommunist insurgents in Nicaragua, Afghanistan, and Cambodia, and was seeking to bankrupt the Soviet Union by pursuing the Strategic Defense Initiative (Star Wars). Moscow found itself caught in the superpower credibility trap of not wanting to be seen as abandoning its allies and thus delivered $6.1 billion worth of armaments to Angola, $3.9 billion to Ethiopia, and $1.1 billion to Mozambique during 1984–1988.[20] In contrast, the United States maintained its influence in sub-Saharan Africa at a fraction of the cost—providing $2.7 billion worth of security assistance to its clients during fiscal years 1984–1988.[21]

Despite Moscow's continued reliance upon arms transfers to its ideological kindred in Africa, top-ranking Soviet policymakers and Third World specialists were, by the end of Gorbachev's first year in office, openly challenging the premises of Moscow's African policy.[22] Radical socialist-oriented Third World states had failed to live up to expectations and remained linked to the world capitalist economy. Gorbachev echoed this view in his February 1986 report to the 27th Party Congress. The Soviet leader continued to attack imperialism, capitalism, and the Strategic Defense Initiative and reaffirmed Moscow's "solidarity with the forces of national and social liberation." Even Kremlin hard-liners agreed that the solution to the problems of impoverishment and neocolonialist exploitation in the Third World was dependent "first and foremost on the policies of the developing countries themselves."[23] In short, the Soviet Union was suffering from the "burdens of empire." To help relieve these burdens, Moscow encouraged its African clients, particularly Ethiopia and Angola, to seek political rather than military solutions to their internal difficulties.

Gorbachev's February 1986 report, in essence, marked a return to a Khrushchev-like policy approach to Africa. While gradually moving to distance Moscow from the security problems of its radical African clients, Gorbachev revived Khrushchev's concept of improving relations with important countries and sought to establish relationships based upon mutual benefit rather than ideological solidarity. Kremlin hard-liners opposed such a shift in emphasis and attacked Gorbachev for abandoning the class-based approach to foreign policy; that is, viewing the world through the lens of capitalist-socialist confrontation. The hard-liners believed that Gorbachev, in rejecting revolution as an instrument of social change and seeking to remove East-West conflict from regional issues, had diminished Moscow's global influence and was "selling us out as a power."[24]

Despite this opposition in the Kremlin, Gorbachev and his associates publicly broke with Brezhnev's class-based approach to the Third World.[25] In November 1987, during his speech commemorating the seventieth anniversary of the Bolshevik Revolution, Gorbachev noted the "decline of the national liberation movement." Soviet foreign minister Eduard Shevardnadze essentially closed the door on the "age of national liberation" in a July 26, 1988, speech to a Foreign Ministry conference in which he proclaimed that "the struggle between the two opposing systems is no longer the defining tendency of the present era." Five months later, the last chapter of decolonization in sub-Saharan Africa—that involving Namibia—ended.

Washington's escalation of the civil war in Angola during the mid-1980s and the increasing military aid burden it placed upon Moscow forced a reassessment of Soviet policy in southern Africa.[26] With the war in Angola in stalemate, Moscow finally accepted in 1987 the concept of linkage between independence for Namibia and the withdrawal of some 50,000 Cuban troops from Angola. Moscow then assumed a supportive role as Washington took the lead in mediating Angolan–Cuban–South African negotiations. In November 1988, the three parties agreed that national elections would be held in Namibia on November 1, 1989, and independence would be granted in March 1990. Cuba, in turn, would begin a phased withdrawal of its troops from Angola, to be completed before July 1991. On December 22, 1988, the United States and the Soviet Union presided at a conference held in New York for the signing of these two agreements.

Soviet policy toward the armed struggle in South Africa also underwent a radical transformation during the Gorbachev years. When the African National Congress (ANC) began armed struggle in November 1961, Moscow provided modest amounts of aid. By the early 1970s, the Soviet Union had become an important source of military and financial aid for the ANC as well as a harsh critic of South Africa's white-minority regime. The Kremlin considered armed struggle to be an indispensable phase in the liberation of South Africa and thus counseled the South African Communist Party (SACP) to cooperate with the ANC (which was deemed an "authentic" NLM) in overthrowing the apartheid regime.[27] Thus, into the mid-1980s, the Soviet Union favored armed struggle and opposed a negotiated settlement in South Africa.

However, when Gorbachev came to power, South Africa seemed to be spinning out of control. The spontaneous outbreak of violence in the black townships in 1984, which had caught even Moscow by surprise, had reached a peak. Moscow and its SACP client feared that the continuation of random acts of violence against civilians, favored by younger ANC militants, would prove counterproductive and destroy South Africa or, in the Kremlin's worst-case analysis, escalate into a world war.[28] Thus, in the spring of 1986, Moscow came out in favor of a political settlement in South Africa, one that would include guarantees for white minority rights.

At the same time that the militants in the townships were shouting revolutionary slogans of violence and socialism, Moscow was discarding such ideas under glasnost and perestroika, and Gorbachev was opening a constructive dialogue with Pretoria. Sandwiched in between secret Soviet–South African discussions held in 1987 and 1989 was an October 1988 meeting in West Germany involving Soviet and ANC officials and South African liberals. Political developments in South Africa in 1989–1990, including the release of Nelson Mandela from prison, led to a softening of Soviet criticism of Pretoria. Even the leadership of the SACP spoke in more moderate terms, favoring the creation of a multiparty system. Few in Moscow seemed alarmed when Nelson Mandela stated that he planned to part ways with the Communists after dismantling apartheid and to preserve market mechanisms in South Africa.[29] In October 1991, two months after surviving the failed hard-liner coup in Moscow, Gorbachev's government welcomed the first South African diplomat allowed in the Soviet Union since 1956; the following month, Moscow restored consular relations with Pretoria. When Gorbachev left office in December 1991, it was only a question of time before full diplomatic relations would be restored between Moscow and Pretoria.

At the same time that Moscow was cooperating with Washington in finding a negotiated settlement in southern Africa, Gorbachev was unloading another one of Moscow's "burdens of empire" in the Horn of Africa—Ethiopia. For several years, the Mengistu regime had been suffering military setback after setback at the hands of the Eritrean People's Liberation Front (EPLF) and the Tigrean People's Liberation Front but refused to negotiate a political settlement despite Moscow's urging. An April 1987 meeting in Moscow had gone badly for Mengistu, as Gorbachev was not impressed by the Ethiopian leader's plea for more arms. At the end of July, a personal message from Gorbachev was delivered to Mengistu, stating that Ethiopia should improve relations with its neighbors despite the fact that they were supporting Ethiopian insurgents. Although Mengistu reached such an accommodation with Somalia's Siad Barre in April 1988, the wars in Eritrea and Tigre continued unabated. An attempt by Mengistu to extract more aid from Moscow by making diplomatic overtures to Washington at the end of 1988 failed; Mengistu subsequently resurrected military ties with Israel. But Gorbachev remained unmoved, and in 1989 he informed Mengistu that Soviet military aid would be cut the following year.

Unfortunately for Mengistu, the Cold War in the Horn of Africa and in the rest of the Third World had ended. Gorbachev's February 1988 announcement that Soviet troops would be withdrawn from Afghanistan provided a clear indication of Moscow's desire to relieve itself of burdensome Marxist-Leninist clients. By the end of 1989, the Soviet Union had withdrawn half of its military advisers from Ethiopia and the Cuban military presence had been decreased significantly. Moreover, during 1989–1990, Moscow's attention was focused on Eastern Europe, which was slipping out of the Soviet orbit. Thus, when the EPLF seized control of the port of Massawa in February 1990, Moscow refused to intervene or, subsequently, to come to the relief of Ethiopian forces under siege in the provincial capital of Asmara.

The Iraqi invasion of Kuwait in August 1990 also diverted Moscow's and Washington's attention from the Horn of Africa. By the time the two superpowers looked back to the Horn in the spring of 1991, Siad Barre had been overthrown and the Mengistu regime was on the verge of collapse.

On May 21, Mengistu resigned as president and fled the country. Because Moscow had seen the end coming and had begun evacuating its nationals from Ethiopia two months earlier, only 170 Soviet nationals and three or four military advisers remained in the country when Addis Ababa fell to the Ethiopian People's Revolutionary Democratic Front on May 28. Reflecting on these developments, Soviet Foreign Ministry officials admitted that the USSR's Ethiopian policy had failed because of the Kremlin's underestimation of the conflict's historical nature.[30]

Mikhail Gorbachev thus presided over the dismantling of Moscow's foreign empire in Africa. By the end of 1991, the Soviet military presence in Africa was virtually nonexistent. Instead, Moscow was focusing upon the economic side of its African relationships. In March 1990, Eduard Shevardnadze had made the first trip ever by a Soviet foreign minister to sub-Saharan Africa to attend Namibia's independence celebration and to explain Moscow's new aid policy. Shevardnadze privately assured African journalists and diplomats that although Washington and Moscow were "successfully moving from rivalry to cooperation," this development would not be to the detriment of Africa. However, the Soviet foreign minister was also in Africa to see if he could collect on some of the debt owed to Moscow.

Gorbachev's "New Thinking" in foreign policy was linked to the domestic debate over glasnost and perestroika.[31] While Shevardnadze was in Africa, a public debate was raging in the Soviet Union over the "squandering of public funds" in the Third World. Given the Soviet Union's own economic problems, Moscow could no longer afford to structure relations on the basis of aid, and this new mood was reflected in Moscow's dealings with Africa. The Soviets were now demanding the repayment of debts and also charging a higher rate of interest on loans. Gorbachev's New Thinking essentially shunned Marxist-Leninist ideology and favored a pragmatic restructuring of Soviet relations in Africa on the basis of mutual economic benefit.

Yeltsin: Constructive Participation in Africa

On December 8, 1991, the president of the Russian Republic, Boris Yeltsin, and the leaders of Ukraine and Belarus signed the Minsk agreement, effectively bringing to an end the Soviet Union. Although the Russian Federation assumed the former Soviet Union's seat on the UN Security Council, Moscow's willingness and ability to act as a great power was questionable. The Warsaw Pact no longer existed, and Moscow's foreign empire had been dismantled. Six years of Gorbachev's New Thinking in foreign policy, coupled with a severe economic crisis and an unstable political situation domestically, had diminished Moscow's military and political influence worldwide.

The demise of the Soviet Union affected not only Moscow's friends in Africa but its adversaries as well. Some countries, such as Angola and Mozambique, lost a major source of aid. Other states that had traditionally obtained aid from the United States now found that it was "no longer pulling its punches in Africa" and was advocating "tough political demands in exchange for assistance."[32] Even anticommunist regimes, such as that of Mobutu Sese Seko in Zaire, lamented the passing away of the Soviet Union, for as their perceived strategic value as strongholds against communism disappeared, so did their ability to extract aid from the West and claim immunity from external pressures to carry out political and economic reforms. The days of right-wing and left-wing dictatorial regimes being lavished with aid and excused for their internal excesses were over.

Russian ties that remained with Africa were largely a product of the Soviet period, which posed a political problem for policymakers and analysts in the Russian Foreign Ministry, who favored maintaining a high-profile role in Africa.[33] Economic pressures had forced Boris Yeltsin to reduce the foreign affairs budget, resulting in the closure of nine embassies and a number of consulates in Africa during 1992. Moreover, there was a dwindling interest in Africa and even a large reservoir of public resentment toward what many Russian people saw as costly and inequitable relationships brought on by the Soviet Union's competition with the United States to establish spheres of influence on the continent. According to Moscow's calculation, the whole of Africa owed the Russian Federation $10 billion, primarily in defense credits.[34] Thus the Foreign Ministry had to combat the attitude at home that Africa was a "loss-making enterprise."

Nonetheless, African experts in the Foreign Ministry argued that Russia could, would, and should continue to act as a great power in Africa.[35] Economically, Africa held promise as a vast market for Russian technical expertise and goods, which, because of their inferior quality, would not be able to break into the U.S. or European consumer markets. Given the bleak economic situation at home, Russian experts might find overseas jobs in education, agriculture, and scientific fields. Moreover, if Moscow hoped to recover its backlog of debt, it had to maintain a political presence in Africa and help the continent develop economically.

The Foreign Ministry also justified a continued Russian presence in Africa on political grounds. Certain rights and responsibilities went with being (or claiming to be) a great power, such as helping resolve regional conflicts. It was especially important that Moscow demonstrate to Africans its dedication to conducting "relations honestly and openly" with no "secret agendas." Moreover, Moscow still had African friends who could not be discarded. According to Russian foreign minister Andrei Kozyrev,

African states had a "manifest interest in [Russia's] political presence" even if there was no aid involved. Moreover, Kozyrev warned, "it is easy to lose ties and influence, but it is extremely difficult to restore them." Thus, the Russian Federation intended to pursue a policy of "constructive participation in the political and economic life . . . [of Africa] just like a normal great power."[36]

The Foreign Ministry's policy of constructive participation came under particular scrutiny in Angola following Kozyrev's February 1992 visit. At that time, only seventy to seventy-five Russian military specialists remained in the country and the MPLA, having shed its Marxist-Leninist ideology, was no longer "the last fortress of communism" in Africa. The Russian foreign minister discovered, however, that the Angolan government—which Moscow claimed still owed it several billion dollars—had no intention of repaying the greater part of its defense debt. Moreover, the prospects for trade between the two countries were limited since Russia did not need Angolan oil or diamonds. Essentially, the choice was between selling the multibillion-dollar debt at fifteen to twenty cents on the dollar and dropping out of Angola or, as the Angolans suggested, writing off part of the debt and receiving the rest in forms other than cash, such as real estate, special offshore fishing contracts, and joint ventures.[37] The Foreign Ministry successfully argued that Russia would never be able to collect the debt in any form if Moscow cut and ran from Angola.

As evidence of its continuing interest in Angola, the Russian Federation along with the United States and Portugal acted as observers of the UNITA-MPLA settlement that resulted in national elections being held in September 1992. The Kozyrev delegation had in fact met with UNITA representatives in February and espoused the view that UNITA was entitled to a full role in Angola's future political system. But after UNITA, dissatisfied with the election results, broke the cease-fire and the UNITA-MPLA war heated up in the spring of 1993, Moscow grew increasingly critical of Jonas Savimbi, depicting him as trying to turn Angola into another Somalia.[38] Savimbi's subsequent attempt to persuade the UN to lift the arms embargo on UNITA was strongly opposed by Moscow.

In 1994 the Russian Federation, the United States, and Portugal brokered another cease-fire between the Angolan government and UNITA. Despite Savimbi's hesitancy over the new Lusaka accord and amid reports that UNITA was burying arms and contacting foreign mercenary groups, the cease-fire was generally being observed into the summer of 1995.[39] In contrast to the East-West split over the UN peacekeeping operation in the Congo in the early 1960s, in the spring of 1995 both Washington and Moscow came out in favor of the UN's launching such an operation in Angola.[40] Besides the political credit the Yeltsin government hopes to claim by helping to put this broken country back together again, Moscow just might be able to collect on some of the huge debt owed it by Luanda.[41]

In the Horn of Africa the Yeltsin government had to respond to political developments involving two former adversaries—the EPLF and Somalia. On May 24, 1993, the EPLF, following the outcome of a UN-supervised referendum the previous month, declared Eritrea an independent state. The Soviet press, which in the past had negatively referred to the EPLF as "mutineers" and "separatists," hailed the precedent set by Eritrea in realizing a nation's right to democratic self-determination in postcolonial Africa.[42] With respect to the humanitarian crisis in Somalia, Moscow supported the UN decision to intervene militarily at the end of 1992, although no Russian troops were involved in Operation Restore Hope. When the confrontation between UN forces and General Mohamed Farah Aidid's militia heated up in the summer of 1993, the Russian Foreign Ministry expressed concern that UN military actions were becoming an end in itself for some of the participants. Nonetheless, Moscow's commitment to the UN operation and the need for "energetic activities . . . to disarm the opposing Somali groups" appeared stronger than that of the United States.[43]

Perhaps the most intriguing relationship that Moscow has developed in Africa as part of its policy of constructive participation, and one that offers the promise of lucrative financial rewards, is with the Republic of South Africa. If Andrei Kozyrev's experience in Angola proved frustrating, the highlight of the Russian foreign minister's February 1992 trip to Africa was his visit to South Africa for the purpose of announcing the restoration of full diplomatic relations between Moscow and Pretoria. Given Moscow's long-standing support for the ANC and SACP, Pretoria attached special importance to the Kozyrev visit. On the same day (February 28) that Kozyrev and South African foreign minister Rulof Botha announced the reopening of relations, the UN Human Rights Commission in Geneva voted 35–15 in favor of continuing sanctions against South Africa until apartheid had been completely dismantled. Nonetheless, the Russian foreign minister justified Moscow's decision on the grounds that it was important to demonstrate support for constructive reformers such as F. W. de Klerk, who seemed fully committed to abolishing apartheid. Moreover, given the violent right-wing opposition to de Klerk's policy, Kozyrev thought that the South African president "could use a foreign policy success."[44]

The Russian Foreign Ministry, however, was concerned about the response of the ANC to the restoration of diplomatic ties between Moscow and Pretoria. Because of the alliance between the ANC and the SACP, and the fact that about one-third of the members of the ANC's Executive Committee were Communists, a period of uncertainty between Moscow and the ANC had developed following the failed hard-line coup the previous

August and the subsequent dissolution of the Soviet Communist party. Still, Kozyrev thought it wise to meet with Mandela at the ANC headquarters in Johannesburg before the official announcement. Although Mandela expressed concern that the move was a bit hasty and that Moscow should wait until a democratically elected postapartheid government came to power, he did not openly condemn the decision. The SACP, however, publicly attacked the move. This criticism did not faze Kozyrev, who responded: "We are used to hearing out advice from communists and doing the opposite."[45]

For President de Klerk, the restoration of diplomatic relations with Moscow would help end South Africa's international isolation. Moscow, however, was less interested in the political significance of the event than in the economic benefits that might be derived from cooperation with Pretoria. Kozyrev and Botha had discussed the possibility of South Africa extending credits to Russia. Russian diplomats and business leaders viewed the development of economic linkages with South Africa as exactly the type of mutually beneficial relationship that Moscow should nurture in Africa. Together, Russia and South Africa controlled 95 percent of the world's output of platinum, 78 percent of vanadium, 67 percent of chromium, 49 percent of manganese, 38 percent of gold, 24 percent of diamonds, and 18 percent of coal.[46] Although this meant that the opportunities for direct bilateral trade or commercial exchange were limited, significant opportunities existed for cooperation and interaction in the development of state-of-the-art technologies in the mining and agricultural sectors, exchanging data on gold and diamond production and sales, and coordinating activities in international markets, particularly with respect to the marketing of gold and diamonds.[47]

The prospect that Russia and South Africa could conceivably dictate the prices of many raw materials on the world market by coordinating their foreign economic policies was on many minds when President de Klerk met with President Yeltsin in Moscow in June 1992. In 1990, Moscow had signed a $5 billion contract with the De Beers company (which controlled 80 percent of the world diamond market) to market Russia's diamonds—bringing into the open a clandestine trade relationship in gold and diamonds that had existed since 1959.[48] When de Klerk arrived in Moscow, he was accompanied by a large group of South African businessmen. Discussions between the Russians and South Africans focused upon ways to promote the exchange of scientific and industrial technology, mainly in the mining industry and in processing and storing farm produce; coordinate action on the world diamond, gold, and platinum markets; and coordinate scientific research, making use of Russian science and South Africa's modern technologies.[49] By the end of de Klerk's visit, two agreements had been made: Direct air flights were to be established between Moscow and Johannesburg, and South Africa agreed to offer Moscow a $50 million revolving credit line to stimulate the growth of trade and economic ties between the two countries.

A visit that a year earlier would have been morally unthinkable for Pretoria while communism still existed in the Soviet Union and politically impossible for Moscow now, ended with the South African president in Moscow standing side by side with the Russian president denying rumors that the two states had signed a secret agreement establishing a cartel. Although some Russian commentators worried that Moscow appeared to have rushed into the arms of South Africa, the ANC response to de Klerk's visit, as it had been the previous February when Kozyrev was in South Africa, was low key.[50] The Russian Foreign Ministry asserted that the Russian Federation's policy was based upon the principle of maintaining an "equidistant" approach to all constructive forces in South Africa and that it therefore expected the South African embassy and ANC representatives to coexist peacefully in Moscow.[51] Following de Klerk's departure, Mandela led a high-level ANC delegation to touch base with Yeltsin—a visit that de Klerk hoped would encourage the ANC to reverse its economic philosophy and policy and "get in step with the rest of the world."[52]

But a year after Moscow reopened its embassy in South Africa, both sides began expressing dissatisfaction with the low level of trade and economic relations. Once the political impact of restoring relations had worn off, de Klerk seemed to have lost interest in Russia. The problem stemmed in part from the fact that both sides were essentially starting from scratch and the development of economic ties would take time. Another factor was that political instability in both countries suggested a cautious business approach. Remarking on this problem, the Russian ambassador to South Africa observed that the "major condition of the development of business in any country is political and economic stability."[53] Although Moscow no longer felt inhibited politically from pursuing constructive economic participation in South Africa, Nelson Mandela's call for the lifting of all economic sanctions against South Africa on September 24, 1993, was seen by the Russian Foreign Ministry as giving "the green light to stepped up relations between Russia and South Africa in every area . . . [except] we intend to strictly abide by the continuing Security Council sanctions on arms supplies to South Africa until a new coalition government has been formed there."[54]

Although Russian officials continue to express a desire to cooperate economically with South Africa, Moscow has not been adverse to taking actions that promote its self-interest at the expense of Pretoria. In 1990 Moscow had signed an agreement to sell the Soviet Union's substantial diamond stockpile (then worth approximately $8 billion) and future production to De Beers in return for a $5 billion loan.[55] But Moscow apparently sold only about $1 billion worth of the stockpile to De Beers. In late 1994, desperate for foreign exchange, Moscow began selling diamonds from its stockpile and current production directly to the open market (allegedly in violation of the 1990 agreement). This action undercut the price of diamonds and forced De Beers to buy up the surplus on the world market in order to maintain its control over diamond prices.[56]

The Russian Federation and South Africa are business competitors in two other lucrative areas—arms and nuclear technology—where cooperation agreements do not exist. Under the Mandela government, South Africa's state-run arms company, ARMSCOR, is able to operate in the open market and is determined to boost sales, which are expected to contribute approximately $500 million in foreign earnings in 1995.[57] During the spring of 1995, Moscow and Pretoria were both wooing Iran with offers of nuclear technology and cooperation, much to the consternation of Washington.[58] In March 1995, South Africa's energy minister, Pik Botha, led a high-level delegation to Tehran to discuss nuclear cooperation. Such an arrangement would help balance the trade relationship between Tehran and Pretoria, as South Africa currently buys 300,000 barrels per day of oil from Iran, or about three-fourths of its national requirements. For Moscow, the deal to sell nuclear reactors to Iran is worth three times the amount of U.S. aid.[59] Thus, the post–Cold War and postapartheid foreign policies of Moscow and Pretoria are motivated by international economics, which will sometimes make them partners and sometimes competitors.

Several observations can be made about Moscow's policy of constructive participation in Africa. First, much of this policy is carried over from Gorbachev's New Thinking, meaning that ideology has been replaced by a pragmatic business approach. Second, the zero-sum competition with the West in Africa has given way to political cooperation. Third, despite a recent reduction in economic ties with Africa owing to Moscow's problems at home (in Chechnya) and the "near-abroad," Russian diplomats recognize that in a continent of half a billion consumers, the potential economic rewards from pursuing cooperation in areas such as geology, construction, agriculture, and mineral prospecting are enormous.[60] Fourth, while Moscow maintains a special interest in such North African countries as Egypt, Libya, and Algeria, in sub-Saharan Africa, its relationship with South Africa will remain especially important, given Pretoria's growing influence on the continent since the lifting of international economic and political sanctions.[61] Fifth, Moscow also appreciates the political weight that Africa carries by its sheer numbers in international organizations and hopes to court that opinion by remaining politically engaged, if not bilaterally, then through multilateral channels.[62] Thus, the new "concept of the African Policy of the Russian Federation" seeks to account for Russia's national interests while weighing Africa's political clout, economic potential, and the specifics of African countries.[63]

Conclusion:
From Zero-Sum to Positive-Sum Game in Africa

Nikita Khrushchev's friendly hands policy in Africa helped transform the Soviet Union from a Eurasian to a global power. Africa was ripe with opportunity as more than two dozen African states became independent between 1956 and 1964. Given the marginal role Africa played in U.S. global strategy, Moscow's policy involved little cost or risk. Soviet economic and military assistance to African governments and NLMs was limited and selective and its impact marginal.

In the mid-1970s, however, Brezhnev raised the stakes in Africa for the West. Increased Soviet military assistance to selected African governments and NLMs eventually produced a Western response and led to a heightening of the Cold War in Africa. Despite the Soviet Union's greater willingness to run risks in Africa, in most instances, Moscow was exploiting opportunities presented by failed Western policies. Moreover, although the Soviets were supporting NLMs, Moscow did not instigate these movements.

Gorbachev's New Thinking in foreign policy was perhaps the most important factor in bringing the Cold War to a close. At the end of the 1980s, both Moscow and Washington were disengaging from troublesome and/or strategically marginal African clients. Moscow's policy toward Africa became more businesslike, expecting a return on its investment and seeking to develop mutually beneficial economic relationships without regard for ideology. With the end of the Cold War, the problem that Africa now confronts is that only a few of its states are of intrinsic economic or strategic interest to outsiders.

In seeking business rather than geopolitical opportunities, the Russian Federation's policy toward Africa has thus far followed the outlines established by Gorbachev. African states, many of which mourned or feared the negative political consequences of the demise of the Soviet Union and the end of the Cold War, have generally responded favorably to developments in Moscow. There have been certain strains in relations, such as the clashes in 1992 between African students and Russian police at Patrice Lumumba University that left a Zimbabwean student dead. Nonetheless, Boris Yeltsin's victory in the April 1993 referendum, which temporarily strengthened his political position, was welcomed in Africa.[64] However, the recent political gains of Vladimir Zhirinovsky—a man who was personally received in Iraq by Saddam Hussein in early 1993—and his ultranationalist party in the December 1993 Russian parliamentary elections is a worrisome trend for those who hope that U.S.-Russian competition and intervention in regional conflicts is a relic of the past.

The most striking aspect in the evolution of Moscow's policy toward Africa is that strategic factors now take a back seat to economic considerations, and political interests are gauged much differently. Whereas the global competition with the United States and support for national liberation struggles once figured prominently in Moscow's foreign policy equation, Washington now is seen as a political partner and a business competitor in Africa.[65] With the national liberation struggle deemed over and Moscow's interest in developing profitable economic ties in Africa on the rise, political stability on the continent is to be promoted, not undermined and then exploited. Russia's Africanist policymakers, like their U.S. counterparts, see Africa as a market of the future that should not be abandoned or forgotten in the present. Given the high growth rates in Africa (7 percent), it is estimated that by the year 2025 the African market will reach $480 billion—the size of the Japanese market today.[66] While there is an element of zero-sum economic competition between the Russian Federation and the West, as well as between Russia and South Africa, from a political-strategic perspective, Moscow's foreign policy calculation toward Africa has evolved from seeing the region in zero-sum terms to viewing Russian-African-Western interaction as a positive-sum game. Thus business opportunity and Moscow's desire to act as a benevolent great power (at least overseas), not the balance of power, are the primary forces underlying Russian policy in Africa today.

Notes

1. Michael MccGwire, *Military Objectives in Soviet Foreign Policy* (Washington, D.C.: Brookings, 1987), pp. 183–185, 220. Africa fell outside of the Soviet Union's "National Security Zone" and was not included in any of the Soviet military theaters of operation.

2. Robert Legvold, "The Soviet Union's Strategic Stake in Africa," in J. Whitaker, ed., *Africa and the United States* (New York: Council on Foreign Relations, 1978), pp. 155–167.

3. See Daniel Kempton, *Soviet Strategy Toward Southern Africa: The National Liberation Connection* (New York: Praeger, 1989), pp. 1–2.

4. See Francis Fukuyama, "Patterns of Soviet Third World Policy," *Problems of Communism* (September–October 1987), pp. 1–13.

5. Gordan Livermore, ed., *Soviet Foreign Policy Today*, 2d ed. (Columbus, Ohio: The Current Digest of the Soviet Press, 1986), pp. 1–7.

6. Zaki Laidi, *The Superpowers and Africa: The Constraints of a Rivalry, 1960–1990* (Chicago: University of Chicago Press, 1990), pp. 20–21.

7. Alvin Rubinstein, *Moscow's Third World Strategy* (Princeton, N.J.: Princeton University Press, 1990), pp. 23–24.

8. See Rubinstein, *Moscow's Third World Strategy*, pp. 85, 104–105, 111–115; and Michael Beschloss, *The Crisis Years* (New York: Edward Burlingame Books, 1991), pp. 60–61. President Eisenhower, who for years had heard boasting and false threats by Khrushchev, was unruffled by the January 1961 "wars of liberation" speech. Eisenhower felt it was merely a reiteration of comments Khrushchev had made in a December 1960 declaration. President Kennedy, on the other hand, saw the January speech as "our clue to the Soviet Union."

9. Laidi, *The Superpowers and Africa*, p. 27. In 1960, the Soviet Union maintained a diplomatic presence in only nine of twenty-two independent African countries, but by the end of 1964, Moscow was represented in twenty-two of thirty-one African states.

10. Nkrumah was overthrown in 1966 and Keita fell in 1968. David Albright, *The USSR and Sub-Saharan Africa in the 1980s* (New York: Praeger, 1983), p. vi.

11. See MccGwire, *Military Objectives in Soviet Foreign Policy*, pp. 214–215; and Legvold, "The Soviet Union's Strategic Stake," pp. 159–160.

12. Legvold, "The Soviet Union's Strategic Stake," pp. 162–163.

13. For background on the Angolan conflict, see Kempton, *Soviet Strategy Toward Southern Africa*, pp. 35–93; and Gillian Gunn, "The Legacy of Angola," in Thomas Weiss and James Blight, eds., *The Suffering Grass: Superpowers and Regional Conflict in Southern Africa and the Caribbean* (Boulder, Colo.: Lynne Rienner, 1992), pp. 39–54. Between 1961 and 1974, the Soviet Union had provided the MPLA with $63 million in aid but then suspended aid to the MPLA in 1973.

14. For background on U.S. and Soviet policy in the Horn, see Jeffrey Lefebvre, *Arms for the Horn: U.S. Security Policy in Ethiopia and Somalia, 1953–1991* (Pittsburgh: University of Pittsburgh Press, 1991); and Robert Pateman, *The Soviet Union in the Horn of Africa* (Cambridge: Cambridge University Press, 1990).

15. For the views of two of the principal foreign policy advisers in the Carter and Reagan administrations, see Zbigniew Brzezinski, *Power and Principle* (New York: Farrar, Straus & Giroux, 1983), pp. 178–182; and Alexander Haig, *Caveat* (New York: Macmillan, 1984), pp. 88–107, 169–172.

16. See U.S. Department of State, Arms Control and Disarmament Agency (ACDA), *World Military Expenditures and Arms Transfers, 1963–1973*, p. 67; and ACDA, *World Military Expenditures and Arms Transfers, 1985*, p. 43.

17. Owen Kahn, ed., *Disengagement from Southwest Africa* (New Brunswick, N.J.: Transaction Publishers, 1991), p. 6.

18. The Chinese reduced their technical aid personnel presence in Africa by more than 10,000 between 1975 and 1979. See CIA, *Communist Aid Activities in Non-Communist Less Developed Countries: A Research Paper, 1979* (Washington, D.C.: CIA, National Foreign Assessment Center, October 1980), pp. iv, 10. Between 1967 and 1976 the People's Republic of China provided $142 million worth of arms to Africa—approximately one-fourteenth the level of Soviet arms transfers ($2.051 billion) to Africa. See ACDA, *World Military Expenditures and Arms Transfers, 1967–1976*, p. 159. During 1979–1983, Chinese arms transfers to Africa increased to $595 million. Nonetheless, this was less than one-twentieth the level of Soviet arms transfers to Africa ($13.9 billion). See ACDA, *World Military Expenditures and Arms Transfers, 1985*, pp. 131–132.

19. Fukuyama, "Soviet Third World Policy," pp. 1–13.

20. See *World Military Expenditures and Arms Transfers, 1989*, pp. 115–116, 120.

21. See Lefebvre, *Arms for the Horn*, pp. 197–240.

22. See Livermore, *Soviet Foreign Policy Today*, pp. 127–128; Gordan Livermore, ed., *Russian Foreign Policy Today*, 5th ed. (Columbus, Ohio: The Current Digest of the Post-Soviet Press, July 1992), p. 141.

23. Livermore, *Soviet Foreign Policy Today*, pp. 130–131.

24. See Livermore, *Russian Foreign Policy Today*, pp. 22–27, 223–228. Gorbachev's policies were also being criticized by the so-called pragmatists and liberal Westernizers.

25. See Livermore, *Russian Foreign Policy Today*, pp. 18–20.

26. See Kahn, *Disengagement from Southwest Africa*, pp. 3–54.

27. See Peter Vanneman, *Soviet Strategy in Southern Africa* (Stanford, Calif.: Hoover Institution Press, 1990), pp. 15–22; and Kempton, *Soviet Strategy Toward Southern Africa*, p. 151.

28. See Vanneman, *Soviet Strategy in Southern Africa*, pp. 18–19; and Kempton, *Soviet Strategy Toward Southern Africa*, pp. 197–203.

29. Alexander Anichkin, "Nelson Mandela: Bidding Farewell to Communism?" *Moscow News*, August 7, 1991. Not only did Mandela put in doubt future cooperation with the SACP, but he raised questions about future relations with Communists in the ANC, who made up one-third of the ANC National Executive Committee.

30. Official Kremlin International News Broadcast (OKINB), "Briefing on Current International Affairs," May 28, 1991.

31. Livermore, *Russian Foreign Policy Today*, pp. 225–226; and Kempton, *Soviet Strategy Toward Southern Africa,* p. 31.

32. Igor Tarutin, "Why There Is No Flag Flying on the Flagpole," *Russian Press Digest*, January 18, 1992.

33. See OKINB, "Contours of Foreign Policy: Should Russia Really Take a Stand in Africa?" November 5, 1992; and OKINB, "New Story of Old Love," May 25, 1993.

34. Alexei Pushkov, "What Should Russia Do in Black Africa?" *Moscow News*, March 11, 1992.

35. See OKINB, "New Story of Old Love"; and OKINB, "Contours of Foreign Policy."

36. See OKINB, "New Story of Old Love"; OKINB, "Contours of Foreign Policy"; OKINB, "Interview with Andrei Kozyrev, Russian Foreign Minister, on the Results of His Visit to Angola, South Africa and Egypt," March 6, 1992; and Z. Nalbandyan, "Diplomacy Not to Be Valued in Dollars," *Russian Press Digest,* March 6, 1992.

37. Pushkov, "What Should Russia Do in Black Africa?" The Angolans offered two arguments: (1) With the breakup of the Soviet Union, who was Angola to pay, since it had received supplies from different Soviet republics that were now independent? and (2) The USSR had been fighting the United States and using Angolan people and soil, so there was no reason to pay. Particularly irritating to the Russians was the fact that Luanda paid its Western creditors on time while dragging out negotiations with Moscow.

38. OKINB, "Press Briefing by RF Foreign Ministry Spokesman Sergei Yastrzemski on the Current Political Situation," June 25, 1993.

39. See "UNITA Burying Arms, Preparing for War," *Agence France Presse,* February 24, 1995.

40. This occurred at a meeting in Lisbon on March 24, 1995. *OKINB*, "Press Briefing by RF Foreign Ministry Deputy Spokesman Mikhail," March 28, 1995.

41. The Yeltsin government has also expressed concern about the fate of three Russian hydropower construction workers who disappeared in November 1992 following a military operation by UNITA. OKINB, "Press Briefing by Mikhail."

42. Seregi Strokan, "African Style Political Divorce," *Moscow News,* May 12, 1993.

43. OKINB, "Press Briefing by Russian Foreign Ministry Department of Information and Press," July 27, 1993.

44. Vladimir Markov, "Andrei Kozyrev's Visit to South Africa," *Russian Press Digest,* February 29, 1992.

45. See Alexei Pushkov, "Support for Reforms at the World's End," *Moscow News,* March 4, 1992; Maxim Yusin, "Russian Diplomacy Discovers South Africa," *Russian Press Digest,* March 2, 1992; and Sergei Velichkin, "Non-alignment: Still Very Much Alive," *Moscow News,* April 15, 1992. Instead, Mandela remarked that the ANC proceeded "from the fact that everything democratic Russia does in the international arena serves to consolidate the process of democratization in South Africa."

46. Andrei Polyakov, "Russia–South Africa: There Is No 'Secret Compact,'" *Biz Ekon News,* July 13, 1992.

47. See OKINB, "Through Stability to Active Business Contacts," February 17, 1993.

48. See Polyakov, "There Is No 'Secret Compact'"; "Russia: South Africa Opens Commercial Center in St. Petersburg," *African Economic Digest,* May 18, 1992; and OKINB, "Press Conference of South African President Frederick de Klerk," June 1, 1992. When asked about the covert relationship, de Klerk replied: "Ask Mr. Harry Oppenheimer."

49. Sergei Kulik and Yuri Leonov, "SAR President in Russia for First Time," *Russian Press Digest,* May 30, 1992.

50. See Velichkin, "Non-alignment: Still Very Much Alive"; and OKINB, "New Story of Old Love."

51. OKINB, "New Story of Old Love."

52. OKINB, "Press Conference of Frederick de Klerk."

53. OKINB, "Through Stability to Active Business Contacts."

54. OKINB, "Press Briefing by RF Spokesman Grigory Karasin," September 28, 1993.

55. See Richard Dowen, "Lucky Escape for the Diamond Company," *The Independent,* April 9, 1995.

56. See Dowen, "Lucky Escape." It is estimated that the Soviet diamond stockpile will run out by 1997.

57. James Adams, "U.S. Fears South Africa Will Sell Nuclear Technology to Teheran," *Sunday Times,* April 23, 1995.

58. Adams, "South Africa Will Sell Nuclear Technology."

59. See "Speech by Russian Foreign Minister Andrei Kozyrev at Nitze School of Advanced International Studies: Russian Foreign Policy and U.S.-Russian Relations," *Federal News Service,* April 28, 1995.

60. Vyacheslav Yelanin, "Do We Need Africa?" *Russian Press Digest,* February 22, 1995.

61. Yelanin, "Do We Need Africa?"

62. Thus, in March 1995, after expressing concern about avoiding a repeat of the crisis that occurred in Burundi the previous September, Moscow backed the idea proposed by the UN Secretary-General to hold a regional conference on peace

and security in Central Africa. See OKINB, "Press Briefing with the RF Foreign Ministry," March 21, 1995.

63. Yelanin, "Do We Need Africa?"

64. This view was expressed by Russian diplomats. OKINB, "Press Briefing by RF Foreign Ministry Spokesman Sergei Yastrzemski," May 12, 1993.

65. During the first half of 1995, all was not well in U.S.-Russian relations. Whereas Washington was concerned about Moscow's policy in Chechnya and its dealings with Iran, Russia had become disillusioned by the West and its failure to deliver a massive aid package from the IMF. See "Speech by Andrei Kozyrev," *Federal News Service;* and David Hearst, "Crumbling Empire Hunts for New Tsar," *The Guardian*, February 27, 1995, p. 7.

66. "Funding African Programs Makes Good Business Sense: State Department," *Agence France Presse,* March 28, 1995.

14
Conclusion: Responding to Africa's Post–Cold War Conflicts

DONALD ROTHCHILD

> A major lacuna in existing subregional and continent-wide political institutions is the lack of viable peacekeeping arrangements, a situation that has led to exacerbation of several intra-State and inter-State African conflicts.
> —*Adebayo Adedeji*[1]

With the end of the Cold War, the threat of international communism diminished, to be replaced in Africa and elsewhere by much more diffuse political challenges—the weakening of the state and the reappearance of vitalized identity group nationalisms. When the former Soviet Union and the United States backed Africa's soft states as a means of enlisting allies in the global struggle against each other, they enabled frail state structures to survive against the challenges of powerful communal groups. The Cold War, Michael Mandelbaum writes, "imposed what can be seen retrospectively as artificial loyalty—or at least obedience—to abstractions: to the principles of democracy and the market or to the precepts of Marxism-Leninism, and to sovereign states."[2] The great powers secured a stability of relations with Africa's countries; meanwhile, the new African leaders, sensitive to their governments' lack of capabilities, achieved their objective of "denationaliz[ing] their states, lest the politics of communalism overwhelm them."[3] As ethnic, religious, and regional interests reemerged in full strength during post–Cold War times, the African states, left more on their own than at any other time in this century, have found it extremely difficult to achieve the tasks of providing security and stability and fulfilling their developmental promises.[4]

Certainly, the present-day African experience is anything but uniform; there are broad distinctions between those relatively hard regimes that have the potential capacity for effective governance (South Africa) and those relatively soft regimes that are unable to exert effective control throughout their realms (Zaire, Angola).

227

In the effectively governed state systems, where ethnic and religious communities have been willing to maintain their connections with the larger society and enter into reciprocal relations with other groups, a normative notion of "civil society" has prevailed.[5] In these states, networks of reciprocity develop that strengthen a belief in the legitimacy of government and its ability to use existing resources effectively to achieve developmental objectives.

In the relatively weak and ineffectively governed states, however, identity politics has often created conflict, defining those included in the community and, by implication, those regarded as outsiders. In worst-case situations where some groups have not been willing to abide by the common rules of relationship, the result has been zero-sum competition and at times a breakdown in the civil order. In such countries as Liberia, Somalia, Sudan, and Zaire, a sense of common fate and overriding societal concerns has collapsed, resulting in violent encounters between state and insurgent armies and widespread brutality and violence by the militia. According to one estimate, sixteen of the thirty-five civil wars with battle deaths exceeding 1,000 a year are currently taking place in Africa.[6] Because Africa generally lacks important economic opportunities and is unable to contain the threat of identity politics in a number of countries, the powerful Western states and Russia have largely lost interest and disengaged from the continent—leaving African states and peoples increasingly to their own devices.

The consequences of this Western disengagement have been devastating in the short term to Africa's economic and social development. Aid levels remain stagnant, Africa's share of European Union trade is declining, and multinational corporations are disinvesting.[7] Indicative of Africa's declining economic importance to the Western countries is Belgium's determination to disengage from its former African territories and France's January 1994 decision to devalue the Communauté Financière Africaine (CFA) franc by 50 percent in relation to the French franc.[8] Devaluation was a relatively small matter for the French economy (though not its image), but it represented a momentous shift in developmental opportunities for the franc zone countries in Africa,[9] resulting in soaring prices for imported manufactured goods and food, causing hardships for many African citizens who were unable to secure compensating wage increases. The consequent strain and political instability (including riots in Dakar in mid-February) were, not surprisingly, reflected in a mood "of resignation and bitterness" among the Francophone African leaders.[10] But the current attitude in Africa has its positive side as well; as Edmond Keller and Olusegun Obasanjo observe in the Introduction and Chapter 1, there is a growing resolve to develop African solutions to African problems and to fight the trend toward the continent's marginalization.

Although foreign countries continue to use their leverage to press for improved governance, democracy, and human rights, they have not displayed a similar urgency to establish the conditions that would enable political liberalization to flourish. In particular, they have not taken adequate steps to build up Africa's economic and social infrastructures. As Peter Schraeder notes in Chapter 12, a lack of symmetry has become evident between Western demands and the resources these countries are prepared to commit to ensure sustained development and regularized intergroup relationships over an extended time period. Under these circumstances, a new Western strategy has become imperative, one that will facilitate a smooth transition to stable democratic regimes. Such predictable patterns of interactions will hopefully lay the basis for balanced economic and social development in the years ahead.

Social Forces at Work: Reemerging Identities and the Implications for the African State System

Internal conflicts within states involving ethnic, religious, and regional identities have been persistent and can be expected to remain a significant factor in the future. Even in the case of Somalia—often cited as one of the rare examples of an ethnically homogeneous country in Africa—"there is nothing ethnically, linguistically, or culturally homogeneous about all the people occupying Somalia," writes Anna Simons in Chapter 5. In large part, this conflictive pattern reflects the power of the state and the intensity of the struggle of identity groups to gain access to state institutions and a better share of publicly controlled resources. When state-ethnic conflicts involve the allocation of tangible resources, the struggle among identity group patrons is normally expressed through interest group politics; as such, these communal brokers are likely to make moderate, negotiable demands to decisionmakers, allowing the conflict to remain at a manageable level.[11] The problem here is not eliminating conflict (since an incompatibility of values and objectives seems ubiquitous) but establishing institutions that reward moderation and encourage compromise among contending interests.

At times, however, the demands of ethnic and religious groups have spilled over from the tangible to the intangible, gaining a symbolic meaning that makes compromise difficult. The call for ethnic self-determination outside the state raises issues of identity championed by its proponents and regarded as threatening and illegitimate by those determined to maintain state unity, as Marina Ottaway observes in Chapter 8. Some of the separatist groups have come to see their security and survival at stake and have thus made more far-reaching demands not easily negotiable by state and substate leaders. In such cases, as Donald Horowitz asserts, "the psychological sources of conflict do not readily lend themselves to modification by the manipulation of material benefits that is so often the stuff of modern policymaking."[12] The emotional dimension of ethnicity takes over in these highly intense encounters, leading to claims for symbolic and substantive rewards (including a restructuring of state rules). In extreme cases, such as Liberia and Rwanda, social situations become suffused with a sense of deprivation and uncertainty about the fate of a group, resulting in extremely hostile behavior toward what is perceived to be an "enemy" ethnic or religious grouping.[13] The effect is to provide incentives for intractable politics and what I. William Zartman (Chapter 4) describes as state collapse.

During the Cold War, these tensions were largely overshadowed by superpower influences on the scene. The role of the great powers in placing parameters on local conflicts is noted by Francis Deng who writes: "Although the end of the Cold War has removed this aggravating external factor [superpower confrontation], it has also removed the moderating role of the superpowers, both as third parties and as mutually neutralizing allies."[14]

With the end of the Cold War, external restraints have been lifted, and old fears and antagonisms have resurfaced. Even as the Cold War raged, Ali Mazrui was already observing that the territory-wide nationalism experienced at the time of decolonization had given way to "the politics of retribalization;" a militant ethnic consciousness had emerged, Mazrui observed, and had become a pole around which people mobilized to make demands on the state.[15] Deng also commented on this process of ethnic renewal: "Old identities, undermined and rendered dormant by the structures and values of the nation-state system, are re-emerging and redefining the standards of participation, distribution, and legitimacy."[16] And not only is resurgent ethnicity causing instability and sometimes violence, but, as Schraeder shows, religion (particularly in the form of Islamic fundamentalism) is currently perceived by neighboring countries and the Western powers as a threat to regional stability.[17] In the worst cases, where this politicization of ethnic and religious sentiment has undermined routines and networks of reciprocity and caused leaders to retreat from their self-declared principles on proportionality and inclusion, the struggle for interests and power may increase in intensity. The resulting distrust and stridency appear likely to lead to bitter confrontations and increased turbulence.

Various factors (resurgent identity politics, the weakening of intergroup reciprocities and linkages, the determination to thwart state repressiveness, the flow of refugees across borders) have resulted in a revised view of the legitimate claims of the state upon society—including the notion of sovereign jurisdiction. Although still valued as protection for the weak, state sovereignty is no longer given single-minded backing. The world community is increasingly unwilling to look aside while dictators, relying upon the protection of the domestic jurisdiction principle, abuse the rights of their citizenry. For UN secretary-general Boutros Boutros-Ghali, "The time of absolute and exclusive sovereignty . . . has passed. . . . It is the task of leaders of States today to understand this and to find a balance between the needs of good internal governance and the requirements of an ever more interdependent world."[18]

The weakening of the African state and the concomitant rise in ethnic, religious, and regional identity politics have meant that powerful subgroups are now in a position to challenge state institutions effectively. As the African state fights back, engaging at times in political and military repression, it tramples on the rights of its citizens and provokes a crisis of international dimensions (for example, in this volume, see Simons on Somalia, Deng and Khalid Medani on Sudan, and Margaret Vogt on Liberia). Under these circumstances, sovereignty is increasingly viewed as a possible refuge for scoundrels. For Nigerian statesman Ibrahim Gambari (Chapter 2), the calculus of sovereignty versus misery is a cruel one for African leaders. Yet it is clear that the international community is currently redefining the notion of state sovereignty to provide for governmental accountability and to legitimize multilateral interventions in situations where misery has become the order of the day. With the end of the Cold War, old principles of international behavior are changing rapidly; as a consequence, today's African leaders appear increasingly inclined to allow regional and global multilateral organizations wider scope in intervening in threatening internal conflicts.

External Third-Party Mediation

The two great powers placed parameters upon Africa's conflicts during the Cold War era. Remedies for internal conflicts had to be sought through them, giving these external actors considerable leverage to regulate relations within and between states.[19] The superpowers were also an integral part of the security equation during the Cold War years, influencing local actors in their relations with the external environment and engaging in extensive arms shipments to their African allies. The disengagement of the great powers from the politics of many of these countries has set primary responsibility on the shoulders of local political leaders to shape the political identities, goals, policies, and practices of their respective states.

With the great powers exhibiting less incentive to intervene in African affairs in the post–Cold War context (with French intervention in Rwanda before and after the genocide being an exception), and with local political actors unable to muster the economic capabilities needed for effective governance, a political space has been created that may allow for considerable disorder, even anarchy. The Russians are overwhelmed by domestic political and economic challenges and quite prepared, as Jeffrey Lefebvre shows in Chapter 13, to throw over the "burdens of empire;" the United States, unconvinced of the need for extensive financial and human sacrifices to preserve the stability of the new world order, is pulling back from a major leadership role in conflicts on the African continent. U.S. policymakers are prepared to allocate limited resources to humanitarian relief efforts (as in Rwanda in 1994) and to give financial support for regional peacekeeping and peace-building initiatives, but there is little apparent will at this time for extensive involvement like that in Somalia. Commenting on the Clinton administration's decision to subordinate foreign policy issues to a domestic reconstruction agenda, Senator Richard Lugar concluded that "the United States can no longer be counted on to take the lead in regional disputes unless it can discern clear national interests at stake."[20]

The failure of the United States to play a more active role as peacekeeper and peacemaker in Liberia, a country it has had long ties with in the past was especially disappointing. U.S. reluctance to become more heavily engaged was a reflection of both domestic constraints and the sense that it lacked a compelling need to offer world leadership in the less threatening circumstances of the post–Cold War environment. To be sure, Russia and the United States did facilitate the negotiations leading up to an agreement between RENAMO and the government in Mozambique and promote acceptance of Angola's ill-fated Bicesse Accords. In other cases, however, such as Sudan and Zaire, the two former adversaries have tended to stay on the sidelines, allowing tensions to gather and situations to deteriorate. And even in those cases where the great powers have been prepared to facilitate agreements, such as Angola, Somalia, and Liberia, they have shown themselves unprepared to make the kind of sustained commitment necessary to ensure successful implementation of these accords.

With the great powers increasingly disinclined to assume a leading role in promoting peace and development, these tasks fall by default on Africa's current leaders. In 1990, African leaders assembled at the Organization of African Unity (OAU) moved cautiously to take the initiative in promoting peace and development. Although Solomon Gomes (Chapter 3), an OAU representative at the UN, describes the institution he represents as unable to impose its will on its members and decidedly constrained in terms of organizational structure, the OAU's leaders have nonetheless resolved to take a more active part in ending conflicts on the continent.[21] Accordingly, in March 1992, the organization established a new Division on Conflict Management within the OAU General Secretariat and subsequently proposed to resuscitate the long-dormant Commission for Mediation, Conciliation and Arbitration. Seeking to defuse crises through active intervention, the OAU agreed to take on a direct role as peacekeepers in the Rwanda conflict, sent sixty-seven military observers to Burundi, raised the possibility of a mediation initiative in Zaire, and authorized peacemaking efforts by the Economic Community of West African States Monitoring Group (ECOMOG) in Liberia.[22] Ruling out the possibility of a separate OAU peace plan for Liberia, the OAU delegation leader, former Zimbabwean president Canaan Banana, stated that his organization was "only complementing" the efforts of the Economic Community of West African States (ECOWAS) in bringing peace to the subregion.[23]

For many observers, peacekeeping efforts were clearly linked to third-party mediation. "To redress the situation where many conflicts in Africa have degenerated to brutal savagery," remarks Adedeji, "it will be important to devise creative and cost-effective arrangements for peacekeeping in Africa in order to give mediation and conciliation a good chance."[24] Mediation may be necessary, but it is hardly sufficient in a majority of instances. When conflict becomes intense and is characterized both by "essentialist" (or fundamentally threatening) perceptions of a rival's intentions and by the presentation of nonnegotiable demands, direct negotiations between state and society often tend to be unproductive. Recent data indicate that the prospects of successful negotiation, particularly in ethnic or religious disputes, are limited, occurring in only one-quarter of the cases in the twentieth century.[25] Daniel Frei, concluding that interstate conflicts tend to be more open to mediation than struggles between a state and an insurgent movement, argues that this difference is explained by the greater legitimacy of the state's ruling coalition.[26]

When certain predisposing conditions are in place—such as the emergence of identifiable bargaining parties, a mutually damaging stalemate, leaders determined to find a political solution, external pressures to reach agreement, and a mediator actively on the scene—third-party mediators have sometimes succeeded in negotiating and implementing an agreement. Such undertakings are more likely to be achieved when the mediator has enormous resources to influence the preferences of the rival parties, but even a mediator with muscle is not likely to prevail in the face of intransigent opposition.

External Actors and the Transition Process

By and large, the literature on mediation concentrates on the prenegotiation and negotiation stages and tends to give short shrift to the implementation stage. Certainly, various African leaders, singly or collectively, have seized favorable opportunities to mediate internal conflicts between the state and an insurgent movement. Among others, Ethiopia's emperor Haile Selassie was an effective arbitrator in the Sudanese government–Southern Sudan Liberation Movement negotiations in 1972; the presidents of Nigeria and other regional powers made a series of partially successful efforts in Chad that resulted in temporary reconciliations among the various internal groupings in the 1979–1986 period; an OAU peacekeeping force (replaced by a UN peacekeeping unit under an August 1993 agreement) has worked alongside a Tanzanian diplomatic team to facilitate negotiations between the Rwanda government and the Rwandese Patriotic Front insurgents; and OAU and UN mediators collaborated in hammering out the 1993 Cotonou Agreement and the follow-up February 28, 1994, agreement between Liberia's Interim Government of National Unity, the National Patriotic Front of Liberia, and the United Liberation Movement for Democracy in Liberia. In other cases, such as Kenya's president Daniel arap Moi's efforts to mediate the Ugandan civil war in 1985–1986 and Zaire's president Mobutu Sese Seko's intervention in the Angolan internal conflict in 1989, the third party mediator proved unable to change the perceptions of the main antagonists. The problem was not a matter of diplomatic skill but the depth of distrust between the adversaries and an inability to exert sufficient pressure to narrow their differences.

Although extracontinental mediators sometimes have an advantage in the leverage they can exercise in facilitating negotiations, their record also leaves much to be desired. U.S. Assistant Secretary of State for African Affairs Chester A. Crocker did succeed against great odds in negotiating an international agreement in Angola in 1988, but the negotiations to end the internal conflict between the Angolan government and the National Union for the Total Independence of Angola (UNITA) rebels proved long and difficult. In 1991, the Portuguese, with U.S. and Soviet backing, managed to work out the Bicesse accords, only to see this agreement fall apart as UNITA leader Jonas Savimbi, fearful of a defeat in the second round of the national election, resumed the civil war. In the case of Mozambique, a laborious Italian-led mediatory initiative, involving both government and private actors, finally produced an agreement in October 1992, but the implementation process has proved complicated and protracted. In other instances, such as various U.S. initiatives in Sudan and Zaire, the results so far have been inconclusive. For all the strategic and economic resources at its command, even the world's last remaining superpower cannot pressure Africa's internal combatants to make peace—or to keep the peace.

The problem of African mediation lies partly in the negotiation of effective agreements and partly in the promotion of regularized routines of relationship in the period that follows. Unless each of these phases in the mediatory process is carried out effectively, the consequences may be unpredictable political routines, irregular rules of encounter, and exacerbated tensions. Clearly a built-in contradiction is often in evidence: Continued external involvement in the peace process is essential; yet in the end a solution—if it is to endure—must be an indigenous, African one. The end of the Cold War raises serious doubts about the developed countries' willingness to play the kind of sustained role in peace building that is essential; hence there is a need to promote a more decentralized system of security maintenance, involving a central role for the UN, the OAU, and Africa's subregional organizations.[27] In this respect, the UN's continuing effort to find a solution in Angola and the roles of the OAU in Rwanda and ECOWAS in Liberia are most encouraging indicators.

The Iterative Process
Leading to Local Acceptance of Basic Norms

The consolidation of agreements during the transition from conflict to peaceful relations has sometimes proven elusive. As Zartman remarks, "African states are becoming increasingly experienced in negotiation, and their negotiating often errs in overaccommodation rather than in overintransigence. They know how to make a deal, more than they know how to keep one."[28] Whereas the implementation process was reasonably effective in Namibia, Eritrea, and Zimbabwe (all of which involved political independence) and thus far seems cautiously hopeful in Mozambique, the transition experiences in Angola, Somalia, and Liberia have been troubled. Moreover, Zaire's internal agreement was never firmed up and the Western Sahara referendum has proven more of a promise than a reality.

Part of the problem lies in the dynamics of external intervention—expanding the decision group from a dyad to a triad. Although external third-party actors can at times facilitate the negotiating process, sustained peace ultimately involves the creation of recognized and legitimate rules of relationship among the contending interests on the scene. In the post–Cold War era, solutions cannot be imposed by external actors and be expected to endure; they must result from a process of mutual dialogue and consent by the local parties themselves. The solution must be perceived to be African mandated.[29]

Reaching such a solution inevitably requires local accommodations on issues of participation and autonomy and an agreement on some form of power sharing. Clearly, if powerful political actors cannot be defeated militarily, then conflict management requires pragmatic perceptions and moderate demands. In such circumstances, effective governance requires a sharing of decisionmaking authority, not exclusivist dominance by one group over another. Without such sharing, there will likely to insufficient stability and thus an inability to compromise on determining the rules of state-society or intergroup relationships. Provided minimum rules exist on such issues as inclusiveness, proportionality, participation, and autonomy, then an iterative process can occur, possibly leading to fully democratic regimes. Colombia's transition from an elite pact to full democracy is encouraging evidence of a possible dynamic at work. In Africa, it may be necessary to open the political process by stages, moving from a broad consensus agreement among elites to multiparty contestation.

Although the depth of suspicion and distrust in ethnic, religious, and nationality group relations often precludes accommodation, it is possible to provide incentives for cooperation among them. Four major arenas of power sharing may be appropriate in Africa: (1) The constitution may provide guidelines on ethnic proportionality in elections, civil service recruitment, resource allocation, the award of scholarships, and so forth; (2) electoral arrangements can be devised to ensure broad minority participation in decisionmaking; (3) leaders at the political center can use a variety of formal and informal strategies to bring the representatives of various identity groups within the ruling coalition; and (4) local initiative can be strengthened by means of decentralization—including constitutional provisions on federalism. Depending upon the context, each of these alternatives may provide inducements to local interests to avoid destructive opposition and to play a constructive role in governing at the local, regional, and national levels.

Proportionality, inclusiveness, and decentralization, then, are guidelines intended to foster interest group accommodation and moderate behavior. They are somewhat broader than political democracy as normally understood and are evident at times in weakly authoritarian, semicompetitive, and genuinely competitive political systems. As such, they can be considered a part of the larger process of democratization. By encouraging various mixes of societal participation and effective state leadership appropriate in each African circumstance, these regime structures help build networks of elite reciprocities that further regularize interactions between state and society.[30]

Successful democratization, then, is the first and most critical dimension in the process of consolidating peace agreements. It cannot be imposed by external actors but must result from the iterative play of local leaders over an extended time period. For democracy to endure, as Obasanjo argues in Chapter 1, it must be "home-induced, home-grown, and home-sustained." At its heart, it depends upon a sense of trust and awareness of common fate—elements that require social learning. When this learning becomes embedded in the social fabric of a wider society, then a structure may develop that can survive the militant outbidding efforts of rejectionist parties bent upon bringing about the collapse of frail agreements.

In South Africa, as Timothy Sisk argues, the elite pact worked out by the core parties at the center (the African National Congress, the National Party, and the Democratic Party) reduced uncertainty by establishing nascent rules of transition.[31] Elite pact making represented a confidence-building mechanism for ethnic, racial, regional, and religious minorities; such an arrangement, as Ottaway and Keller show, encourages a sense of well-being and security among these minority interests through power sharing in the national cabinet and other decisionmaking bodies. Whether this inclusive coalition and its elite pact can hold in the face of new (and possibly deepening) pressures in the posttransition period remains to be seen. One distinguished South African scholar, Hermann Giliomee, wrote recently of a possible trend in that country toward a one-party dominant system.[32] What does seem likely, however, is that such rules of relationship will be critical during the transition phase and that they will have to be enlarged upon (albeit in modified form) over time, or the consolidation of the agreement will likely prove difficult to carry through. Democratization, then, must be seen as an ongoing process that requires nurturing. If negotiated and renegotiated over the years, it can prove indispensable in laying the basis for persistent and stable intergroup relations.

The Inescapable Role of the International Community to Act as Peacemaker and Peace Enforcer

When the iterative process culminates in a broadly accepted elite pact, the effect is to encourage moderate political encounters and stable group relations. In achieving a measure of predictability and regularity of relationships, they build confidence and, in certain circumstances, preempt legitimate international intervention. State-societal conflict becomes an international concern only when local actors fail to develop self-sustaining rules of encounter—and allow their conflicts to spill over into the region around them. In recent years, as authoritarian regimes have declined and ethnic dominance has been overthrown by society's disadvantaged, the old order has sometimes been undermined without the emergence of a new consensus (such as in Liberia, Somalia, and Zaire). When the state's structure of authority and organizing rules have disintegrated, the state sometimes collapses.[33] This collapse may well entail a terrifying descent into anarchy, requiring in extreme cases the intercession of regional or international actors. Not surprisingly, these worst-case scenarios may be just the ones that the international community will avoid (as was the case for Rwanda until the fait accompli in July 1994).

Intercessions by regional and global organizations have not always influenced the course of state-subnational or micronational disputes. While these transstate bodies proved largely ineffective in resolving conflicts in Angola, Somalia, Western Sahara, and elsewhere, the ECOMOG experience in Liberia, as described by Robert Mortimer (Chapter 10) and Vogt, has shown the African states to be making serious efforts in mobilizing and launching a collective military operation to deal with a regional security problem.[34] When the regional and global actors have been prepared to respond to a local crisis with overwhelming force, they have managed to exert profound leverage. Thus the deployment of significant UN monitoring units during the implementation stage in Namibia and in the period prior to the "founding" elections in Mozambique had a decisive impact on the actions of local parties, ensuring a smooth transition to peaceful relations.

By contrast, the deployment in 1991 of a small international monitoring force to deal with the disarming of rival military units and the integration of a new, unified army in strife-ridden Angola (combined with indecisive leadership) contributed to a faulty consolidation of the successes made earlier at the peace table.[35] For a limited time, the dispatch to Somalia in December 1992 of a sizable U.S.-led international force did much to improve security in many parts of the country;[36] however, as the United States began to withdraw its troops and heavy equipment from the area and to turn over its functions to various UN forces, security in South Mogadishu quickly deteriorated, culminating in sharp attacks in 1993 by General Mohamed Farah Aidid's supporters upon Pakistani and U.S. peacekeeping units.

The dilemma of international peacekeeping became apparent to all. On the one hand, it was necessary to provide overwhelming force to ensure security in situations where the state was gravely weakened or had broken down; on the other, such irresistible power is difficult to muster in all but the most unique confrontations. As an alternative, some new institutional arrangement arising from such initiatives as the Africa Leadership Forum's proposed Conference on Security, Stability, Development and Cooperation in Africa may come to play a significant role in the reduction of conflict, but, as Terrence Lyons (Chapter 6) and Denis Venter (Chapter 9) suggest, these are possibilities for the future, not effective conflict management mechanisms in the present.

Ethnic and religious wars continue to be waged across Africa and Eastern Europe, and the will and the means to cope with these post–Cold War disorders are simply not in evidence. Objecting to the U.S. paralysis of will in the face of the massacres in Rwanda, former assistant secretary of state for African Affairs Herman Cohen wrote:

> By standing in the way of African troops intervening in Rwanda under "combat" terms of engagement, the United States is effectively imposing upon the Security Council the same rule that it applies to itself. That is to

> say, the administration sees no vital American interest engaged in Rwanda, and therefore does not want U.N. troops to have a muscular mandate even though African troops would be willing to take on such a difficult and dangerous assignment. . . . the United States and other important powers should start working to give the United Nations the ability to put out fires while they are still smoldering.[37]

The problem of resoluteness is compounded by the inexplicit nature of the guidelines under which the UN and regional organizations operate. The post–Cold War institutions lack the rules and regulations necessary to prepare them in advance of the collapse of states and to determine how to respond by means of peacemaking and peace enforcement initiatives. The result, as John Gerald Ruggie observes, is that "the United Nations has entered a domain of military activity—a vaguely defined no-man's-land lying somewhere between traditional peacekeeping and enforcement—for which it lacks any guiding operational concept."[38] Ruggie goes on to note that UN peacekeeping forces are not designed to engage in military enforcement activities; either the major military countries will increase the capability of the international community to undertake such assignments quickly and effectively, something they are most reluctant to do at this juncture, or these organizations will witness a decline in their credibility.[39] The signs are not encouraging. As an organization of states, to make use of Gomes's phrase, the UN structure tends to place firm boundaries on the kind of decisive action required in these situations.

Conclusion

"The collapse of Soviet communism," writes former U.S. secretary of state Henry Kissinger, "marked the intellectual vindication of American ideals and, ironically, brought America face to face with the kind of world it had been seeking to escape throughout its history."[40] The vindication of U.S. ideals may prove to be a temporary phenomenon, but clearly the United States' long-standing penchant for a stable and moderate world order is now endangered anew by a rise in ethnic and religious nationalism in Africa and the rest of the world. At times, these new forces of ethnic identity nationalism have been accommodated within the political system. Nevertheless, when communal interests and state elites are deeply distrustful and make nonnegotiable demands on each other, the gap between them widens and conflict within the state may become intense and spill over into the region around it.

At this point, regional and international peacemaking initiatives become essential, although they are not always sufficient to the task at hand. The conciliation and mediation efforts required under these circumstances involve three intertwined and overlapping stages: prenegotiation, negotiation, and implementation. Much of the current literature on peacemaking concentrates on the negotiation stage, giving only limited attention to the prenegotiation stage and even less to the implementation of agreements. These are serious oversights: A failure to agree on basic principles or to set a realizable agenda early on may contribute to imprecise negotiating outcomes; the inability to implement peace agreements effectively may lead, as in Angola, to the resurfacing of menacing perceptions and a resumption of internal strife and warfare. With each break of interelite and intergroup connections, it becomes more difficult to reestablish the networks of reciprocities necessary for regularized relations to take place among political leaders.

The consolidation of agreements involves the process of regularizing rules of relationship and, when this is incomplete, international peacemaking and peacekeeping initiatives. Successful regularizing of the rules (which reaches its highest level of predictability with democratization) preempts the need for international intervention, but when democratic norms and routines are slow to develop, external regional and global peacemaking efforts become essential to provide stability through the turbulent encounters of the transitional period.

In light of financial constraints, fear of troop losses, and general lack of will and determination on the part of many member states, most notably the major powers, there is no guarantee that the UN will be able to shoulder its full peacekeeping responsibilities in the years ahead. Evidence abounds of great power fatigue with peacekeeping burdens. The West is currently retreating from extended commitments, and it remains unclear whether this will prove a short- or long-term disengagement. In the years ahead, the West may well become a precarious redoubt, as Obasanjo asserts, should it try to isolate itself from the Third World. Rather, its interests lie in decentralizing global responsibility and redefining security in the post–Cold War era so that it offers effective leadership in alliance with others to promote world peace. These objectives involve developing a realistic strategy to strengthen the UN and various regional bodies to enable them to provide incentives for political moderation and democracy and to help manage the peace.

Notes

I wish to thank Edmond Keller, Michael Bratton, and Letitia Lawson for comments on the first draft of this chapter.

1. Statement by Adebayo Adedeji to the Kampala Forum on Security, Stability, Development and Cooperation in Africa, in Olusegun Obasanjo and Felix G. N. Mosha, eds., *Africa: Rise to Challenge* (New York: Africa Leadership Forum, 1993), p. 302.

2. Michael Mandelbaum, "The Reluctance to Intervene," *Foreign Policy* 95 (Summer 1994), p. 6.

3. Mark R. Beissinger, "Demise of an Empire-State: Identity, Legitimacy, and the Deconstruction of Soviet Politics," in Crawford Young, ed., *The Rising Tide of Cultural Pluralism* (Madison: University of Wisconsin Press, 1993), p. 95.

4. On this, see Robert D. Kaplan, "The Coming Anarchy," *Atlantic Monthly* 273,2 (February 1994), p. 70.

5. On this, see Victor Azarya, "Civil Society and Disengagement in Africa," in John W. Harbeson, Donald Rothchild, and Naomi Chazan, eds., *Civil Society and the State in Africa* (Boulder, Colo.: Lynne Rienner, 1994), p. 91.

6. Desmond Davies, "Conflicts in Africa," *West Africa,* January 24–30, 1994, p. 114.

7. Thomas M. Callaghy reports that 43 of 139 British companies with industrial developments in Africa withdrew their holdings during the 1980s. See his "Africa and the World Political Economy: Still Caught Between a Rock and a Hard Place," in John W. Harbeson and Donald Rothchild, eds., *Africa in World Politics*, 2d ed. (Boulder, Colo.: Westview Press, 1995), pp. 41–68.

8. Correspondent, "Belgium: The End of an Affair," *Africa Confidential* 35,5 (March 4, 1994), p. 3.

9. See Charles Debbasch, "L'Afrique sans la France," *Jeune Afrique* 1734 (March 31–April 6, 1994), pp. 74–75.

10. Editorial, "The Future of the Franc Zone," *West Africa*, February 21–27, 1994, p. 295.

11. This is discussed at length in Donald Rothchild, "An Interactive Model for State-Ethnic Relations," in Francis M. Deng and I. William Zartman, eds., *Conflict Resolution in Africa* (Washington, D.C.: Brookings, 1991), pp. 195–197.

12. Donald L. Horowitz, *Ethnic Groups in Conflict* (Berkeley: University of California Press, 1985), p. 566.

13. Donald Rothchild and Alexander Groth, "Domestic and International Aspects of Pathological Ethnicity," *Political Science Quarterly* 110,1 (Spring 1995), pp. 73–75.

14. Francis M. Deng, "Africa and the New World Dis-Order," *The Brookings Review* 11,2 (Spring 1993), p. 34.

15. Ali A. Mazrui, "Violent Contiguity and the Politics of Retribalization in Africa," *Journal of International Affairs* 23,1 (1969), pp. 89–105.

16. Deng, "Africa and the New World Dis-Order," p. 34.

17. Also see the discussion in Peter J. Schraeder, *United States Foreign Policy Toward Africa: Incrementalism, Crisis and Change* (Cambridge: Cambridge University Press, 1994), pp. 253–256.

18. Boutros Boutros-Ghali, *An Agenda for Peace* (New York: UN, 1992), p. 9. Also see Francis M. Deng and Larry Minear, *The Challenges of Famine Relief* (Washington, D.C.: Brookings, 1992), p. 131.

19. Deng, "Africa and the New World Dis-Order," p. 32.

20. Richard G. Lugar, "American Foreign Policy in the Post–Cold War Period," *Presidential Studies Quarterly* 24,1 (Winter 1994), p. 23.

21. Organization of African Unity, *Resolving Conflicts in Africa: Proposals for Action* (Addis Ababa: OAU, 1992), p. 4.

22. On the possibility of a Zairian initiative, see *Foreign Broadcast Information Service (FBIS)*, Sub-Saharan Africa, 93,087 (May 7, 1993), p. 2.

23. *FBIS* 93,037 (February 26, 1993), p. 1; also see the contributions by Robert A. Mortimer and Margaret Aderinsola Vogt to this volume.

24. Adedeji, "Statement to the Kampala Forum," p. 302.

25. Stephen John Stedman, *Peacemaking in Civil Wars: International Mediation in Zimbabwe, 1974–1980* (Boulder, Colo.: Lynne Rienner, 1987), pp. 5–9.

26. Daniel Frei, "Conditions Affecting the Effectiveness of International Mediation," *Papers of the Peace Science Society* (International) 26 (1976), p. 70. Also see Paul R. Pillar, *Negotiating Peace: War Termination as a Bargaining Process* (Princeton, N.J.: Princeton University Press, 1983), pp. 5–7.

27. On this, see Charles William Maynes, "A Workable Clinton Doctrine," *Foreign Policy,* 93 (Winter 1993–1994), p. 11.

28. I. William Zartman, "Inter-African Negotiation," in Harbeson and Rothchild, eds., *Africa in World Politics,* 2d ed., pp. 234–249.

29. Peter Wallensteen, "Conflict Resolution After the Cold War: Five Implications," Carter Center, *Resolving Intra-national Conflicts: A Strengthened Role for Intergovernmental Organizations,* Conference Report Series 5,1 (Atlanta: Carter Center, 1993), p. 40.

30. These mixes of societal participation and forms of state control are explored in Donald Rothchild and Letitia Lawson, "The Interactions Between State and Civil Society in Africa: From Deadlock to New Routines," in Harbeson, Rothchild, and Chazan, eds., *Civil Society and the State in Africa,* pp. 255–281.

31. Timothy D. Sisk, *Democratization in South Africa: The Elusive Social Contract* (Princeton, N.J.: Princeton University Press, 1995). As Stephen Stedman notes, such a centrist coalition could act in an authoritarian manner when faced with a militant opposition following the transition. See his "South Africa: Transition and Transformation," in Stephen John Stedman, ed., *South Africa: The Political Economy of Transformation* (Boulder, Colo.: Lynne Rienner, 1994), p. 20.

32. Hermann Giliomee, "Democratization in South Africa," *Political Science Quarterly* 110,1 (Spring 1995), p. 104.

33. I. William Zartman, "Putting the State Back Together," *SAIS Review* 13,2 (Summer–Fall 1993), p. 50.

34. Not all West African states support the ECOMOG initiative. In addition to such open opponents as Burkina Faso, some states that participated in the ECOMOG action, such as Ghana, have expressed strong reservations about the Liberian venture as a precedent. For a statement of African reservations about ECOWAS becoming "a forum for crisis management," see the interview with Ghana's president Jerry John Rawlings in *West Africa,* January 10–16, 1994, p. 15.

35. Donald Rothchild, "The United States and Conflict Management in Africa," in Harbeson and Rothchild, eds., *Africa in World Politics*, 2d ed., chap. 10.

36. Raymond W. Copson and Theodros S. Dagne, "Somalia: Operation Restore Hope," *Congressional Research Service Issue Brief,* January 19, 1993, p. 1.; and Ken Menkhaus and Terrence Lyons, "What Are the Lessons to Be Learned From Somalia?" *CSIS Africa Notes* 144 (January 1993), p. 5.

37. Herman Cohen, "Getting Rwanda Wrong," *Washington Post,* June 3, 1994, quoted in *Congressional Record—Senate* 140, 72 (June 10, 1994), pp. S6786–S6787.

38. John Gerald Ruggie, "The U.N.: Between Peacekeeping and Enforcement," *Foreign Affairs: Agenda 1994,* p. 99.

39. Ruggie, "The U.N.," p. 101. See also Boutros Boutros-Ghali, "Supplement to an Agenda for Peace: Position Paper of the secretary-general on the Occasion of the Fifteenth Anniversary of the United Nations," UN, General Assembly, 50th sess. (January 3, 1995), A/50/60, p. 11.

40. Henry Kissinger, *Diplomacy* (New York: Simon and Schuster, 1994), pp. 18–19.

ABOUT THE CONTRIBUTORS

Francis M. Deng is a senior fellow of the Brookings Institution in the African Studies division of the Foreign Policy Studies Program. He is a former ambassador for Sudan and a former human rights officer at the United Nations.

Ibrahim A. Gambari is the ambassador and Permanent Representative of Nigeria to the United Nations.

Solomon Gomes is Special Affairs Officer, Organization of African Unity Mission to the United Nations.

Edmond J. Keller is professor of political science and director of the James S. Coleman African Studies Center at the University of California, Los Angeles. He is past president of the African Studies Association and a specialist on the politics of northeast Africa.

Jeffrey A. Lefebvre is associate professor of political science and director of the Middle Eastern Languages and Area Studies Program at the University of Connecticut.

Terrence Lyons is a research associate at the Foreign Policy Studies Program of the Brookings Institute.

Khalid M. Medani is currently a Ph.D. student in political science at the University of California, Berkeley. He has worked as a research assistant at the Brookings Institution and as a free-lance journalist in Africa.

Robert A. Mortimer is a professor of political science at Haverford College.

Olusegun Obasanjo is the former head of state of Nigeria and the founding chairman of the African Leadership Forum. In addition, he was co-chairman of the Commonwealth Eminent Persons Group on South Africa in 1985–1986. He is currently a political prisoner in Nigeria.

Marina Ottaway is visiting professor in the African Studies Program, Georgetown University.

Donald Rothchild is professor of political science at the University of California, Davis.

Peter J. Schraeder is associate professor of political science, Loyola University, Chicago, and is currently a Fulbright scholar with the Faculte de Sciences Juridiques et Politiques at Cheikh Anta Diop University in Senegal.

Anna Simons is assistant professor of anthropology at the University of California, Los Angeles.

Denis Venter is executive director and head, Academic Programmes at the Africa Institute of South Africa in Pretoria. He is the immediate past president of the African Studies Association of South Africa.

Margaret Aderinsola Vogt is a senior associate, International Peace Academy.

I. William Zartman is Jacob Blaustein Professor of International Organization and Conflict Resolution Director of African Studies at the Johns Hopkins School of Advanced International Studies.

INDEX

245

ABOUT THE BOOK

With Africa in a period of rapid change, its leaders are faced with both re-thinking old notions of state sovereignty and establishing new guidelines governing when and how international actors should intervene in domestic conflicts. This collection explores the increasing interrelationship of the domestic and international security environments of African states—a trend that surprisingly has accelerated with the end of the Cold War.

Combining theoretical and policy analyses with rich case studies, the book addresses critical questions: Will the OAU and the UN, in the interest of regional security, be able to redefine notions of sovereignty, state responsibility, and norms of external intervention? Can Africa develop a regional capacity for conflict prevention and management? What roles will external actors be expected to play in African peacekeeping? The authors critically examine traditional modalities for conflict management, as well as new ideas for coping with Africa's security dilemma.

Edmond J. Keller is professor of political science at the University of California, Los Angeles. He has edited numerous collections, among them (with Louis A. Picard) *South Africa in Southern Africa: Domestic Change and International Conflict*. **Donald Rothchild** is professor of political science at the University of California, Davis. His publications include *Ghana: The Political Economy of Recovery*.